LIFE IS STRANGE

– STRINGS –

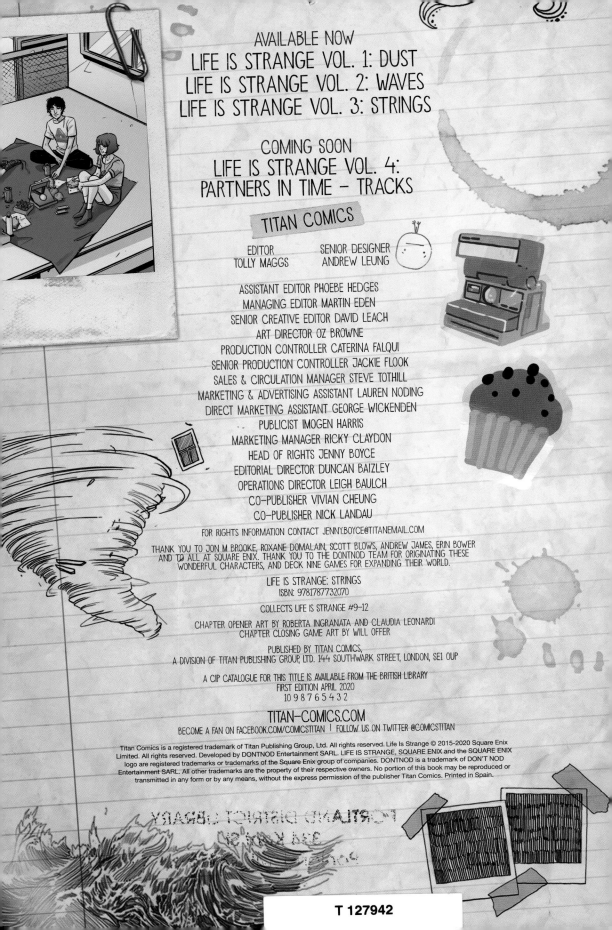

AVAILABLE NOW
LIFE IS STRANGE VOL. 1: DUST
LIFE IS STRANGE VOL. 2: WAVES
LIFE IS STRANGE VOL. 3: STRINGS

COMING SOON
LIFE IS STRANGE VOL. 4:
PARTNERS IN TIME – TRACKS

TITAN COMICS

EDITOR
TOLLY MAGGS

SENIOR DESIGNER
ANDREW LEUNG

ASSISTANT EDITOR PHOEBE HEDGES
MANAGING EDITOR MARTIN EDEN
SENIOR CREATIVE EDITOR DAVID LEACH
ART DIRECTOR OZ BROWNE
PRODUCTION CONTROLLER CATERINA FALQUI
SENIOR PRODUCTION CONTROLLER JACKIE FLOOK
SALES & CIRCULATION MANAGER STEVE TOTHILL
MARKETING & ADVERTISING ASSISTANT LAUREN NODING
DIRECT MARKETING ASSISTANT GEORGE WICKENDEN
PUBLICIST IMOGEN HARRIS
MARKETING MANAGER RICKY CLAYDON
HEAD OF RIGHTS JENNY BOYCE
EDITORIAL DIRECTOR DUNCAN BAIZLEY
OPERATIONS DIRECTOR LEIGH BAULCH
CO-PUBLISHER VIVIAN CHEUNG
CO-PUBLISHER NICK LANDAU

FOR RIGHTS INFORMATION CONTACT JENNY.BOYCE@TITANEMAIL.COM

THANK YOU TO JON M BROOKE, ROXANE DOMALAIN, SCOTT BLOWS, ANDREW JAMES, ERIN BOWER
AND TO ALL AT SQUARE ENIX. THANK YOU TO THE DONTNOD TEAM FOR ORIGINATING THESE
WONDERFUL CHARACTERS, AND DECK NINE GAMES FOR EXPANDING THEIR WORLD.

LIFE IS STRANGE: STRINGS
ISBN: 9781787732070

COLLECTS LIFE IS STRANGE #9-12

CHAPTER OPENER ART BY ROBERTA INGRANATA AND CLAUDIA LEONARDI
CHAPTER CLOSING GAME ART BY WILL OFFER

PUBLISHED BY TITAN COMICS,
A DIVISION OF TITAN PUBLISHING GROUP, LTD. 144 SOUTHWARK STREET, LONDON, SE1 0UP

A CIP CATALOGUE FOR THIS TITLE IS AVAILABLE FROM THE BRITISH LIBRARY
FIRST EDITION APRIL 2020
10 9 8 7 6 5 4 3 2

TITAN-COMICS.COM
BECOME A FAN ON FACEBOOK.COM/COMICSTITAN | FOLLOW US ON TWITTER @COMICSTITAN

T 127942

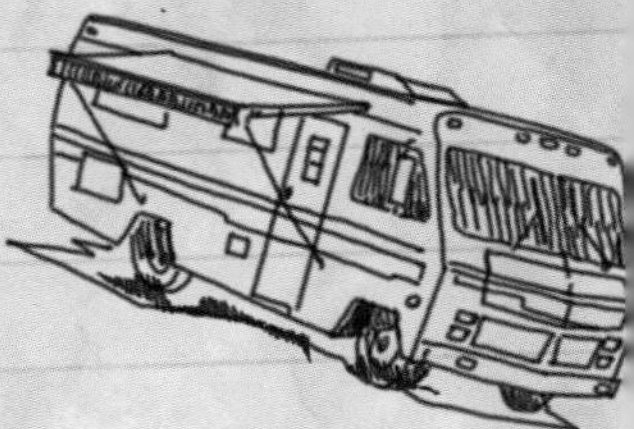

LIFE IS STRANGE

– STRINGS –

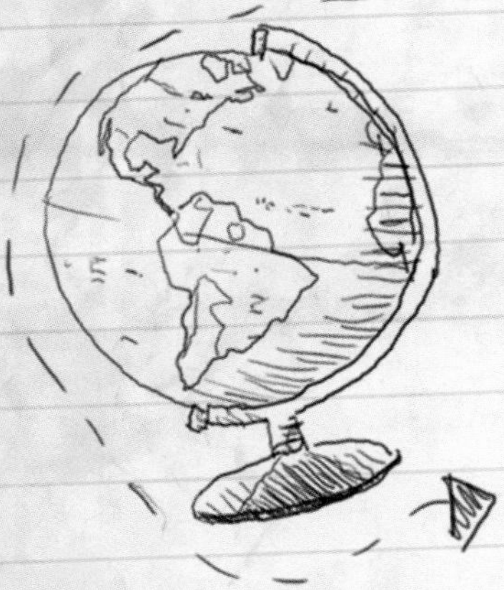

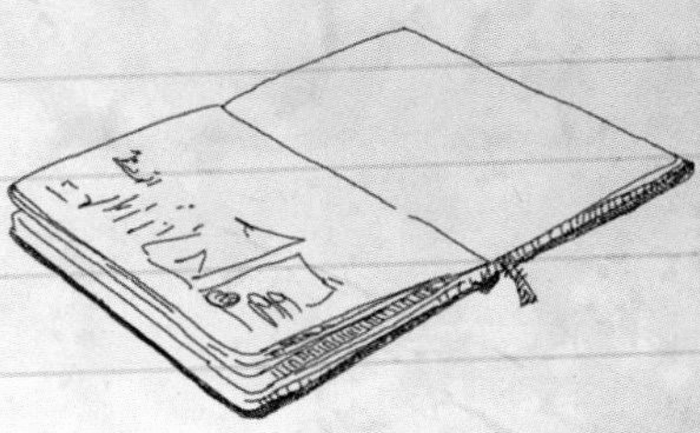

WRITTEN BY
EMMA VIECELI

ARTWORK BY
CLAUDIA LEONARDI

COLORS BY
ANDREA IZZO

LETTERS BY
RICHARD STARKINGS & COMICRAFT'S
JIMMY BETANCOURT

ORIGINAL STORY AND CHARACTERS BY
RAOUL BARBET, JEAN-LUC CANO
AND MICHEL KOCH.

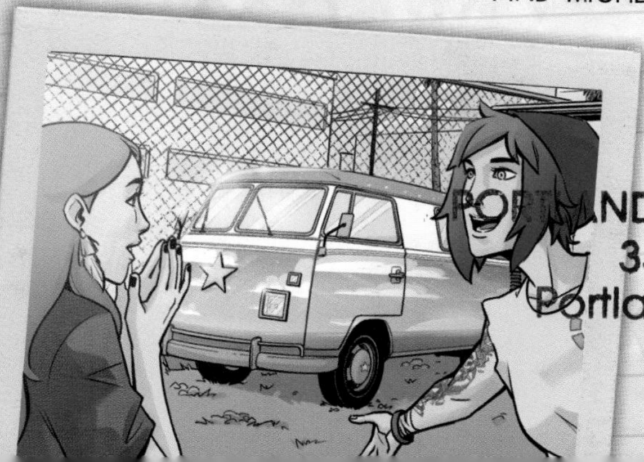

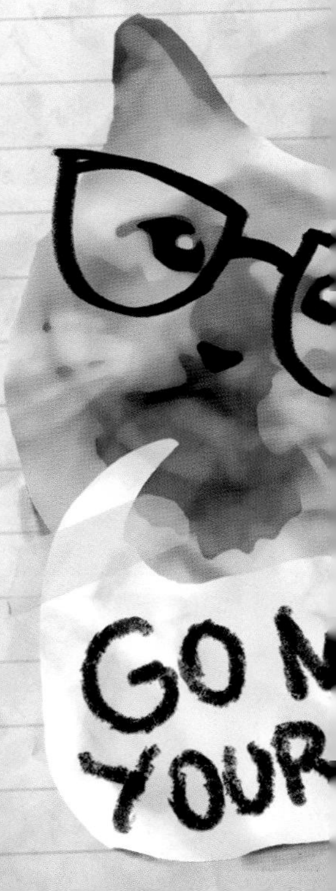
GO
YOUR

PREVIOUSLY...

Mysteriously gifted with the power to rewind time, young photography student Max Caulfield became entangled in the secrets of Arcadia Bay. She used her strange new abilities to reconnect with her oldest friend, Chloe Price, and to bring to justice the men who had murdered Chloe's closest confidante, Rachel Amber. Max's abilities came at a cost, however, creating a hurricane that threatened to destroy the town. In one reality, Max chose to save Chloe's life, sacrificing Arcadia Bay. After a year by Chloe's side, temporal stresses from all her time-jumping started to pull Max apart, and it was only by jumping away from her original timeline, into one where both Chloe and Rachel were still alive, that Max could survive...

After being torn away from her world, time traveler Max found a reality where Rachel Amber was still alive, and with Chloe Price. As time passed, Max continued to struggle to adjust.

Chloe has been working in a garage, while picking up her first commission as a sculptor -- one that has brought this reality's version of The High Seas to play a gig in California. She has called the sculpture "The Storm".

Rachel, who's a livestreamer and influencer, as well as an aspiring actor, has been offered a touring theatrical gig that will take her away from home for six months -- to the dismay and eventual support of Chloe.

Max met the distant and isolated Tristan, a mysterious young man living on the streets, who seemingly has the power to disappear at will.

MEMORIES IN TIME

Two Whales

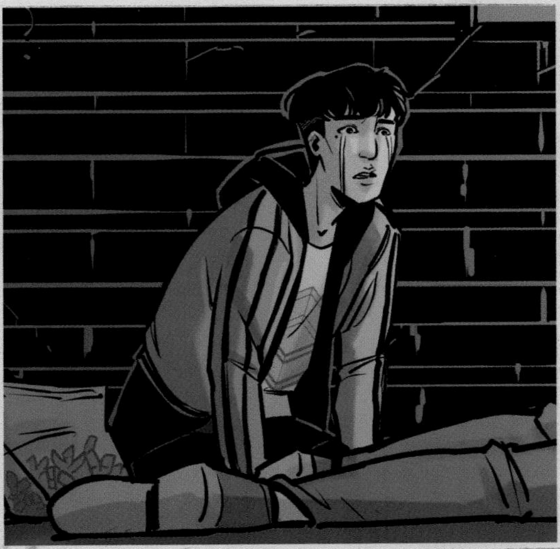

Detailing the night his ability manifested, Tristan explained how he saw his best friend get shot when a drug deal went bad. His friend's final words cursed Tristan for abandoning him, even though Tristan was right there -- but invisible.

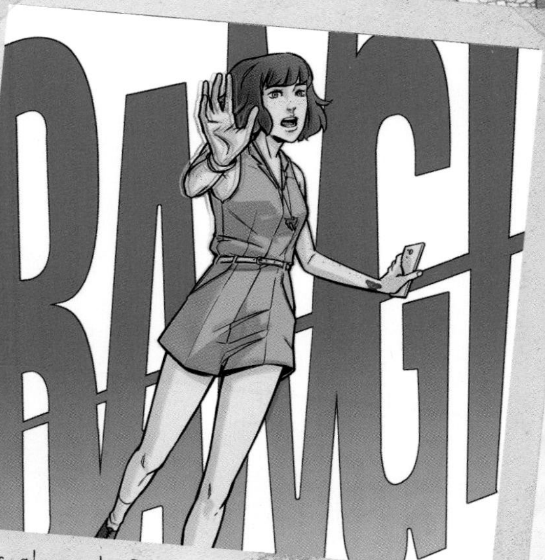

BANG!

Later, at a party, Rachel's friend overdosed. When Max stepped outside to call an ambulance, she saw Tristan get shot by the same dealers who shot his friend! Instinctively, Max reached out and rewound time!

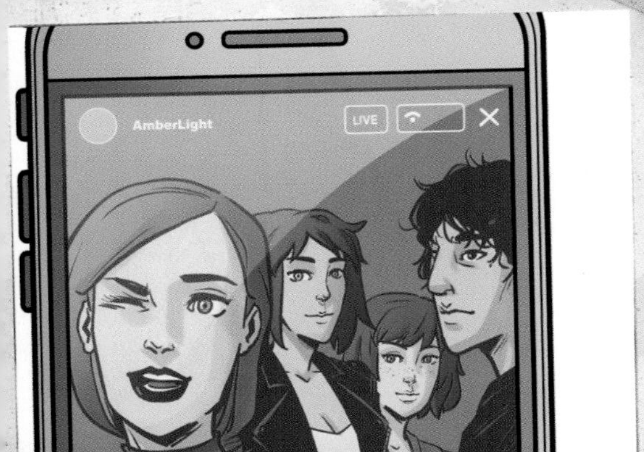

AmberLight
LIVE
DrowneDrone
ScienceBoi01
be careful...

By using her power, Max saved both Tristan and Rachel's friend, but ended up getting caught by the drug dealers. A joint effort from Tristan, Chloe and Rachel saved Max from a horrible fate, with the entire incident being broadcast on Rachel's livestream!

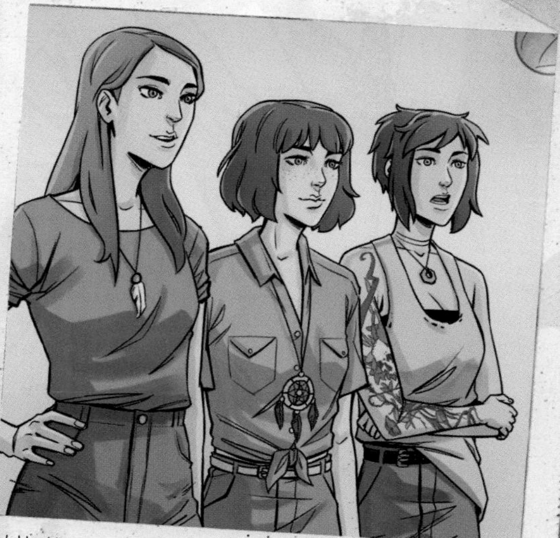

With the drug dealers brought to justice, Max made the decision to talk to Chloe and Rachel, and tell them the truth of her past...

ShOOSH I'm dreaming

CHAPTER 1

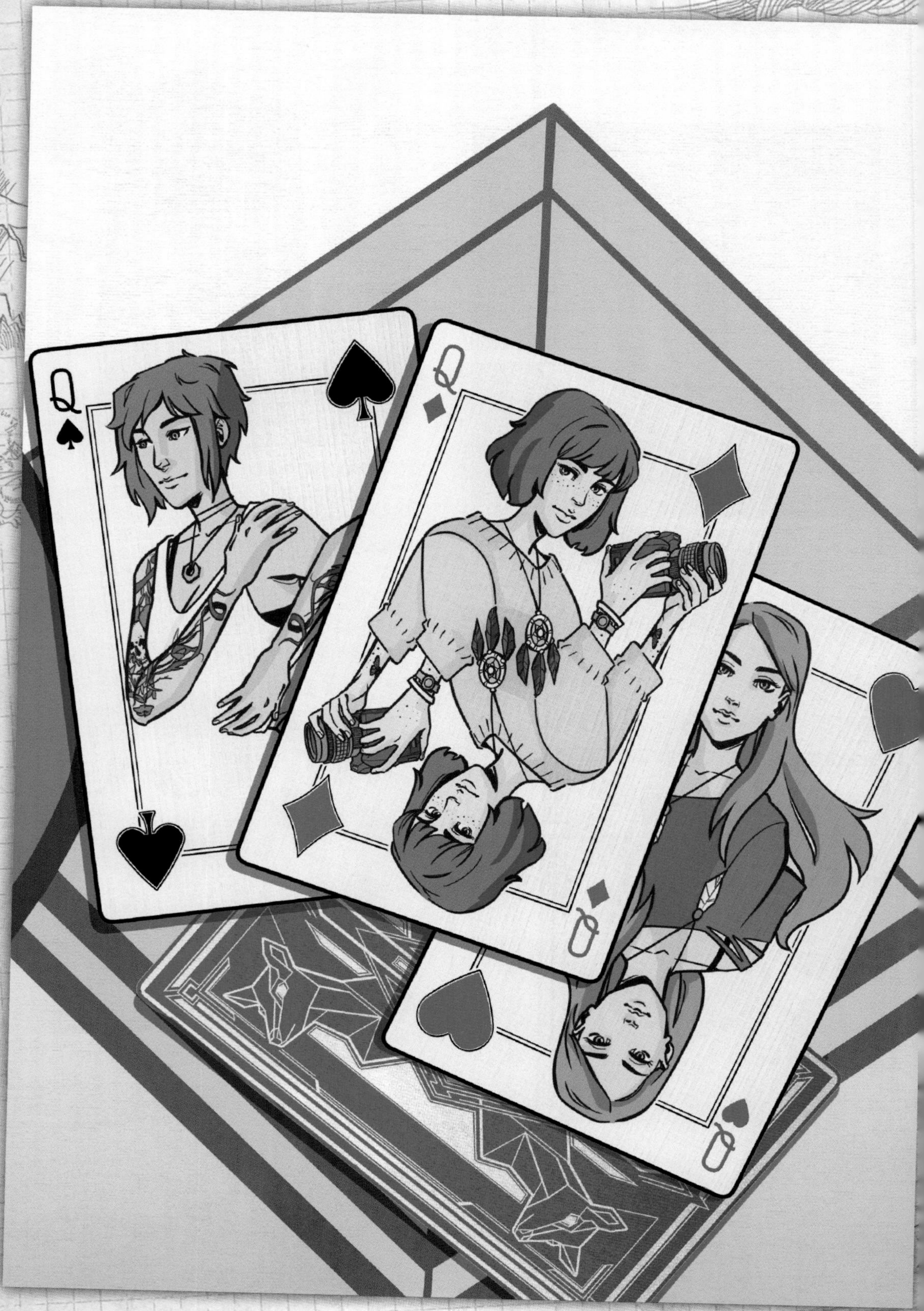

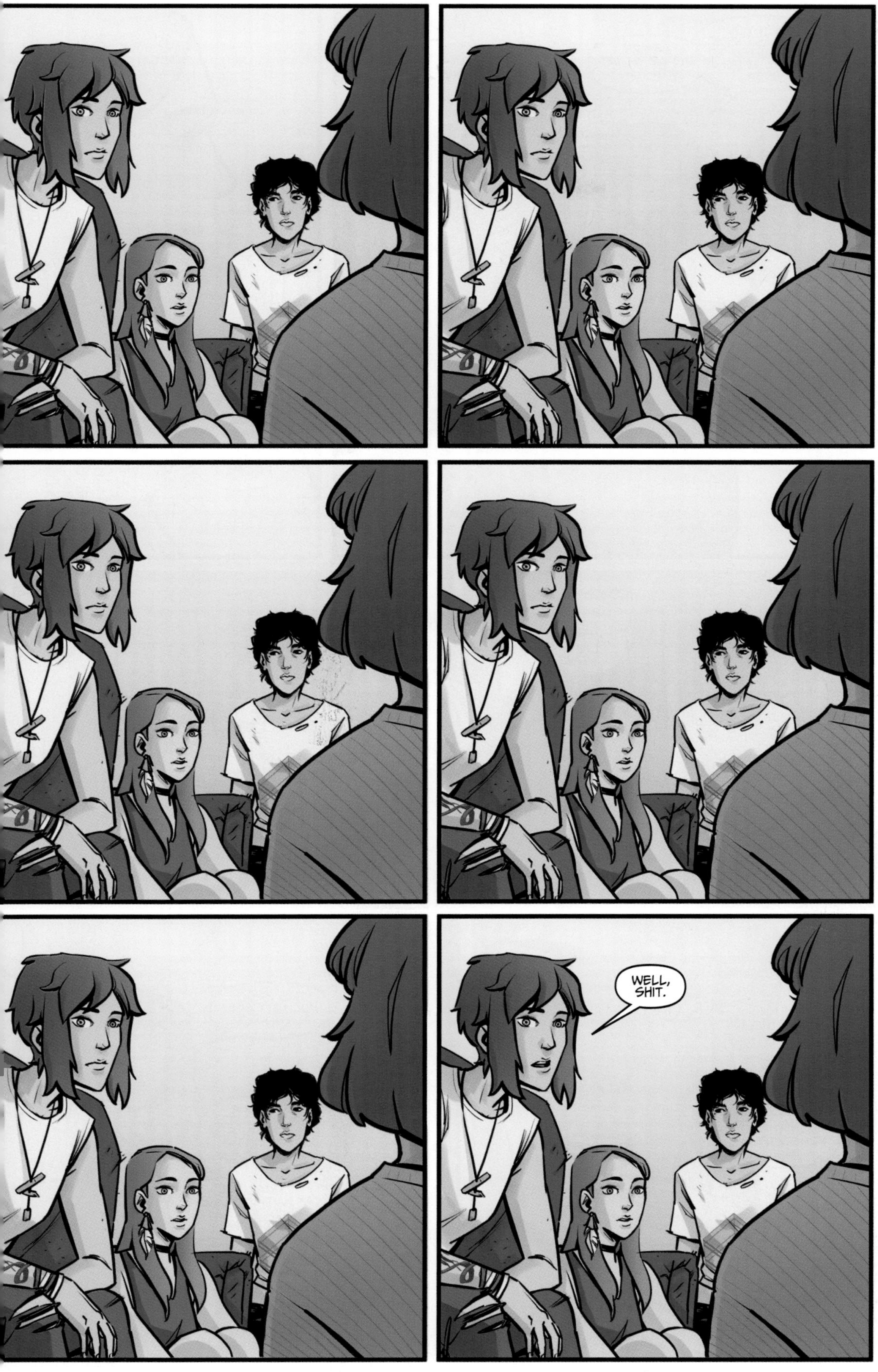
WELL, SHIT.

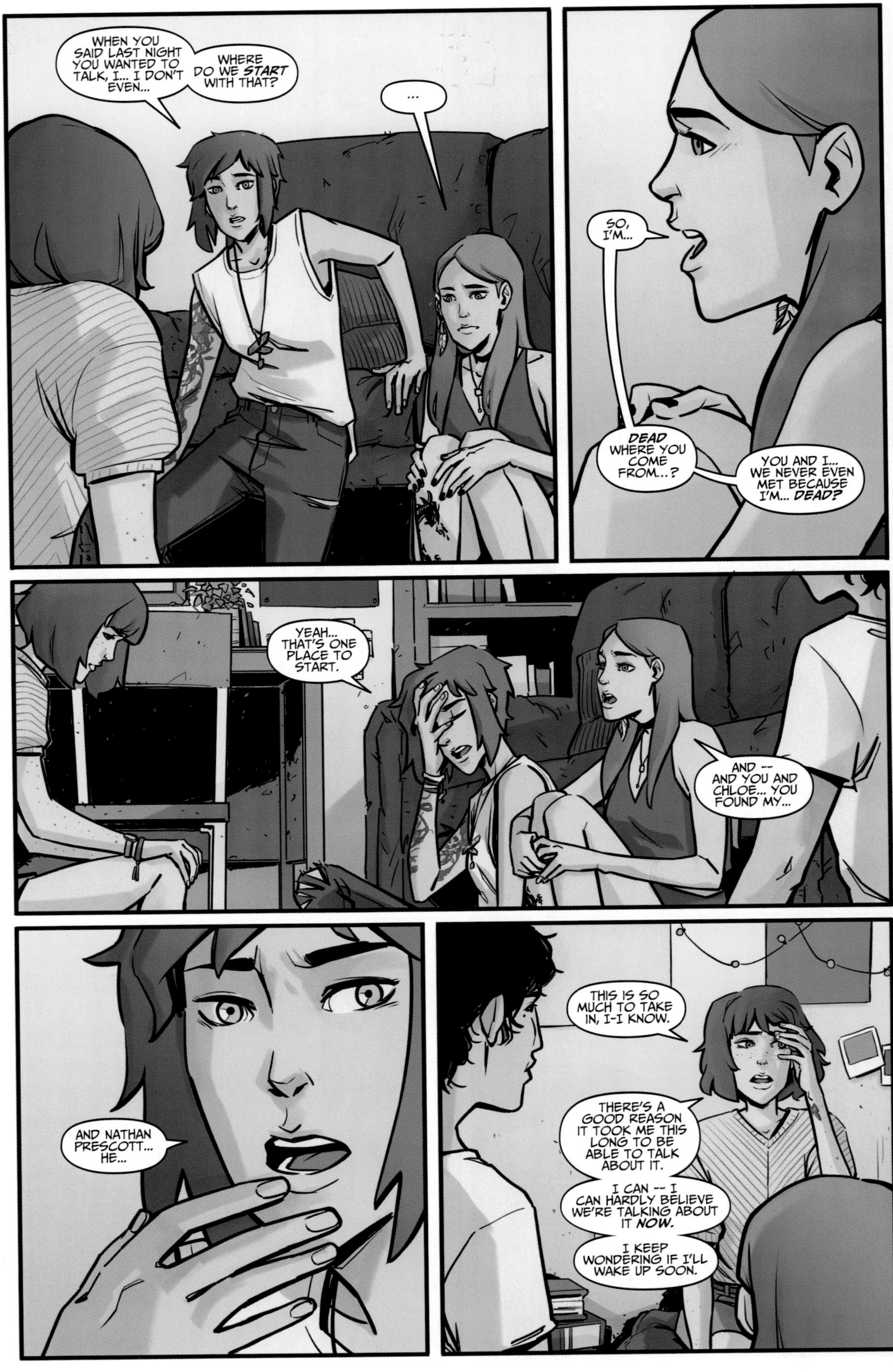
WHEN YOU SAID LAST NIGHT YOU WANTED TO TALK, I... I DON'T EVEN...
WHERE DO WE *START* WITH THAT?
...
SO, I'M...
DEAD WHERE YOU COME FROM...?
YOU AND I... WE NEVER EVEN MET BECAUSE I'M... *DEAD?*
YEAH... THAT'S ONE PLACE TO START.
AND -- AND YOU AND CHLOE... YOU FOUND MY...
AND NATHAN PRESCOTT... HE...
THIS IS SO MUCH TO TAKE IN, I-I KNOW.
THERE'S A GOOD REASON IT TOOK ME THIS LONG TO BE ABLE TO TALK ABOUT IT.
I CAN -- I CAN HARDLY BELIEVE WE'RE TALKING ABOUT IT *NOW.*
I KEEP WONDERING IF I'LL WAKE UP SOON.

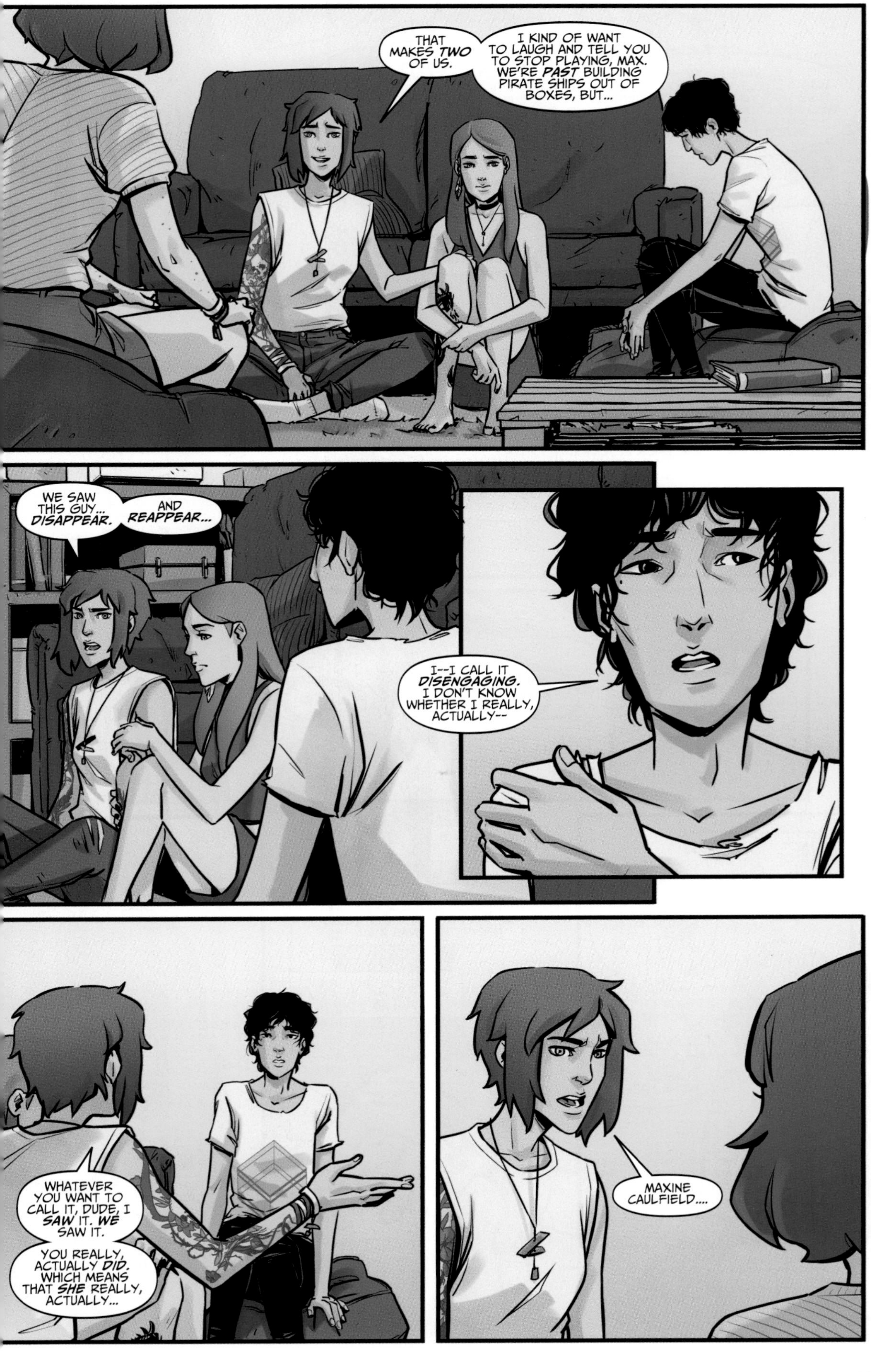
THAT MAKES *TWO* OF US.
I KIND OF WANT TO LAUGH AND TELL YOU TO STOP PLAYING, MAX. WE'RE *PAST* BUILDING PIRATE SHIPS OUT OF BOXES, BUT...
WE SAW THIS GUY... *DISAPPEAR.*
AND *REAPPEAR...*
I--I CALL IT *DISENGAGING.* I DON'T KNOW WHETHER I REALLY, ACTUALLY--
WHATEVER YOU WANT TO CALL IT, DUDE, I *SAW* IT. *WE* SAW IT.
YOU REALLY, ACTUALLY *DID.* WHICH MEANS THAT *SHE* REALLY, ACTUALLY...
MAXINE CAULFIELD....

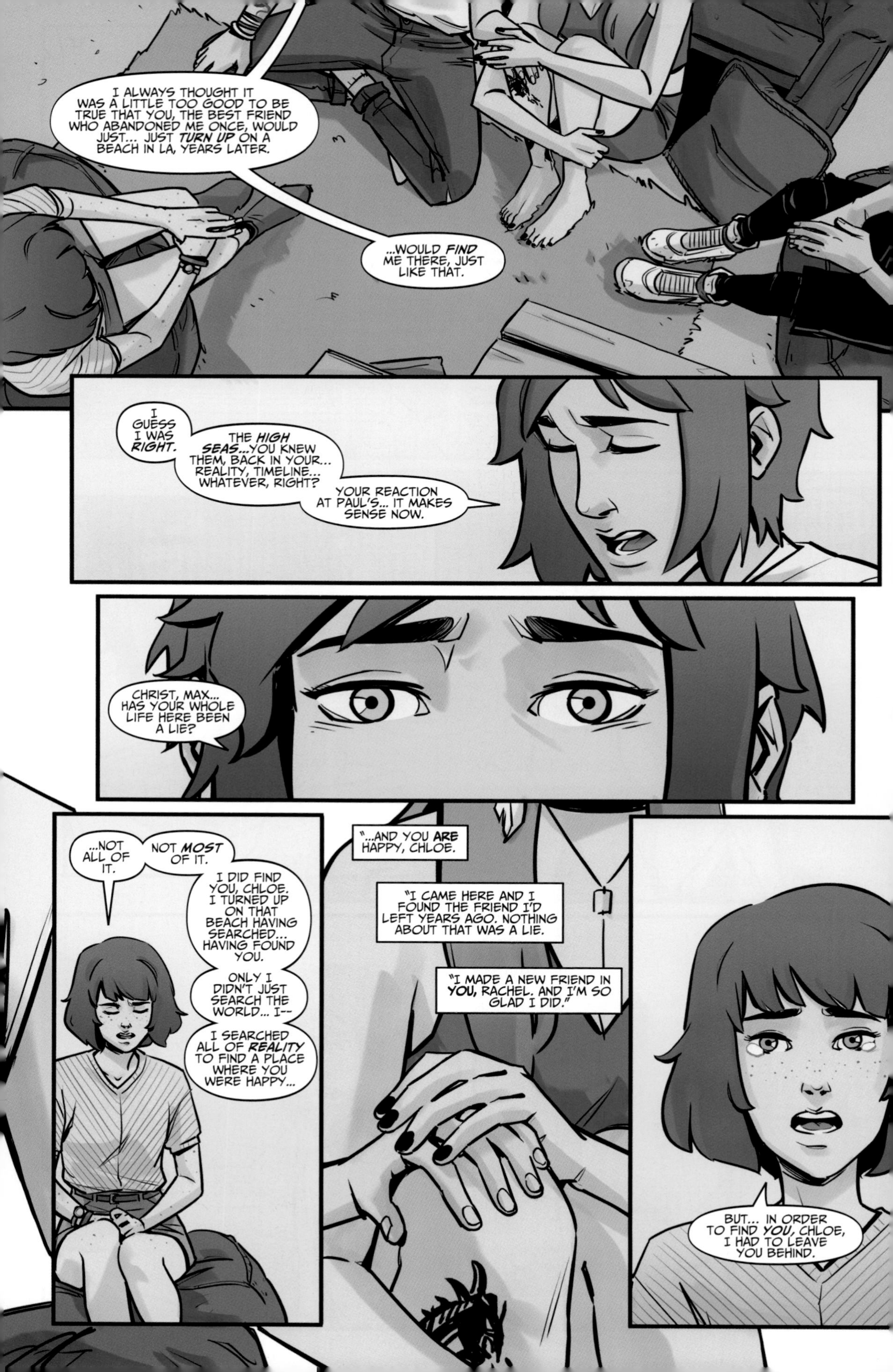
I ALWAYS THOUGHT IT WAS A LITTLE TOO GOOD TO BE TRUE THAT YOU, THE BEST FRIEND WHO ABANDONED ME ONCE, WOULD JUST... JUST TURN UP ON A BEACH IN LA, YEARS LATER.
...WOULD FIND ME THERE, JUST LIKE THAT.
I GUESS I WAS RIGHT.
THE HIGH SEAS...YOU KNEW THEM, BACK IN YOUR... REALITY, TIMELINE... WHATEVER, RIGHT?
YOUR REACTION AT PAUL'S... IT MAKES SENSE NOW.
CHRIST, MAX... HAS YOUR WHOLE LIFE HERE BEEN A LIE?
...NOT ALL OF IT.
NOT MOST OF IT.
I DID FIND YOU, CHLOE. I TURNED UP ON THAT BEACH HAVING SEARCHED... HAVING FOUND YOU.
ONLY I DIDN'T JUST SEARCH THE WORLD... I--
I SEARCHED ALL OF REALITY TO FIND A PLACE WHERE YOU WERE HAPPY...
"...AND YOU ARE HAPPY, CHLOE.
"I CAME HERE AND I FOUND THE FRIEND I'D LEFT YEARS AGO. NOTHING ABOUT THAT WAS A LIE.
"I MADE A NEW FRIEND IN YOU, RACHEL. AND I'M SO GLAD I DID."
BUT... IN ORDER TO FIND YOU, CHLOE, I HAD TO LEAVE YOU BEHIND.

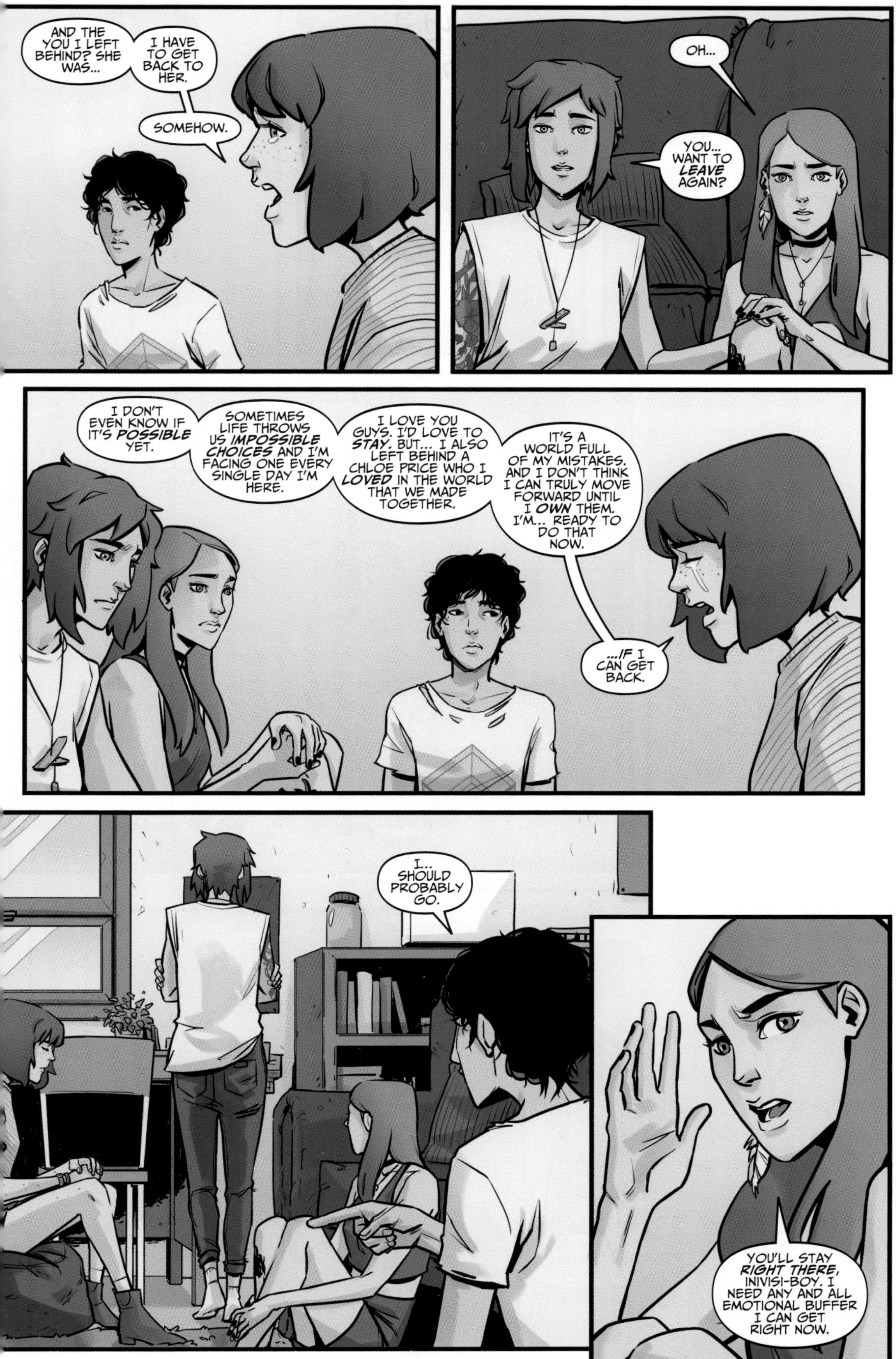

AND THE YOU I LEFT BEHIND? SHE WAS...
I HAVE TO GET BACK TO HER.
SOMEHOW.
OH...
YOU... WANT TO *LEAVE* AGAIN?
I DON'T EVEN KNOW IF IT'S *POSSIBLE* YET.
SOMETIMES LIFE THROWS US *IMPOSSIBLE CHOICES* AND I'M FACING ONE EVERY SINGLE DAY I'M HERE.
I LOVE YOU GUYS. I'D LOVE TO *STAY*. BUT... I ALSO LEFT BEHIND A CHLOE PRICE WHO I *LOVED* IN THE WORLD THAT WE MADE TOGETHER.
IT'S A WORLD FULL OF MY MISTAKES. AND I DON'T THINK I CAN TRULY MOVE FORWARD UNTIL I *OWN* THEM. I'M... READY TO DO THAT NOW.
...*IF* I CAN GET BACK.
I... SHOULD PROBABLY GO.
YOU'LL STAY *RIGHT THERE,* INIVISI-BOY. I NEED ANY AND ALL EMOTIONAL BUFFER I CAN GET RIGHT NOW.

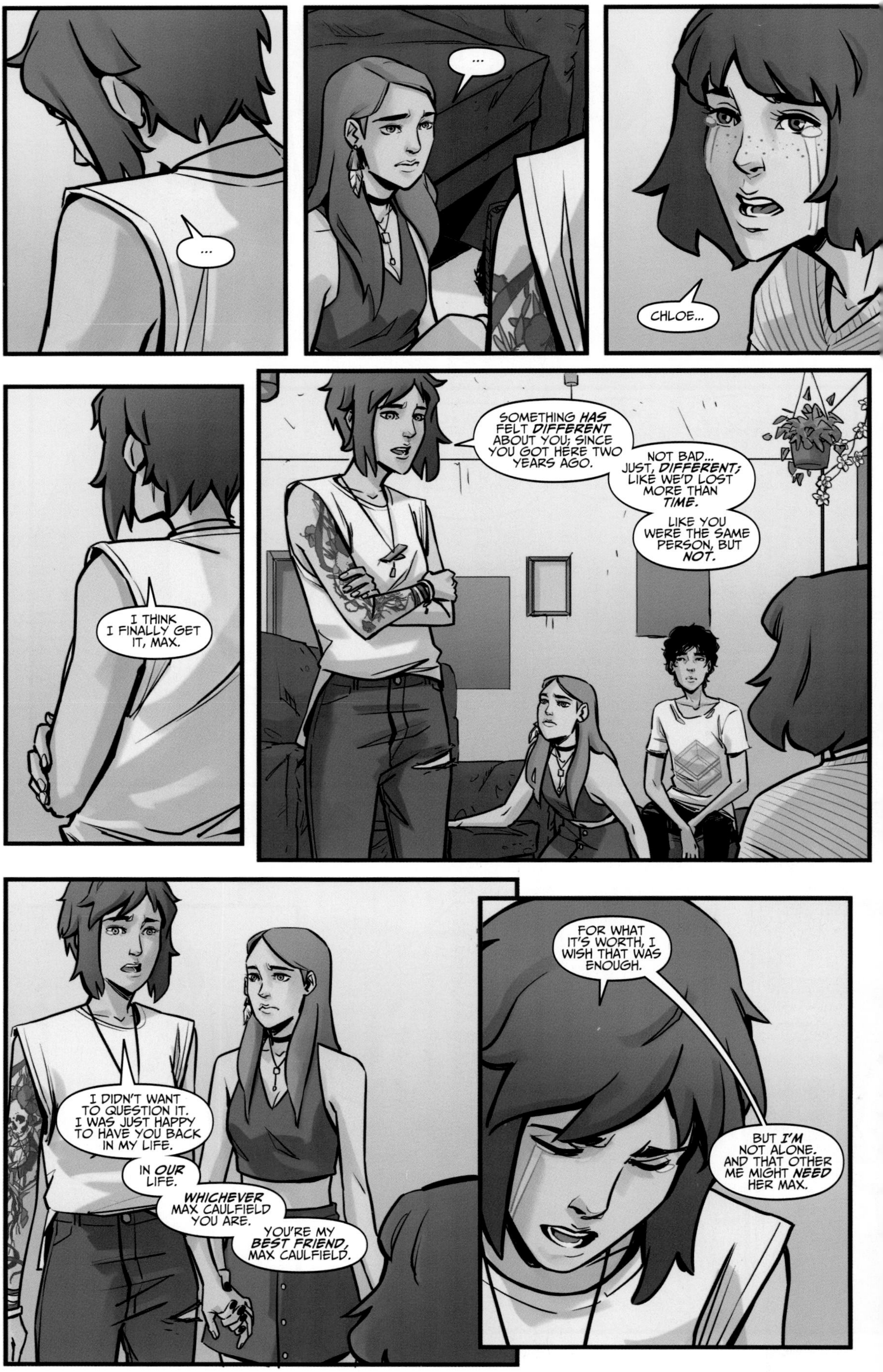
...
...
CHLOE...
I THINK I FINALLY GET IT, MAX.
SOMETHING HAS FELT DIFFERENT ABOUT YOU; SINCE YOU GOT HERE TWO YEARS AGO.
NOT BAD... JUST, DIFFERENT; LIKE WE'D LOST MORE THAN TIME.
LIKE YOU WERE THE SAME PERSON, BUT NOT.
I DIDN'T WANT TO QUESTION IT. I WAS JUST HAPPY TO HAVE YOU BACK IN MY LIFE.
IN OUR LIFE.
WHICHEVER MAX CAULFIELD YOU ARE.
YOU'RE MY BEST FRIEND, MAX CAULFIELD.
FOR WHAT IT'S WORTH, I WISH THAT WAS ENOUGH.
BUT I'M NOT ALONE. AND THAT OTHER ME MIGHT NEED HER MAX.

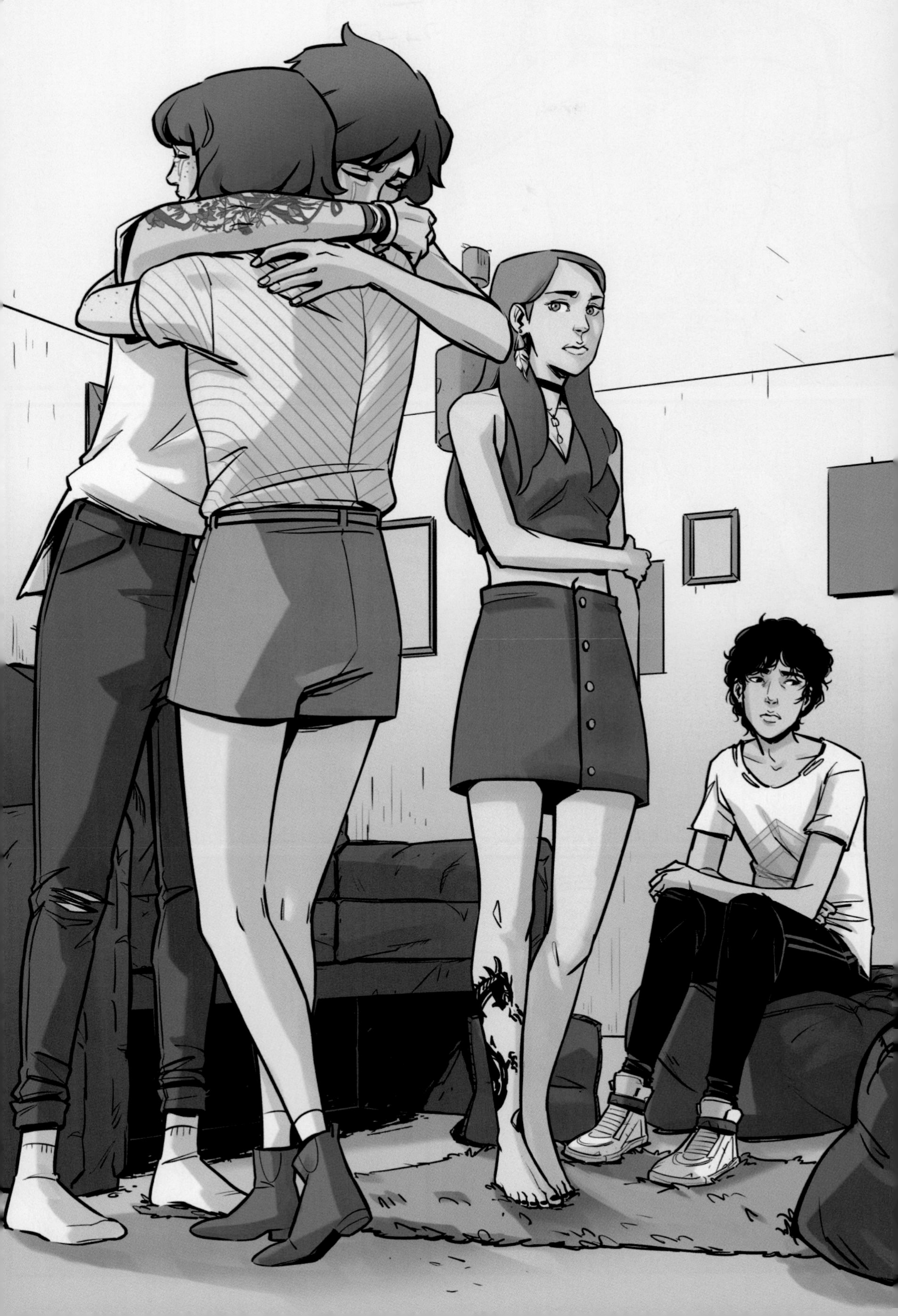

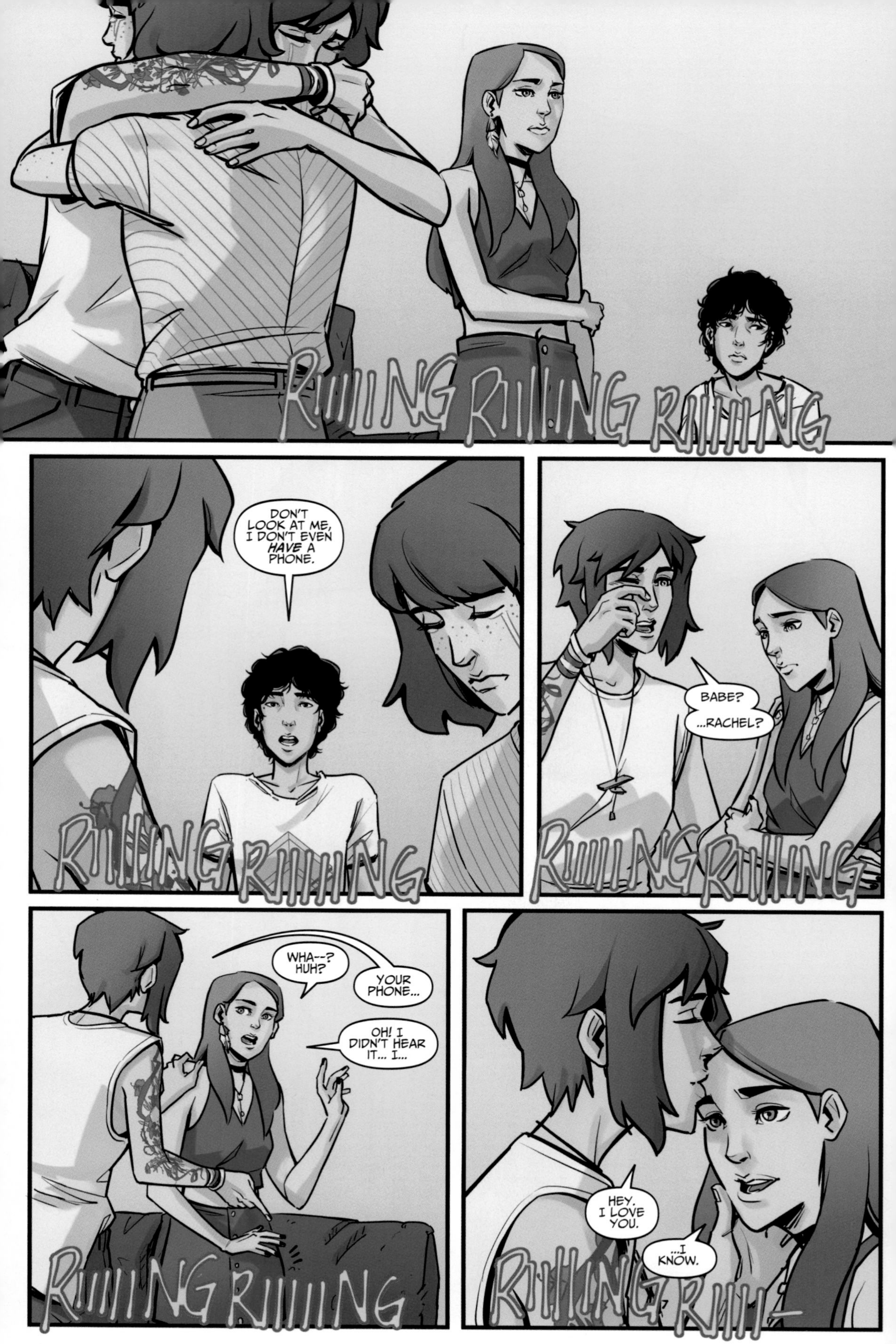
RIIIING RIIIING RIIIING
DON'T LOOK AT ME, I DON'T EVEN *HAVE* A PHONE.
RIIIING RIIIING
BABE?
...RACHEL?
RIIIING RIIIING
WHA--? HUH?
YOUR PHONE...
OH! I DIDN'T HEAR IT... I...
RIIIING RIIIING
HEY. I LOVE YOU.
...I KNOW.

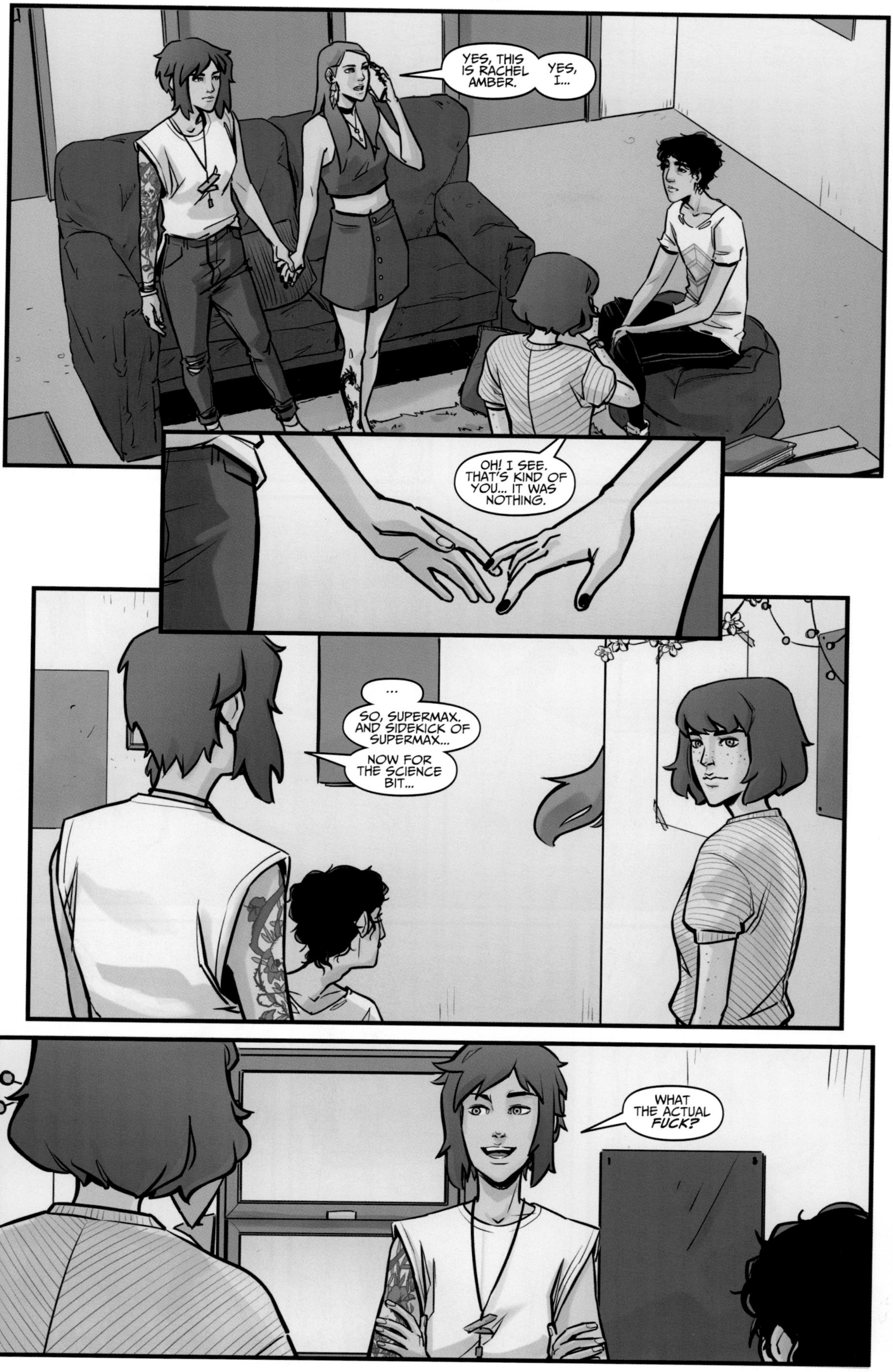
YES, THIS IS RACHEL AMBER.
YES, I...
OH! I SEE. THAT'S KIND OF YOU... IT WAS NOTHING.
...
SO, SUPERMAX. AND SIDEKICK OF SUPERMAX...
NOW FOR THE SCIENCE BIT...
WHAT THE ACTUAL *FUCK?*

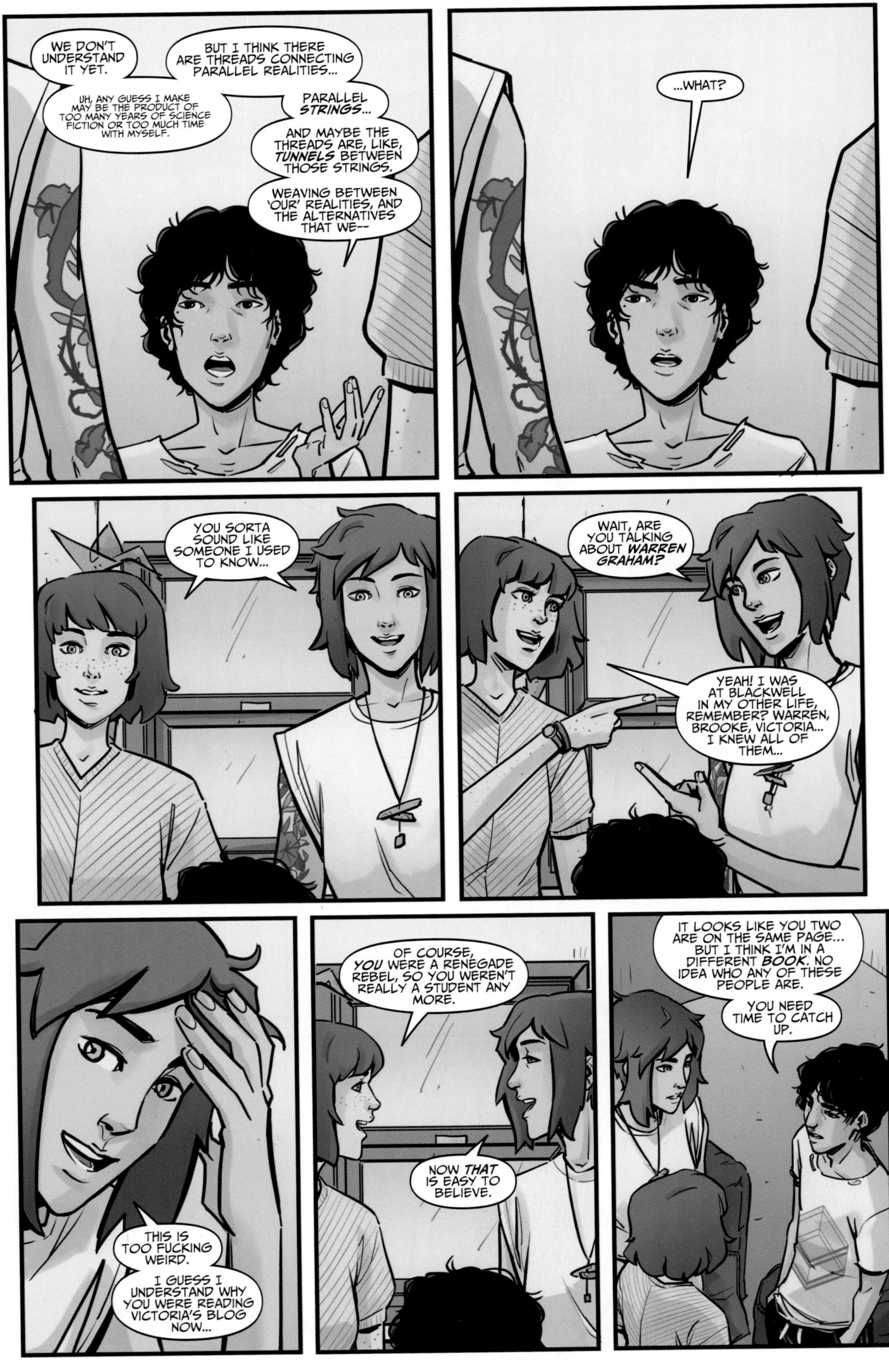
WE DON'T UNDERSTAND IT YET.
BUT I THINK THERE ARE THREADS CONNECTING PARALLEL REALITIES...
UH, ANY GUESS I MAKE MAY BE THE PRODUCT OF TOO MANY YEARS OF SCIENCE FICTION OR TOO MUCH TIME WITH MYSELF.
PARALLEL STRINGS...
AND MAYBE THE THREADS ARE, LIKE, TUNNELS BETWEEN THOSE STRINGS.
WEAVING BETWEEN 'OUR' REALITIES, AND THE ALTERNATIVES THAT WE--
...WHAT?
YOU SORTA SOUND LIKE SOMEONE I USED TO KNOW...
WAIT, ARE YOU TALKING ABOUT WARREN GRAHAM?
YEAH! I WAS AT BLACKWELL IN MY OTHER LIFE, REMEMBER? WARREN, BROOKE, VICTORIA... I KNEW ALL OF THEM...
THIS IS TOO FUCKING WEIRD.
I GUESS I UNDERSTAND WHY YOU WERE READING VICTORIA'S BLOG NOW...
OF COURSE, YOU WERE A RENEGADE REBEL, SO YOU WEREN'T REALLY A STUDENT ANY MORE.
NOW THAT IS EASY TO BELIEVE.
IT LOOKS LIKE YOU TWO ARE ON THE SAME PAGE... BUT I THINK I'M IN A DIFFERENT BOOK. NO IDEA WHO ANY OF THESE PEOPLE ARE.
YOU NEED TIME TO CATCH UP.

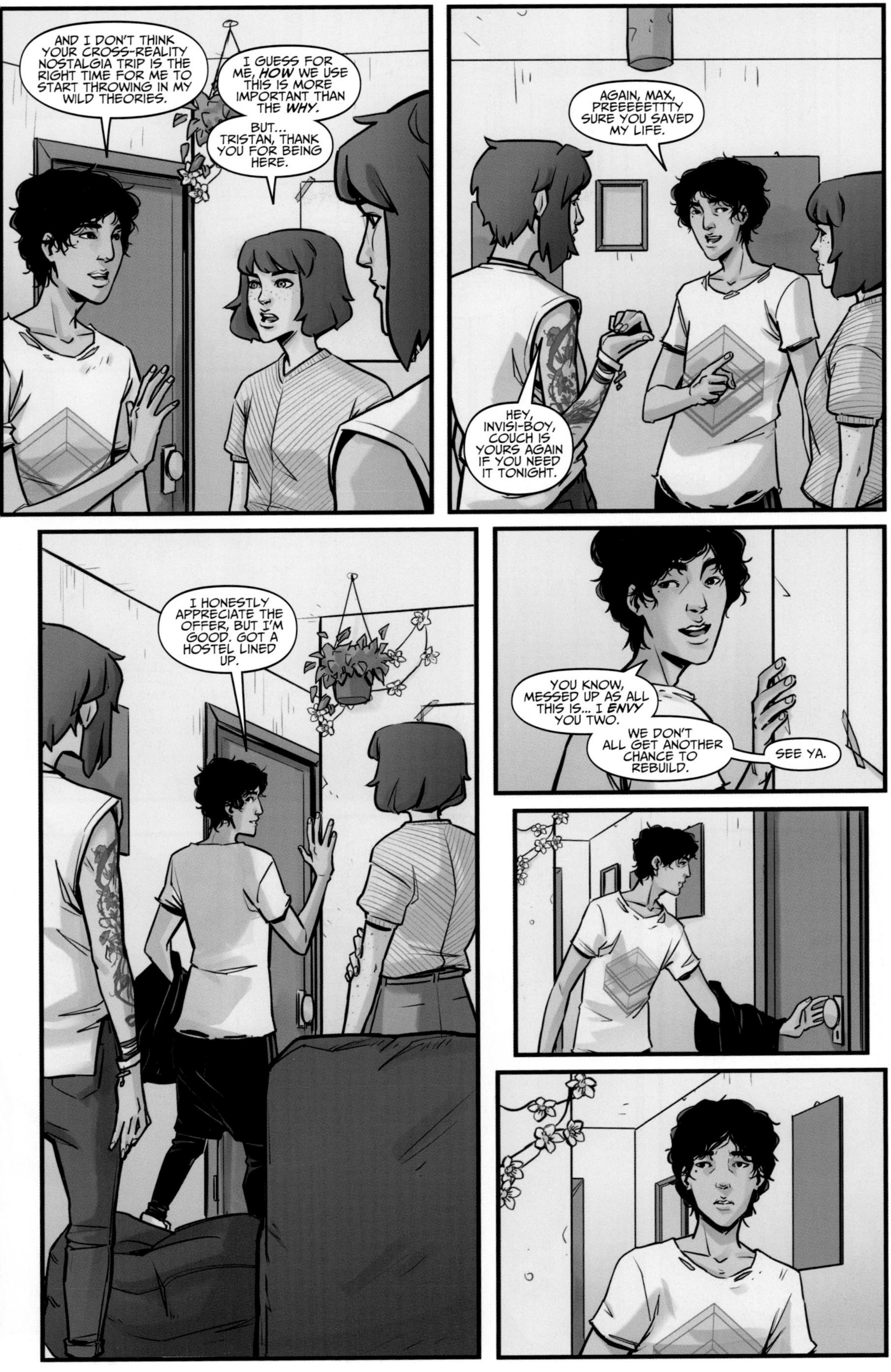

AND I DON'T THINK YOUR CROSS-REALITY NOSTALGIA TRIP IS THE RIGHT TIME FOR ME TO START THROWING IN MY WILD THEORIES.
I GUESS FOR ME, **HOW** WE USE THIS IS MORE IMPORTANT THAN THE ***WHY.***
BUT... TRISTAN, THANK YOU FOR BEING HERE.
AGAIN, MAX, PREEEEETTTY SURE YOU SAVED MY LIFE.
HEY, INVISI-BOY, COUCH IS YOURS AGAIN IF YOU NEED IT TONIGHT.
I HONESTLY APPRECIATE THE OFFER, BUT I'M GOOD. GOT A HOSTEL LINED UP.
YOU KNOW, MESSED UP AS ALL THIS IS... I ***ENVY*** YOU TWO.
WE DON'T ALL GET ANOTHER CHANCE TO REBUILD.
SEE YA.

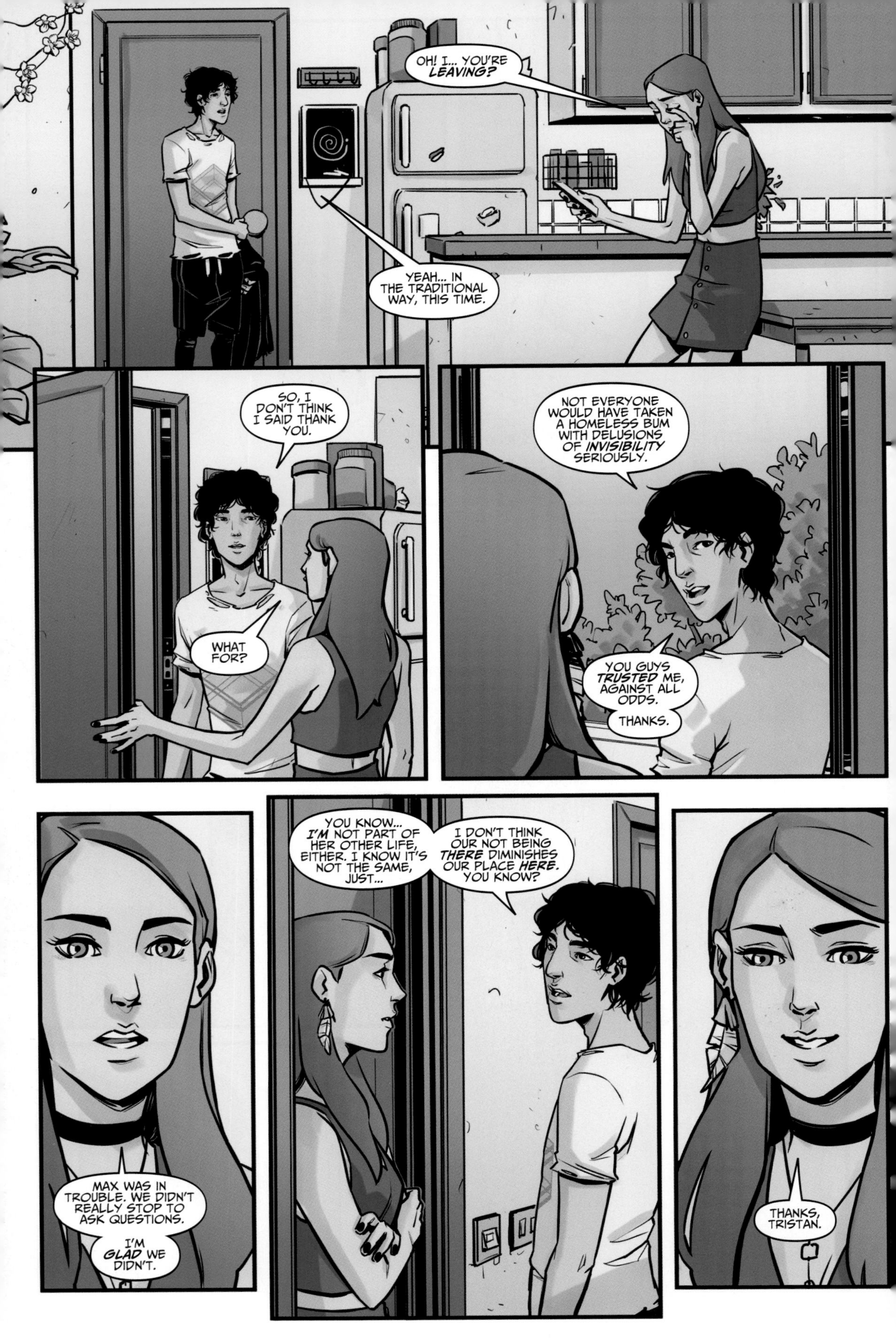
OH! I... YOU'RE LEAVING?
YEAH... IN THE TRADITIONAL WAY, THIS TIME.
SO, I DON'T THINK I SAID THANK YOU.
WHAT FOR?
NOT EVERYONE WOULD HAVE TAKEN A HOMELESS BUM WITH DELUSIONS OF INVISIBILITY SERIOUSLY.
YOU GUYS TRUSTED ME, AGAINST ALL ODDS.
THANKS.
MAX WAS IN TROUBLE. WE DIDN'T REALLY STOP TO ASK QUESTIONS.
I'M GLAD WE DIDN'T.
YOU KNOW... I'M NOT PART OF HER OTHER LIFE, EITHER. I KNOW IT'S NOT THE SAME, JUST...
I DON'T THINK OUR NOT BEING THERE DIMINISHES OUR PLACE HERE. YOU KNOW?
THANKS, TRISTAN.

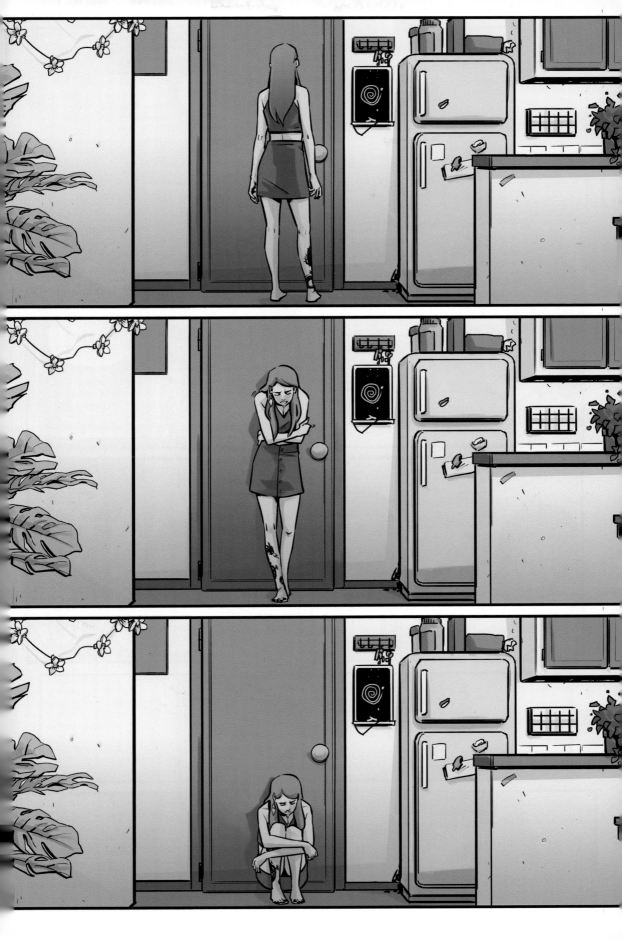

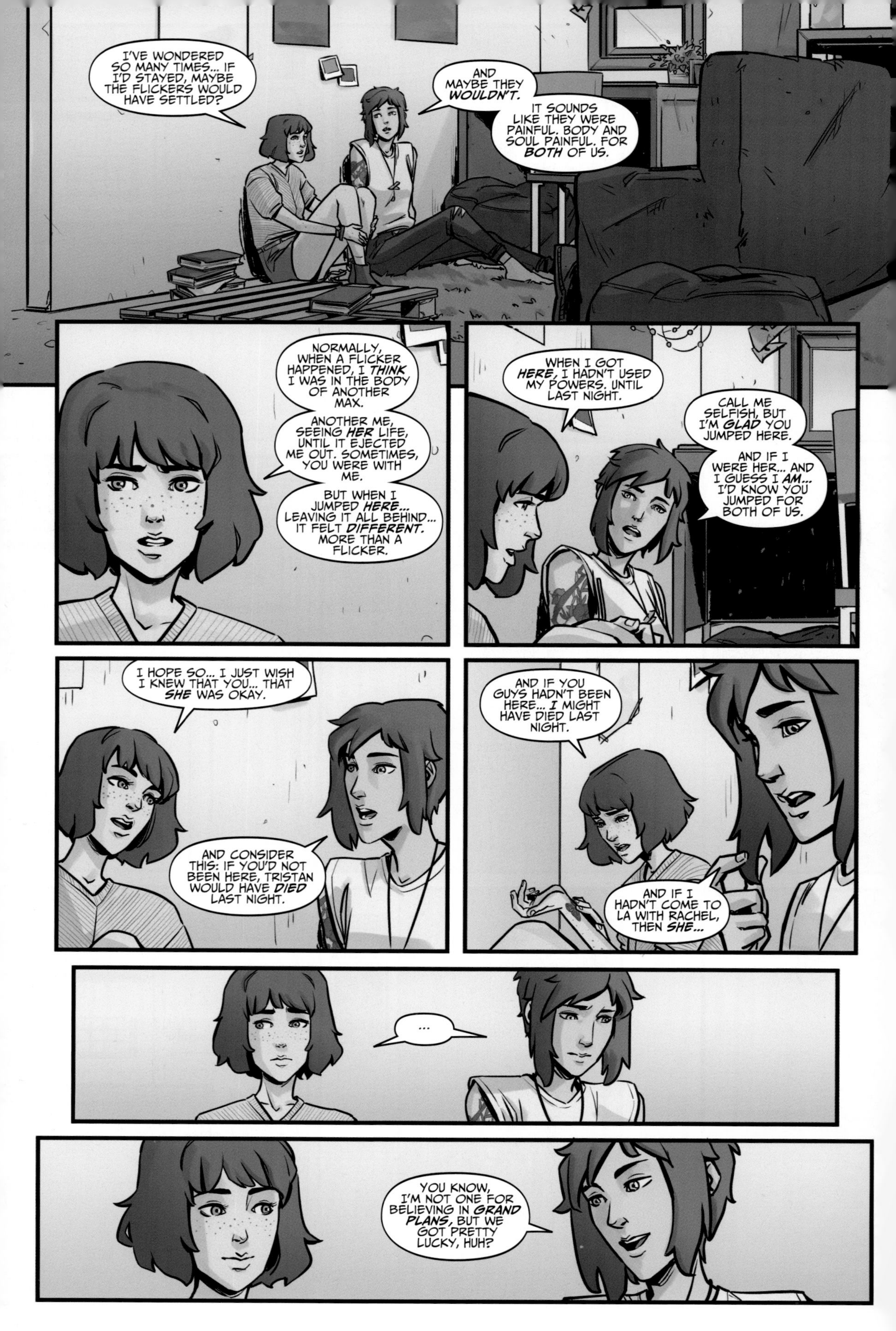
I'VE WONDERED SO MANY TIMES... IF I'D STAYED, MAYBE THE FLICKERS WOULD HAVE SETTLED?
AND MAYBE THEY *WOULDN'T.*
IT SOUNDS LIKE THEY WERE PAINFUL. BODY AND SOUL PAINFUL. FOR *BOTH* OF US.
NORMALLY, WHEN A FLICKER HAPPENED, I *THINK* I WAS IN THE BODY OF ANOTHER MAX.
ANOTHER ME, SEEING *HER* LIFE, UNTIL IT EJECTED ME OUT. SOMETIMES, YOU WERE WITH ME.
BUT WHEN I JUMPED *HERE...* LEAVING IT ALL BEHIND... IT FELT *DIFFERENT.* MORE THAN A FLICKER.
WHEN I GOT *HERE,* I HADN'T USED MY POWERS. UNTIL LAST NIGHT.
CALL ME SELFISH, BUT I'M *GLAD* YOU JUMPED HERE.
AND IF I WERE HER... AND I GUESS I *AM...* I'D KNOW YOU JUMPED FOR BOTH OF US.
I HOPE SO... I JUST WISH I KNEW THAT YOU... THAT *SHE* WAS OKAY.
AND CONSIDER THIS: IF YOU'D NOT BEEN HERE, TRISTAN WOULD HAVE *DIED* LAST NIGHT.
AND IF YOU GUYS HADN'T BEEN HERE... *I* MIGHT HAVE DIED LAST NIGHT.
AND IF I HADN'T COME TO LA WITH RACHEL, THEN *SHE...*
...
YOU KNOW, I'M NOT ONE FOR BELIEVING IN *GRAND PLANS,* BUT WE GOT PRETTY LUCKY, HUH?

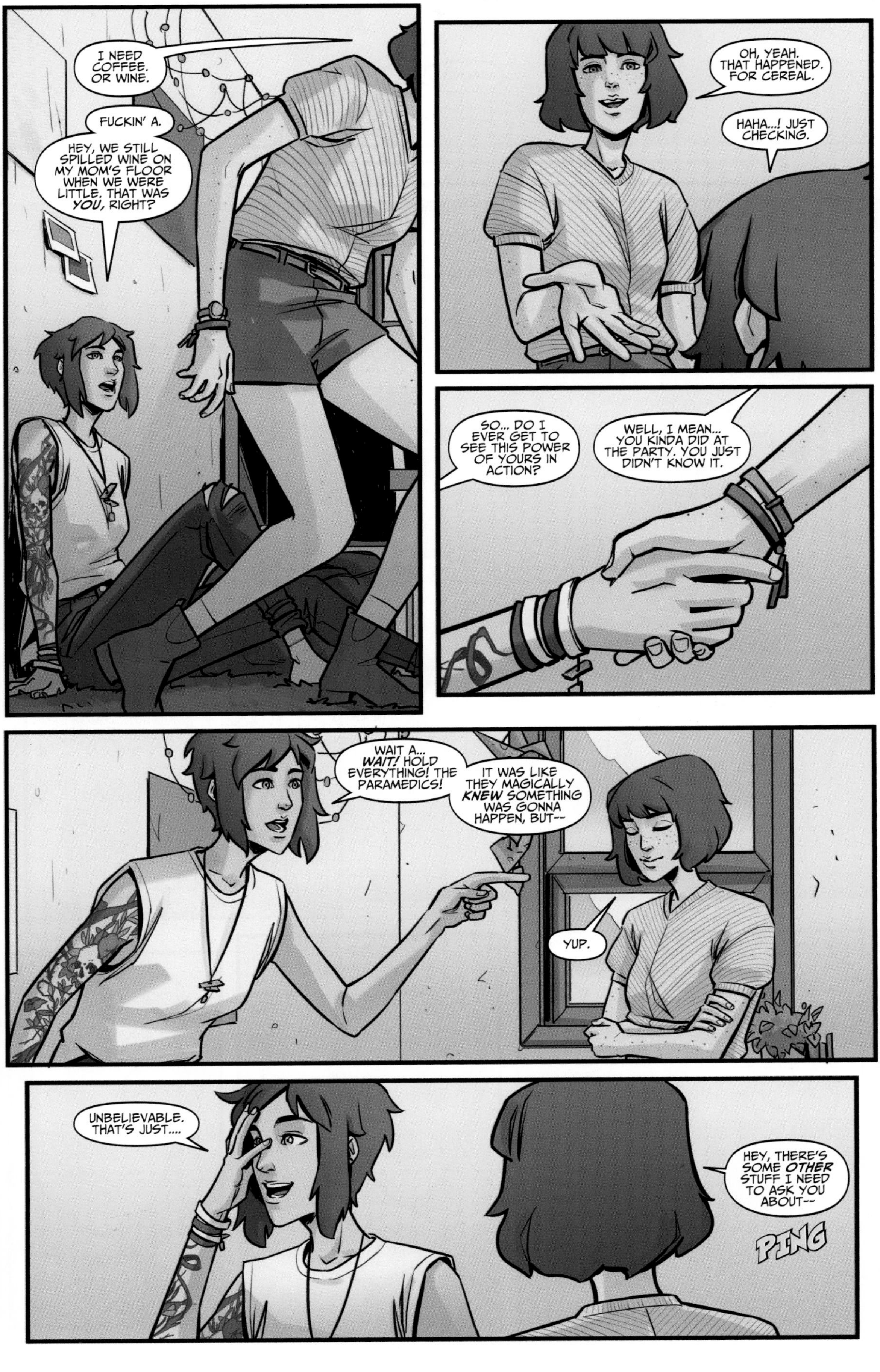
I NEED COFFEE. OR WINE.
FUCKIN' A.
HEY, WE STILL SPILLED WINE ON MY MOM'S FLOOR WHEN WE WERE LITTLE. THAT WAS *YOU,* RIGHT?
OH, YEAH. THAT HAPPENED. FOR CEREAL.
HAHA...! JUST CHECKING.
SO... DO I EVER GET TO SEE THIS POWER OF YOURS IN ACTION?
WELL, I MEAN... YOU KINDA DID AT THE PARTY. YOU JUST DIDN'T KNOW IT.
WAIT A... *WAIT!* HOLD EVERYTHING! THE PARAMEDICS!
IT WAS LIKE THEY MAGICALLY *KNEW* SOMETHING WAS GONNA HAPPEN, BUT--
YUP.
UNBELIEVABLE. THAT'S JUST....
HEY, THERE'S SOME *OTHER* STUFF I NEED TO ASK YOU ABOUT--
PING

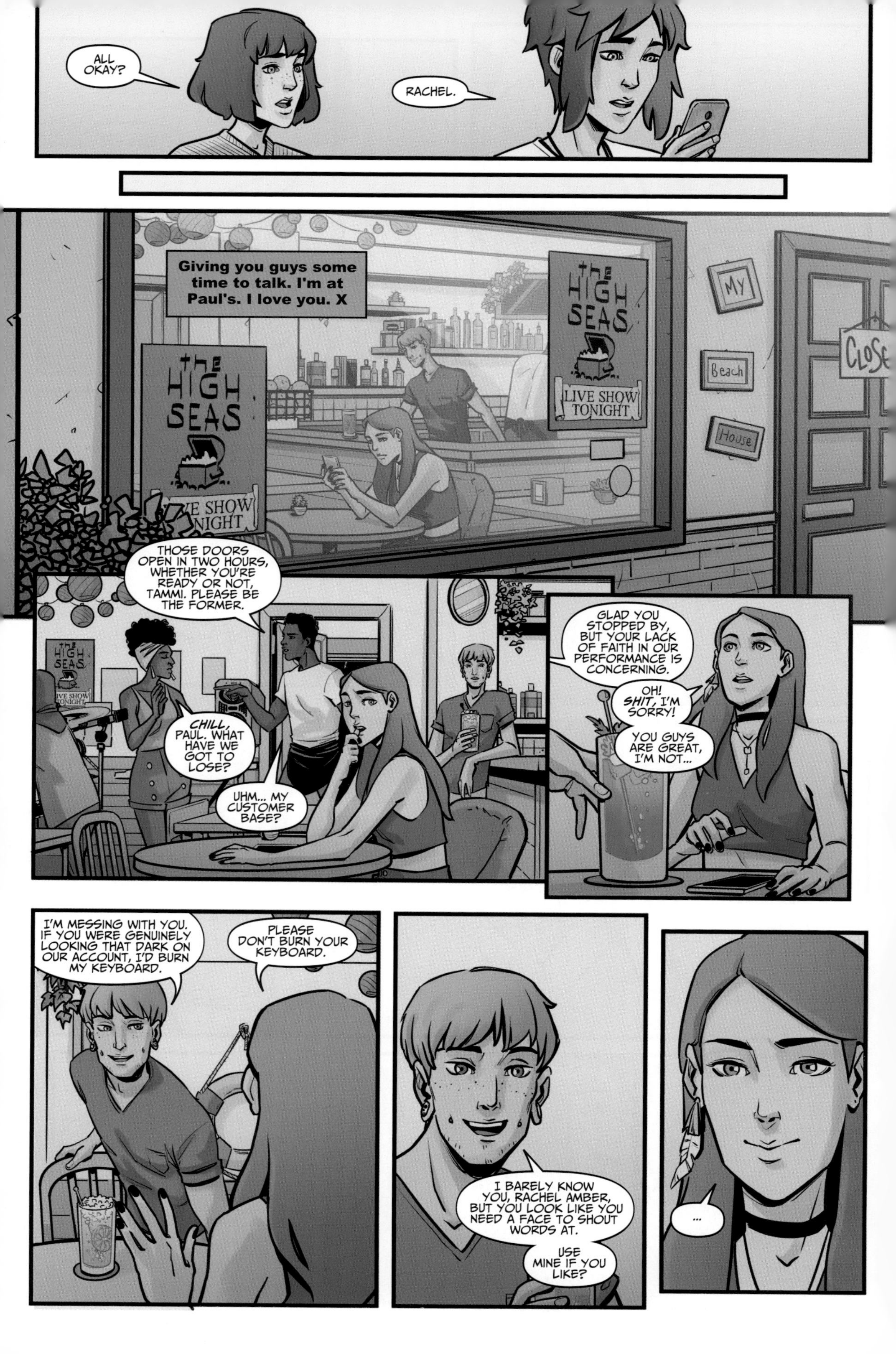
ALL OKAY?
RACHEL.
Giving you guys some time to talk. I'm at Paul's. I love you. X
the HIGH SEAS
LIVE SHOW TONIGHT
the HIGH SEAS
LIVE SHOW TONIGHT
My
Beach
House
CLOSE
THOSE DOORS OPEN IN TWO HOURS, WHETHER YOU'RE READY OR NOT, TAMMI. PLEASE BE THE FORMER.
CHILL, PAUL. WHAT HAVE WE GOT TO LOSE?
UHM... MY CUSTOMER BASE?
GLAD YOU STOPPED BY, BUT YOUR LACK OF FAITH IN OUR PERFORMANCE IS CONCERNING.
OH! SHIT, I'M SORRY!
YOU GUYS ARE GREAT, I'M NOT...
I'M MESSING WITH YOU. IF YOU WERE GENUINELY LOOKING THAT DARK ON OUR ACCOUNT, I'D BURN MY KEYBOARD.
PLEASE DON'T BURN YOUR KEYBOARD.
I BARELY KNOW YOU, RACHEL AMBER, BUT YOU LOOK LIKE YOU NEED A FACE TO SHOUT WORDS AT.
USE MINE IF YOU LIKE?
...

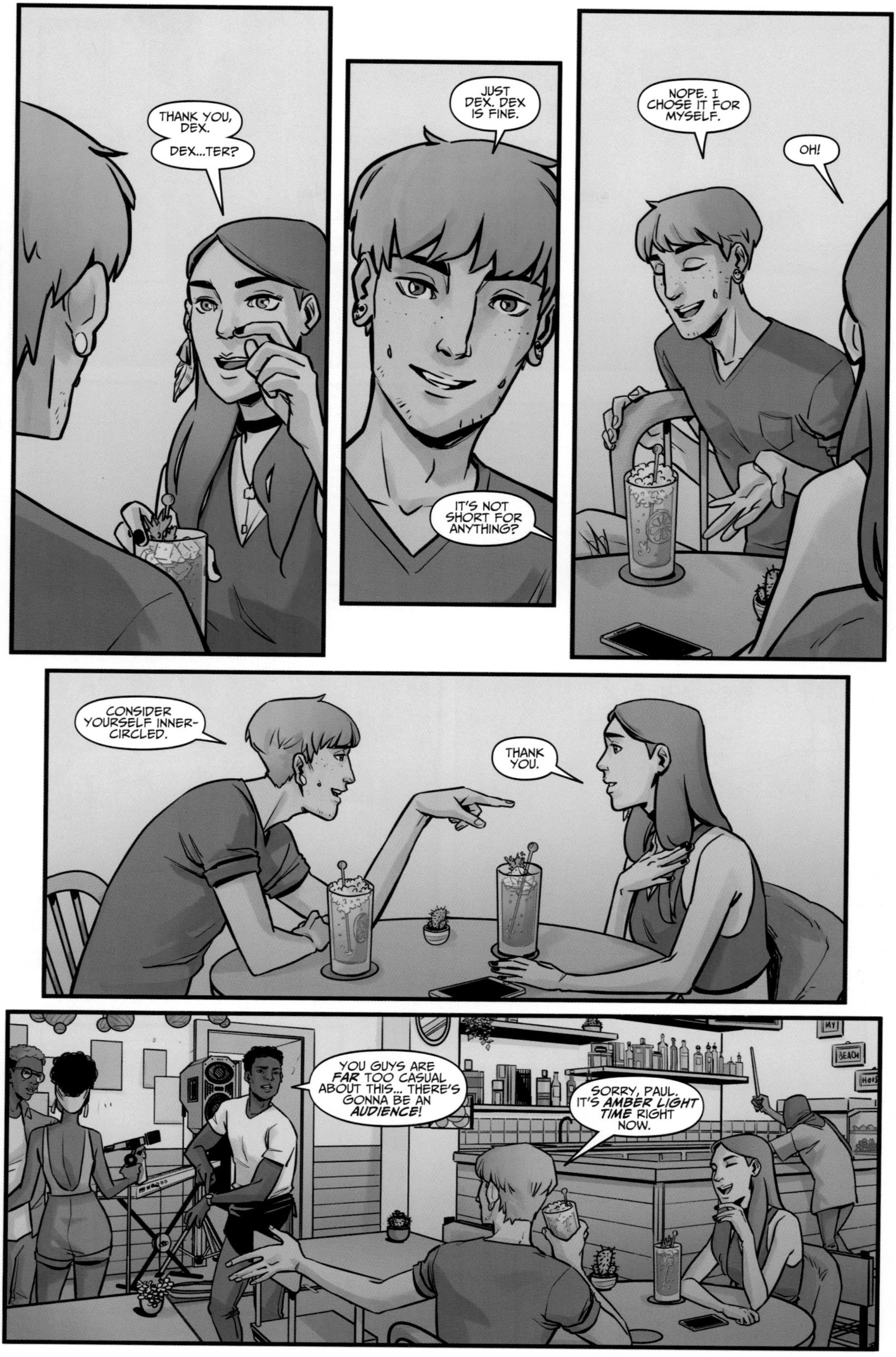
THANK YOU, DEX.
DEX...TER?
JUST DEX. DEX IS FINE.
IT'S NOT SHORT FOR ANYTHING?
NOPE. I CHOSE IT FOR MYSELF.
OH!
CONSIDER YOURSELF INNER-CIRCLED.
THANK YOU.
YOU GUYS ARE *FAR* TOO CASUAL ABOUT THIS... THERE'S GONNA BE AN *AUDIENCE*!
SORRY, PAUL. IT'S *AMBER LIGHT TIME* RIGHT NOW.
MY
BEACH

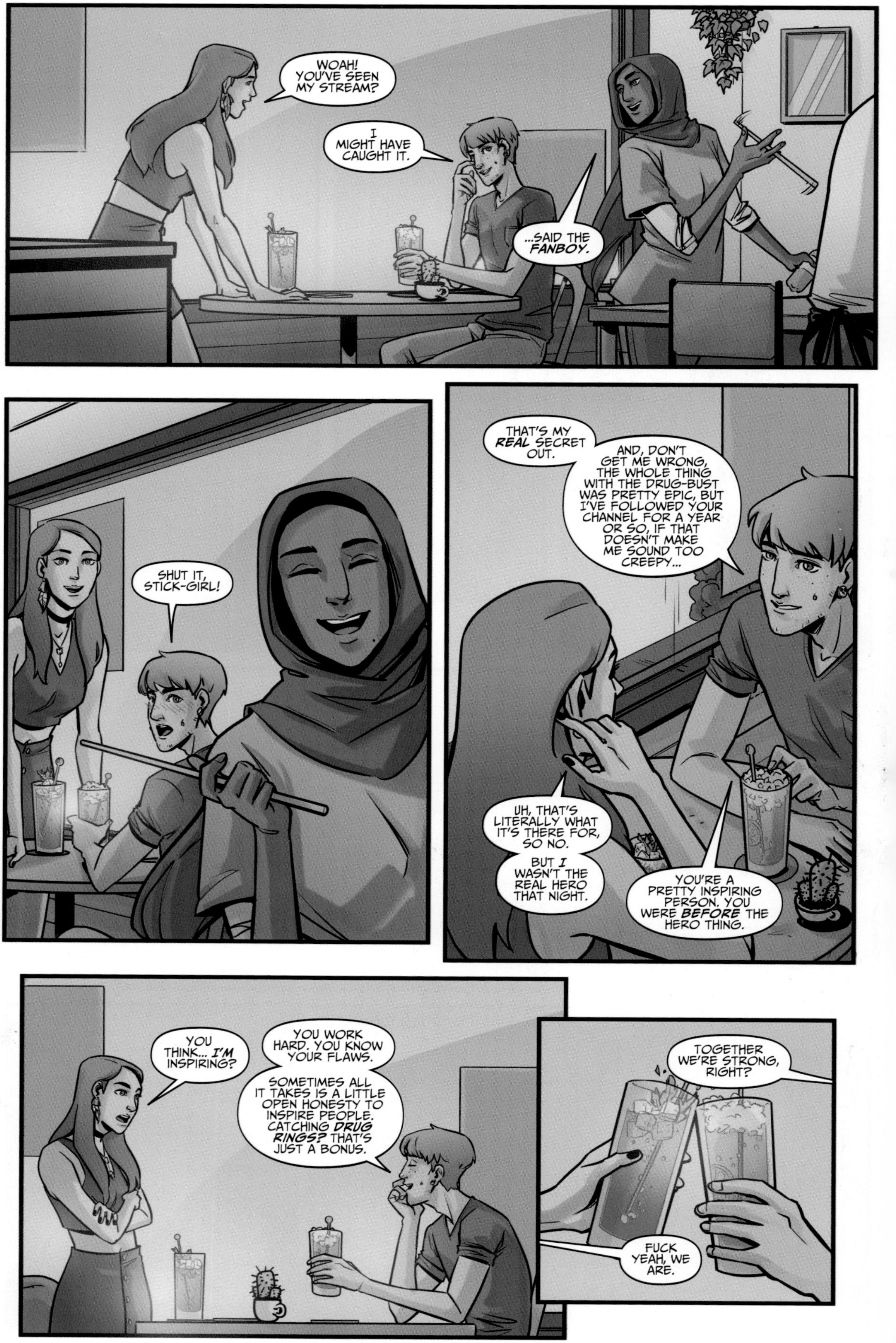

WOAH! YOU'VE SEEN MY STREAM?
I MIGHT HAVE CAUGHT IT.
...SAID THE FANBOY.
SHUT IT, STICK-GIRL!
THAT'S MY REAL SECRET OUT.
AND, DON'T GET ME WRONG, THE WHOLE THING WITH THE DRUG-BUST WAS PRETTY EPIC, BUT I'VE FOLLOWED YOUR CHANNEL FOR A YEAR OR SO, IF THAT DOESN'T MAKE ME SOUND TOO CREEPY...
UH, THAT'S LITERALLY WHAT IT'S THERE FOR, SO NO.
BUT I WASN'T THE REAL HERO THAT NIGHT.
YOU'RE A PRETTY INSPIRING PERSON. YOU WERE BEFORE THE HERO THING.
YOU THINK... I'M INSPIRING?
YOU WORK HARD. YOU KNOW YOUR FLAWS.
SOMETIMES ALL IT TAKES IS A LITTLE OPEN HONESTY TO INSPIRE PEOPLE. CATCHING DRUG RINGS? THAT'S JUST A BONUS.
TOGETHER WE'RE STRONG, RIGHT?
FUCK YEAH, WE ARE.

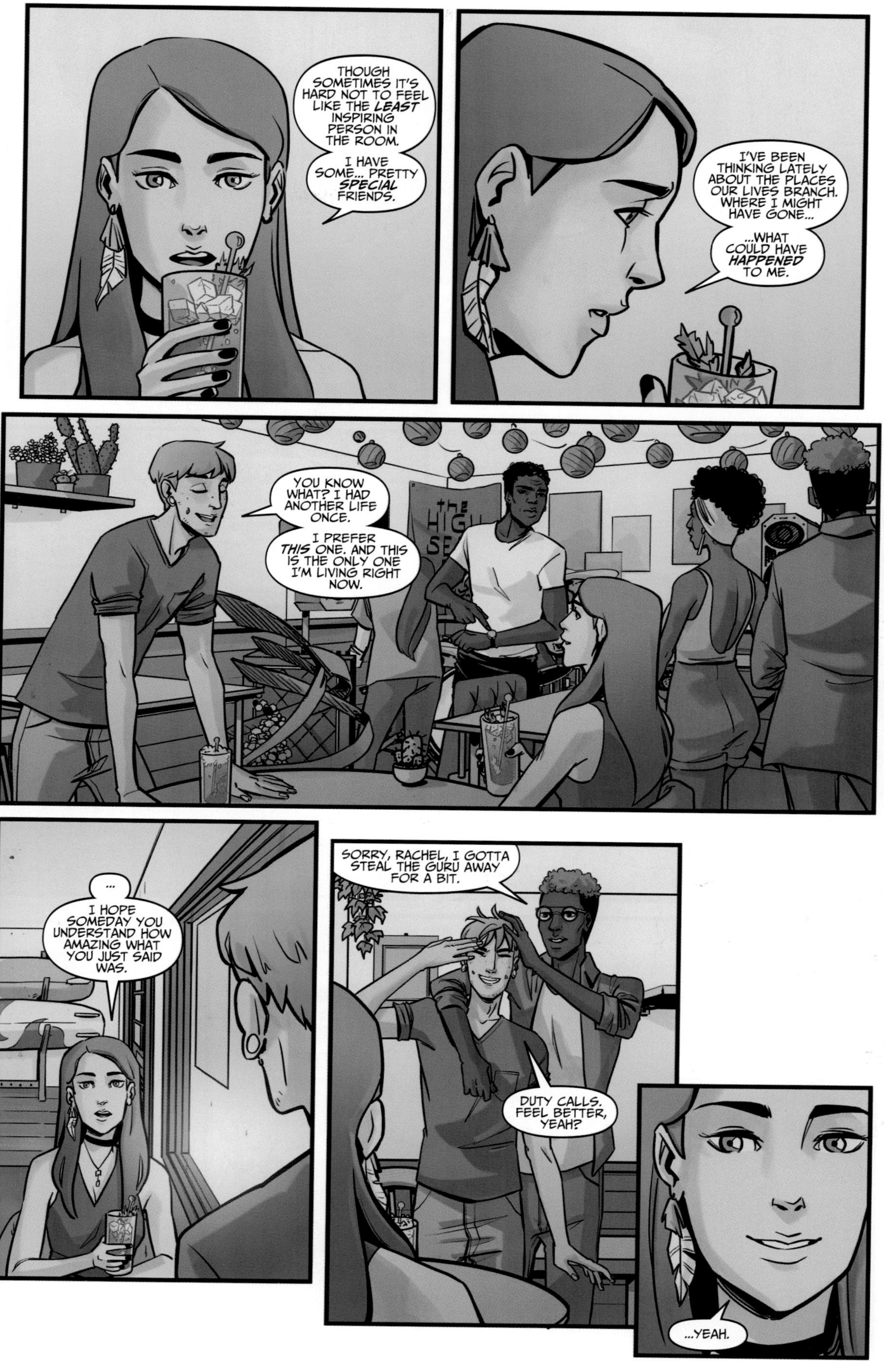
THOUGH SOMETIMES IT'S HARD NOT TO FEEL LIKE THE *LEAST* INSPIRING PERSON IN THE ROOM.
I HAVE SOME... PRETTY ***SPECIAL*** FRIENDS.
I'VE BEEN THINKING LATELY ABOUT THE PLACES OUR LIVES BRANCH. WHERE I MIGHT HAVE GONE...
...WHAT COULD HAVE ***HAPPENED*** TO ME.
YOU KNOW WHAT? I HAD ANOTHER LIFE ONCE.
I PREFER ***THIS*** ONE. AND THIS IS THE ONLY ONE I'M LIVING RIGHT NOW.
...
I HOPE SOMEDAY YOU UNDERSTAND HOW AMAZING WHAT YOU JUST SAID WAS.
SORRY, RACHEL, I GOTTA STEAL THE GURU AWAY FOR A BIT.
DUTY CALLS. FEEL BETTER, YEAH?
...YEAH.

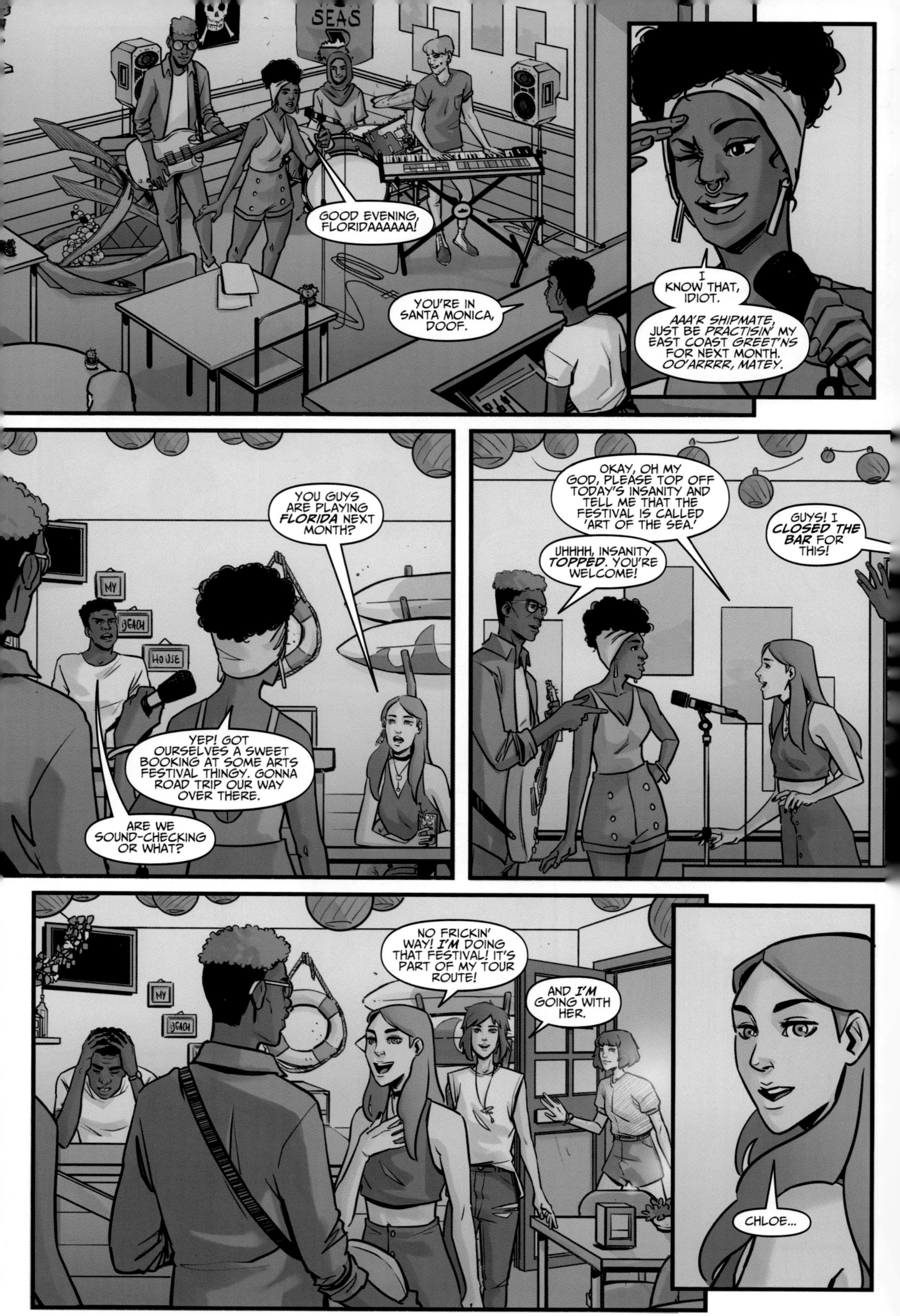
SEAS
GOOD EVENING, FLORIDAAAAAA!
YOU'RE IN SANTA MONICA, DOOF.
I KNOW THAT, IDIOT.
AAA'R SHIPMATE, JUST BE PRACTISIN' MY EAST COAST GREET'NS FOR NEXT MONTH. OO'ARRRR, MATEY.
MY
BEACH
HOUSE
YOU GUYS ARE PLAYING FLORIDA NEXT MONTH?
YEP! GOT OURSELVES A SWEET BOOKING AT SOME ARTS FESTIVAL THINGY. GONNA ROAD TRIP OUR WAY OVER THERE.
ARE WE SOUND-CHECKING OR WHAT?
OKAY, OH MY GOD, PLEASE TOP OFF TODAY'S INSANITY AND TELL ME THAT THE FESTIVAL IS CALLED 'ART OF THE SEA.'
UHHHH, INSANITY TOPPED. YOU'RE WELCOME!
GUYS! I CLOSED THE BAR FOR THIS!
NO FRICKIN' WAY! I'M DOING THAT FESTIVAL! IT'S PART OF MY TOUR ROUTE!
AND I'M GOING WITH HER.
CHLOE...

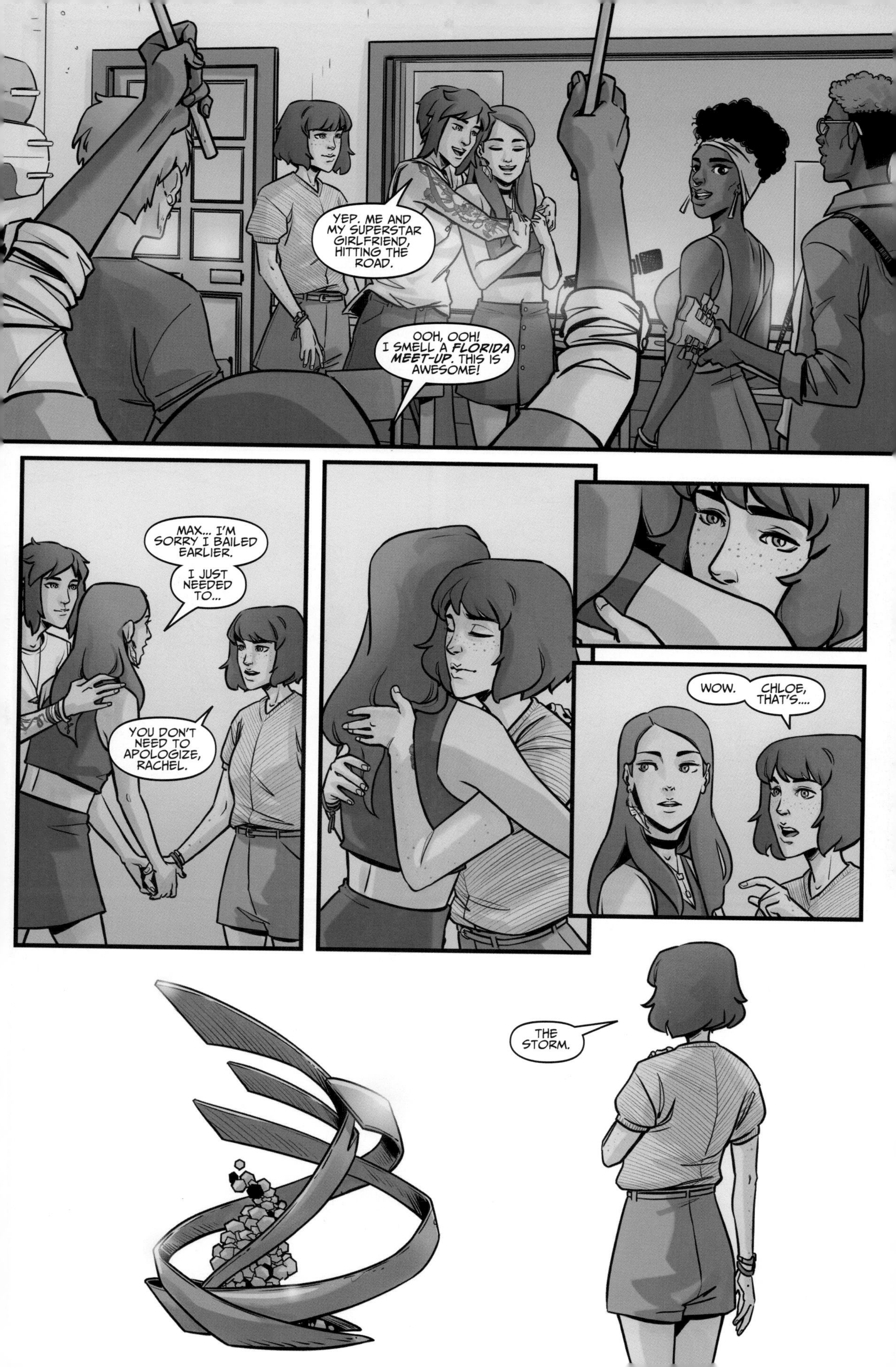
YEP. ME AND MY SUPERSTAR GIRLFRIEND, HITTING THE ROAD.
OOH, OOH! I SMELL A *FLORIDA MEET-UP*. THIS IS AWESOME!
MAX... I'M SORRY I BAILED EARLIER.
I JUST NEEDED TO...
YOU DON'T NEED TO APOLOGIZE, RACHEL.
WOW.
CHLOE, THAT'S....
THE STORM.

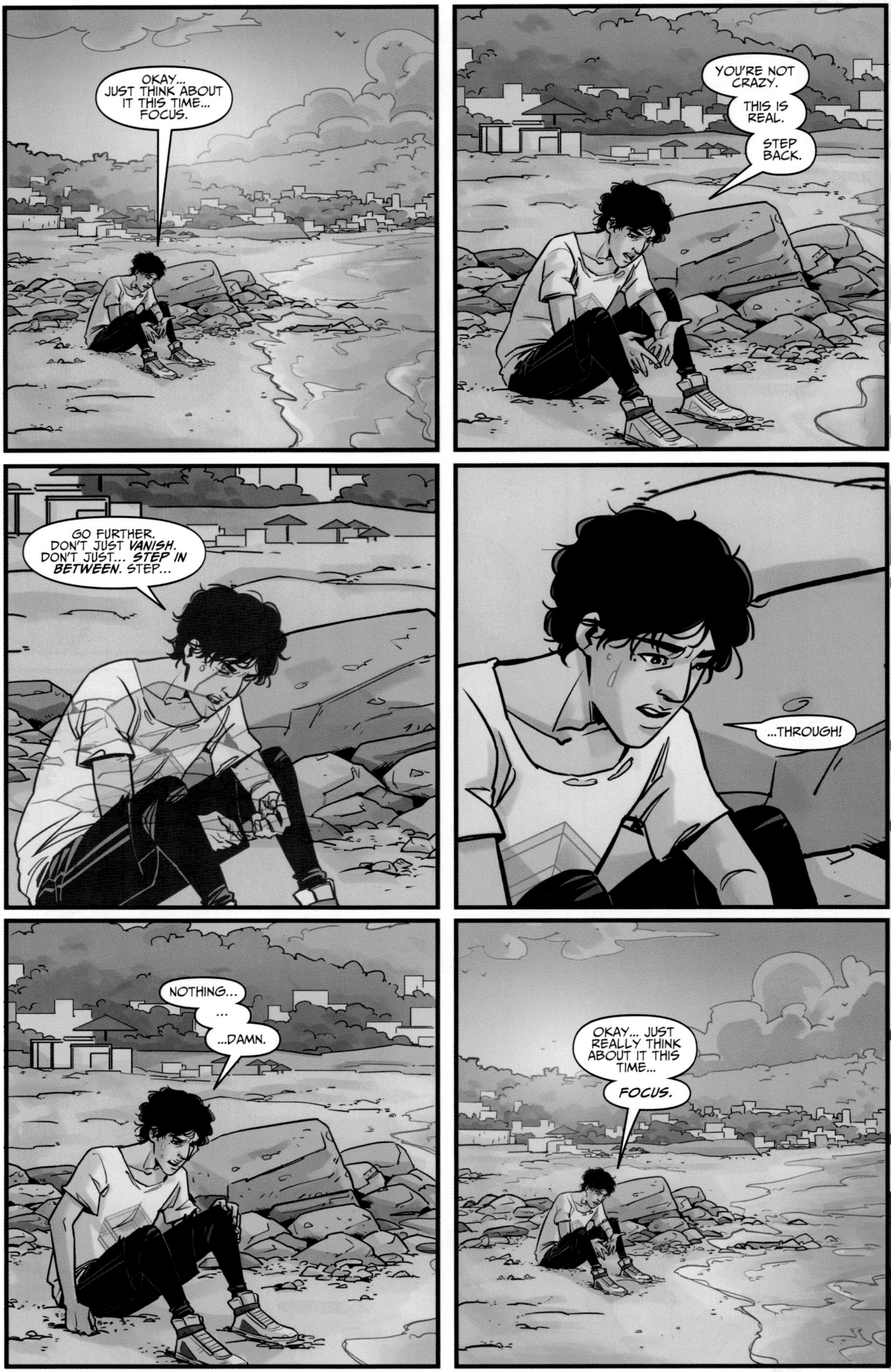
OKAY... JUST THINK ABOUT IT THIS TIME... FOCUS.
YOU'RE NOT CRAZY.
THIS IS REAL.
STEP BACK.
GO FURTHER. DON'T JUST VANISH. DON'T JUST... STEP IN BETWEEN. STEP...
...THROUGH!
NOTHING...
...
...DAMN.
OKAY... JUST REALLY THINK ABOUT IT THIS TIME...
FOCUS.

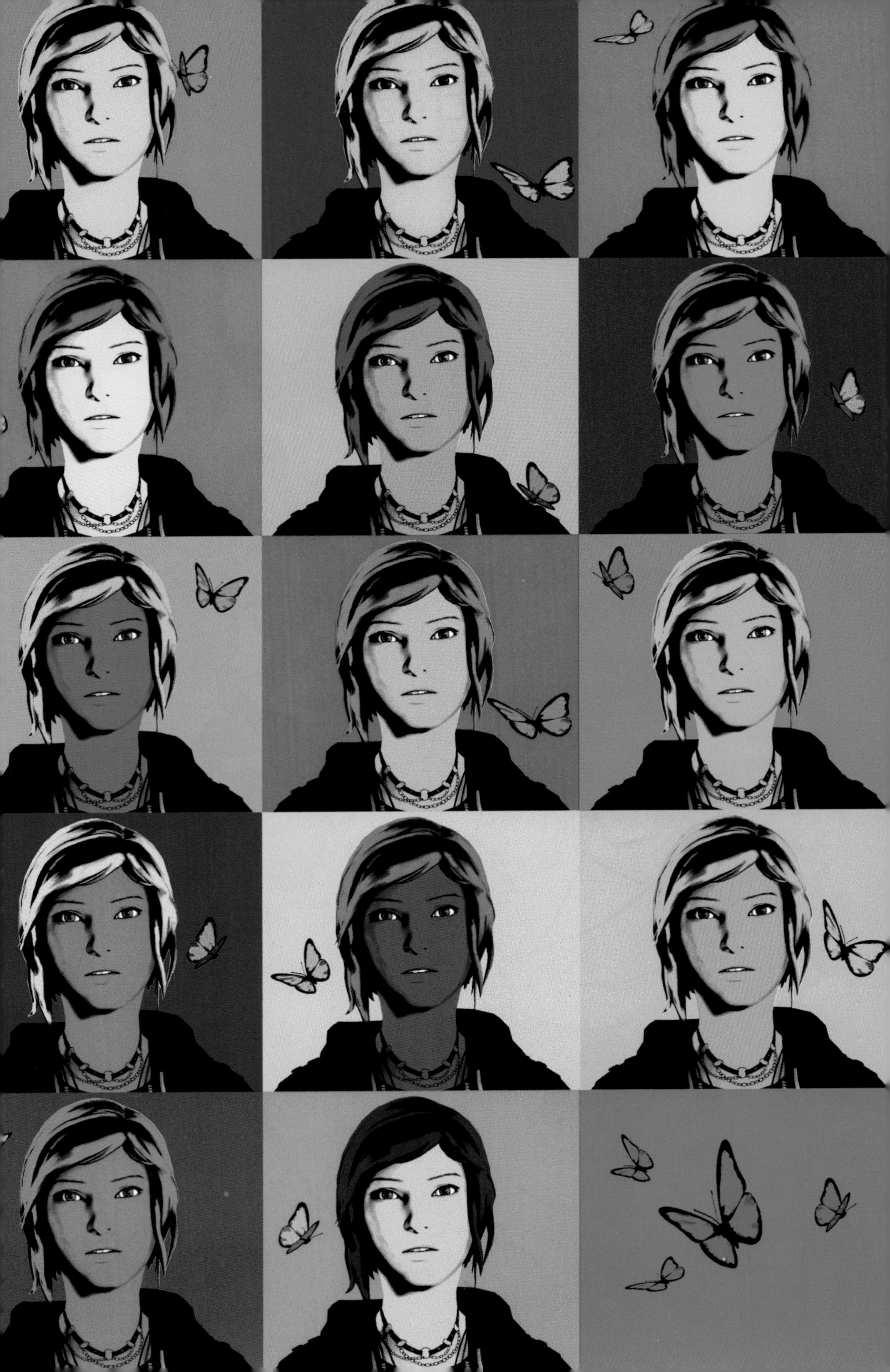

CHAPTER 2

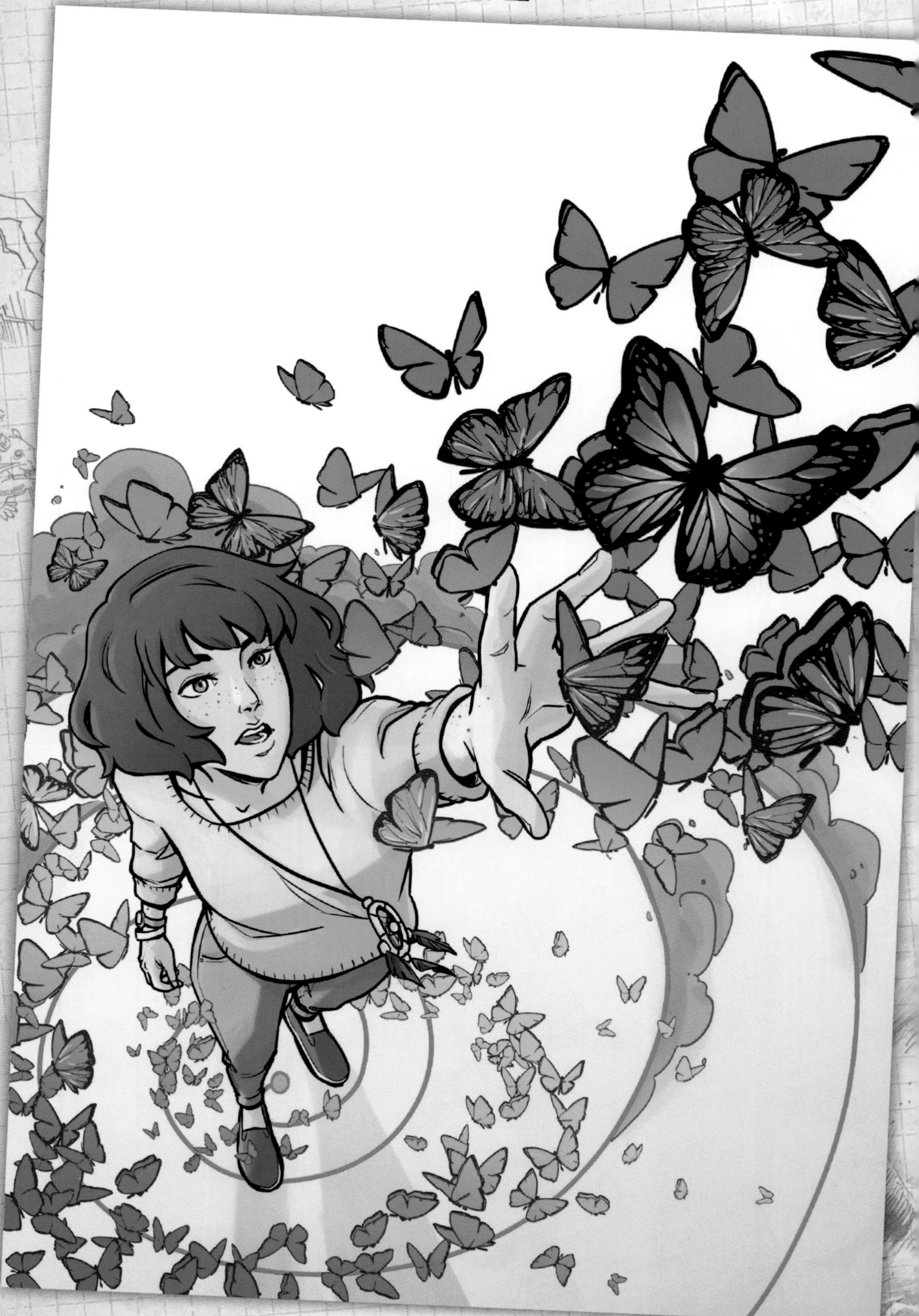

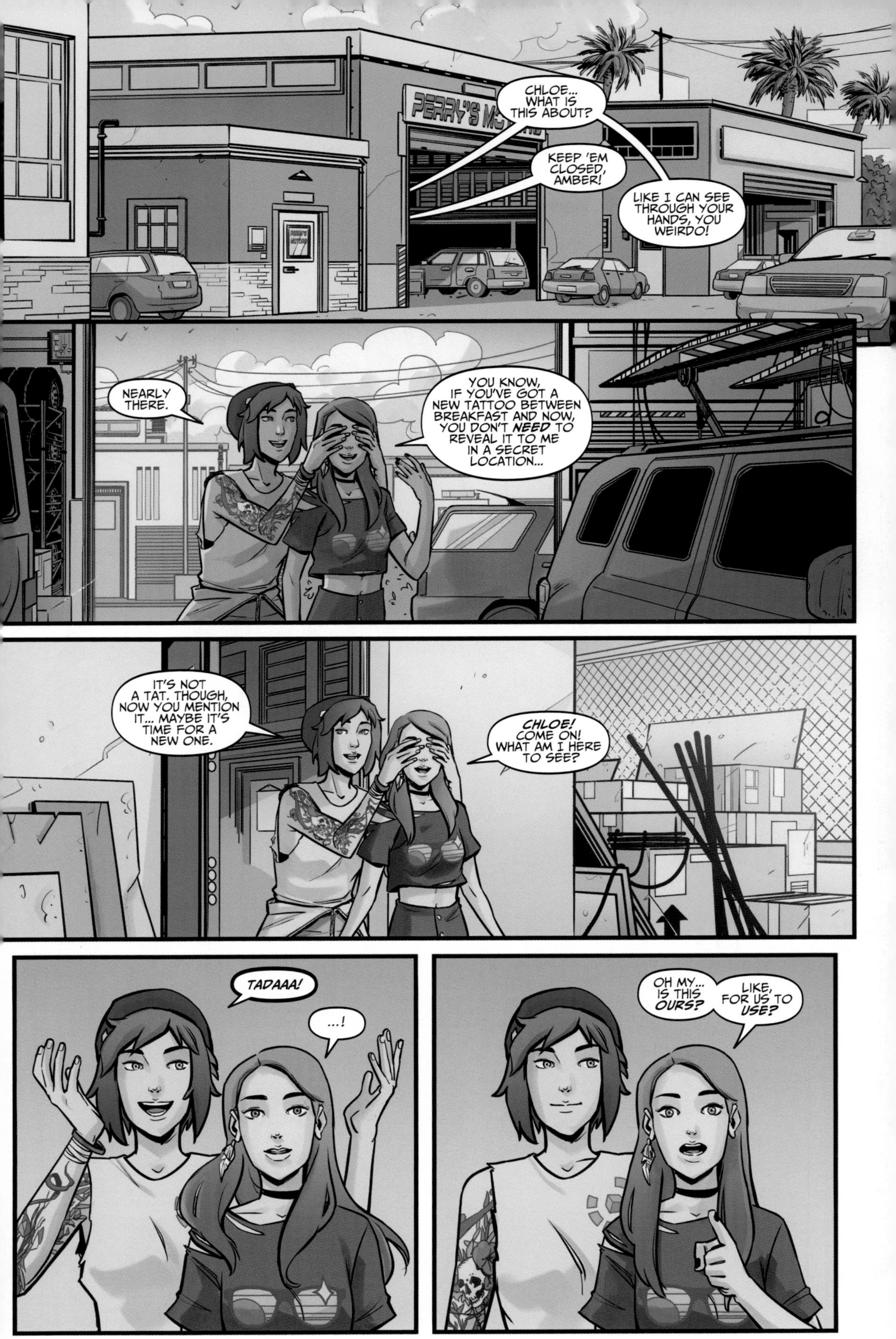
PERRY'S MOTORS
CHLOE... WHAT IS THIS ABOUT?
KEEP 'EM CLOSED, AMBER!
LIKE I CAN SEE THROUGH YOUR HANDS, YOU WEIRDO!
NEARLY THERE.
YOU KNOW, IF YOU'VE GOT A NEW TATTOO BETWEEN BREAKFAST AND NOW, YOU DON'T *NEED* TO REVEAL IT TO ME IN A SECRET LOCATION...
IT'S NOT A TAT. THOUGH, NOW YOU MENTION IT... MAYBE IT'S TIME FOR A NEW ONE.
CHLOE! COME ON! WHAT AM I HERE TO SEE?
TADAAA!
...!
OH MY... IS THIS *OURS?*
LIKE, FOR US TO *USE?*

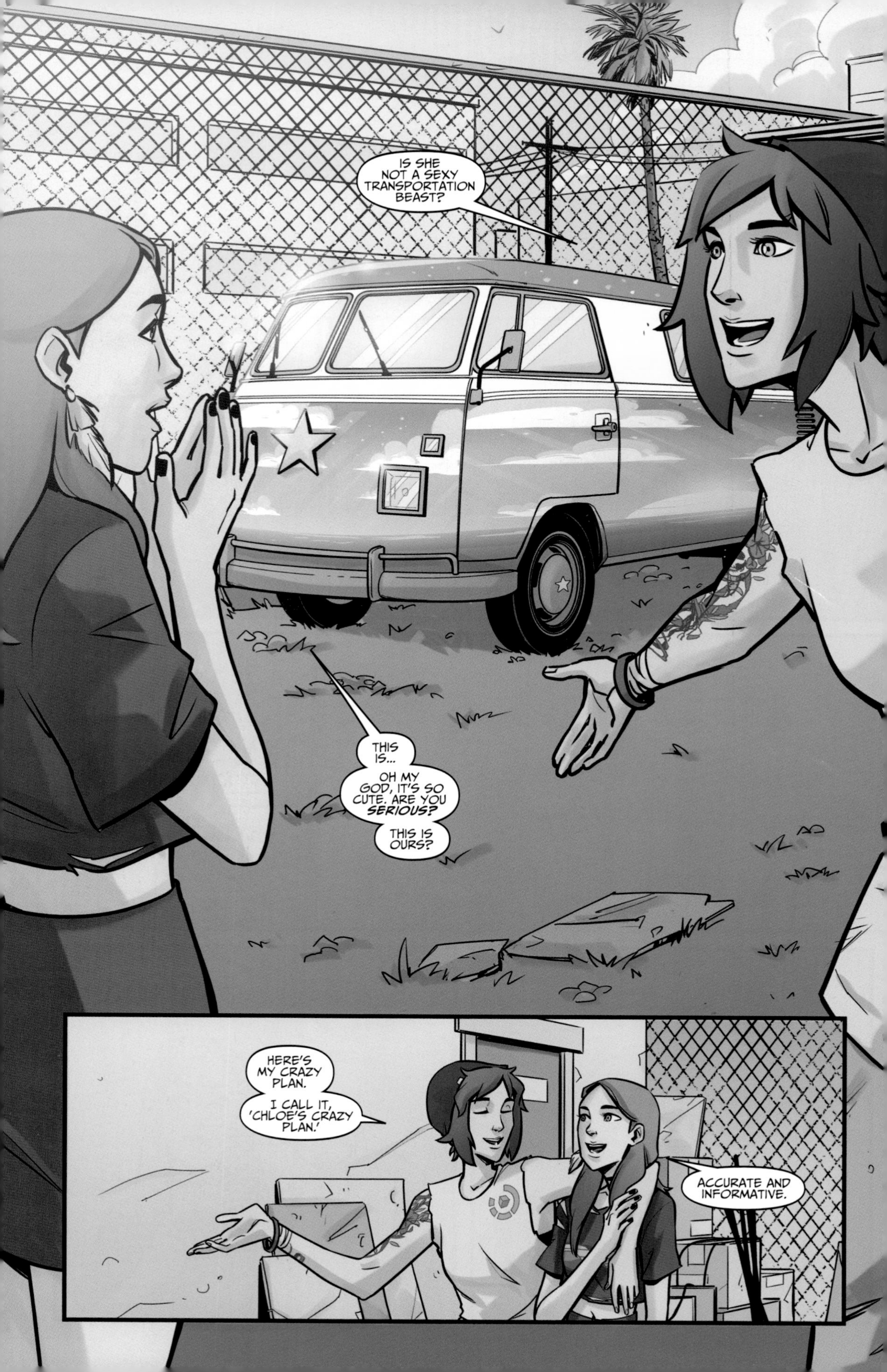
IS SHE NOT A SEXY TRANSPORTATION BEAST?
THIS IS...
OH MY GOD, IT'S SO CUTE. ARE YOU ***SERIOUS?***
THIS IS OURS?
HERE'S MY CRAZY PLAN.
I CALL IT, 'CHLOE'S CRAZY PLAN.'
ACCURATE AND INFORMATIVE.

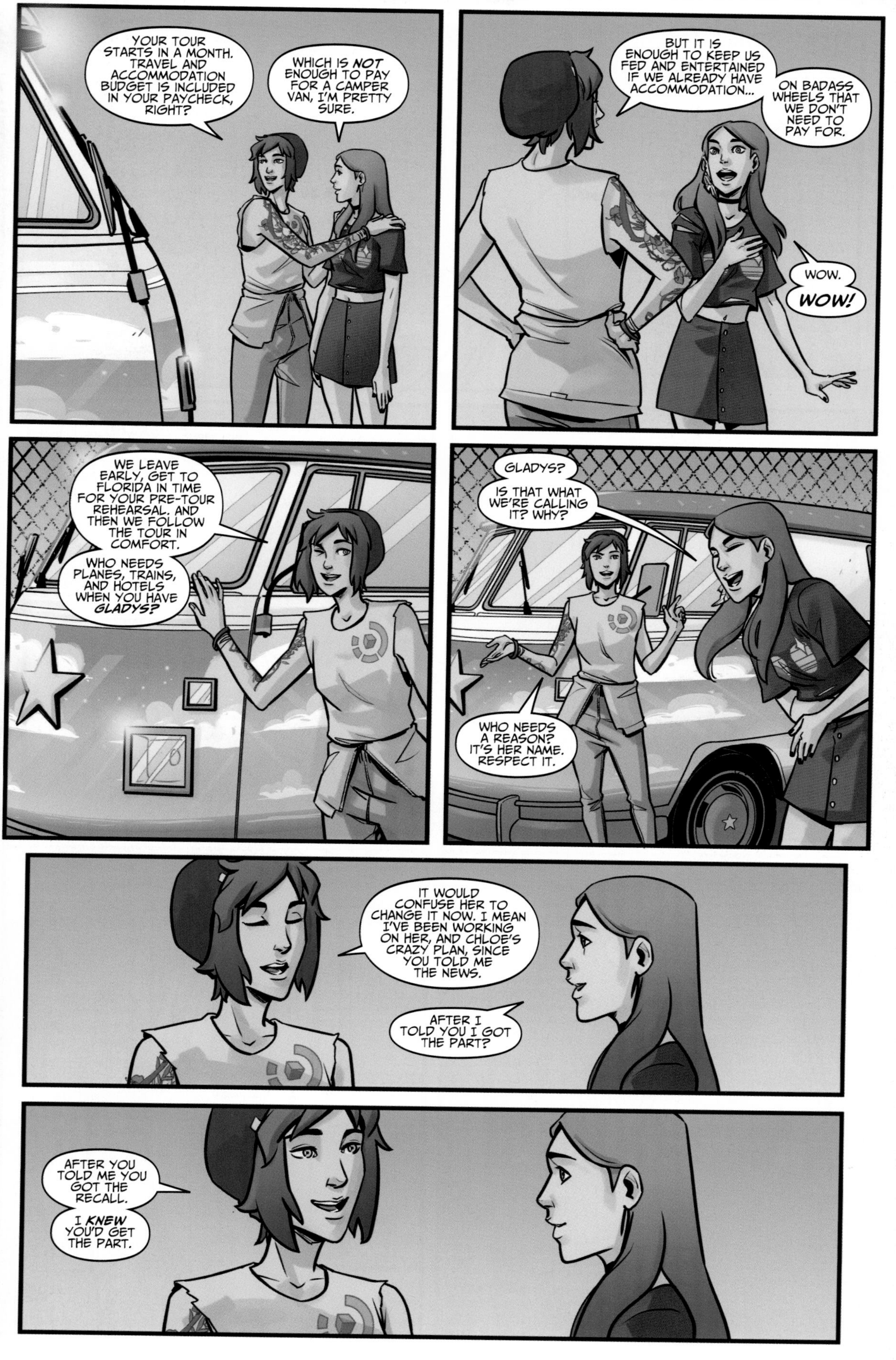
YOUR TOUR STARTS IN A MONTH. TRAVEL AND ACCOMMODATION BUDGET IS INCLUDED IN YOUR PAYCHECK, RIGHT?
WHICH IS *NOT* ENOUGH TO PAY FOR A CAMPER VAN, I'M PRETTY SURE.
BUT IT IS ENOUGH TO KEEP US FED AND ENTERTAINED IF WE ALREADY HAVE ACCOMMODATION...
ON BADASS WHEELS THAT WE DON'T NEED TO PAY FOR.
WOW.
WOW!
WE LEAVE EARLY, GET TO FLORIDA IN TIME FOR YOUR PRE-TOUR REHEARSAL. AND THEN WE FOLLOW THE TOUR IN COMFORT.
WHO NEEDS PLANES, TRAINS, AND HOTELS WHEN YOU HAVE *GLADYS?*
GLADYS?
IS THAT WHAT WE'RE CALLING IT? WHY?
WHO NEEDS A REASON? IT'S HER NAME. RESPECT IT.
IT WOULD CONFUSE HER TO CHANGE IT NOW. I MEAN I'VE BEEN WORKING ON HER, AND CHLOE'S CRAZY PLAN, SINCE YOU TOLD ME THE NEWS.
AFTER I TOLD YOU I GOT THE PART?
AFTER YOU TOLD ME YOU GOT THE RECALL.
I *KNEW* YOU'D GET THE PART.

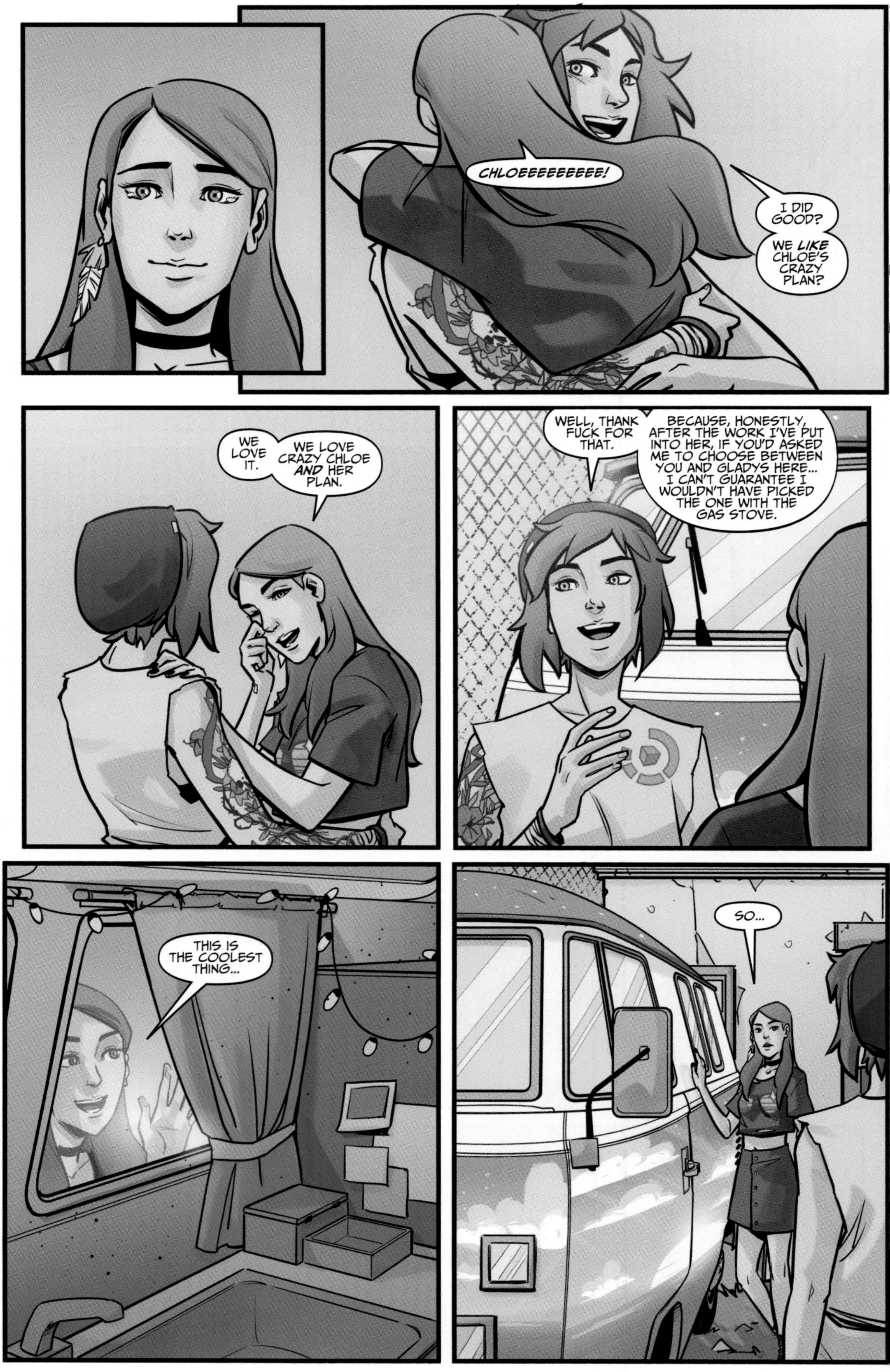
CHLOEEEEEEEEE!
I DID GOOD?
WE *LIKE* CHLOE'S CRAZY PLAN?
WE LOVE IT.
WE LOVE CRAZY CHLOE *AND* HER PLAN.
WELL, THANK FUCK FOR THAT.
BECAUSE, HONESTLY, AFTER THE WORK I'VE PUT INTO HER, IF YOU'D ASKED ME TO CHOOSE BETWEEN YOU AND GLADYS HERE... I CAN'T GUARANTEE I WOULDN'T HAVE PICKED THE ONE WITH THE GAS STOVE.
THIS IS THE COOLEST THING...
SO...

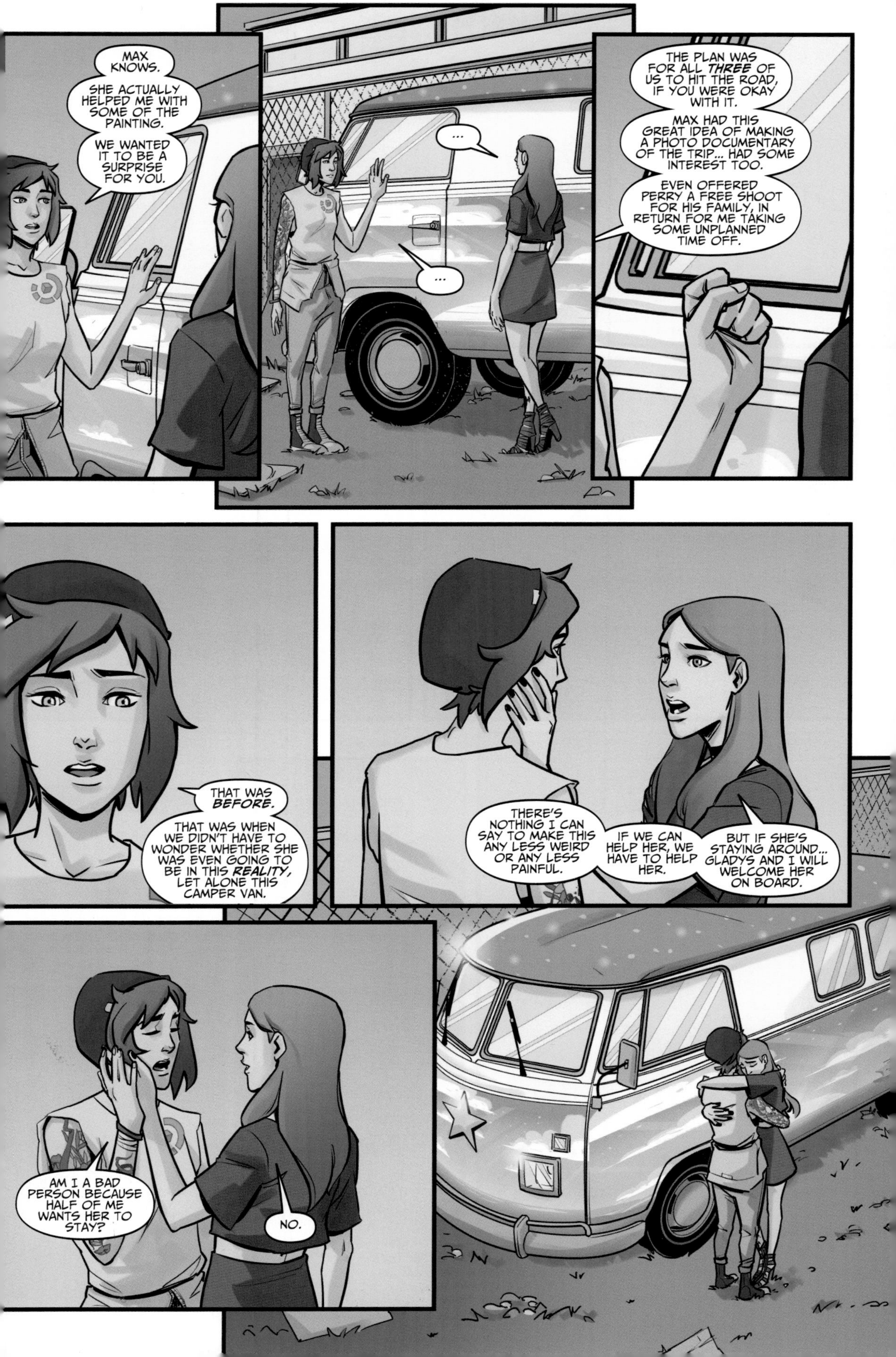
MAX KNOWS.
SHE ACTUALLY HELPED ME WITH SOME OF THE PAINTING.
WE WANTED IT TO BE A SURPRISE FOR YOU.
...
...
THE PLAN WAS FOR ALL THREE OF US TO HIT THE ROAD, IF YOU WERE OKAY WITH IT.
MAX HAD THIS GREAT IDEA OF MAKING A PHOTO DOCUMENTARY OF THE TRIP... HAD SOME INTEREST TOO.
EVEN OFFERED PERRY A FREE SHOOT FOR HIS FAMILY, IN RETURN FOR ME TAKING SOME UNPLANNED TIME OFF.
THAT WAS BEFORE.
THAT WAS WHEN WE DIDN'T HAVE TO WONDER WHETHER SHE WAS EVEN GOING TO BE IN THIS REALITY, LET ALONE THIS CAMPER VAN.
THERE'S NOTHING I CAN SAY TO MAKE THIS ANY LESS WEIRD OR ANY LESS PAINFUL.
IF WE CAN HELP HER, WE HAVE TO HELP HER.
BUT IF SHE'S STAYING AROUND... GLADYS AND I WILL WELCOME HER ON BOARD.
AM I A BAD PERSON BECAUSE HALF OF ME WANTS HER TO STAY?
NO.

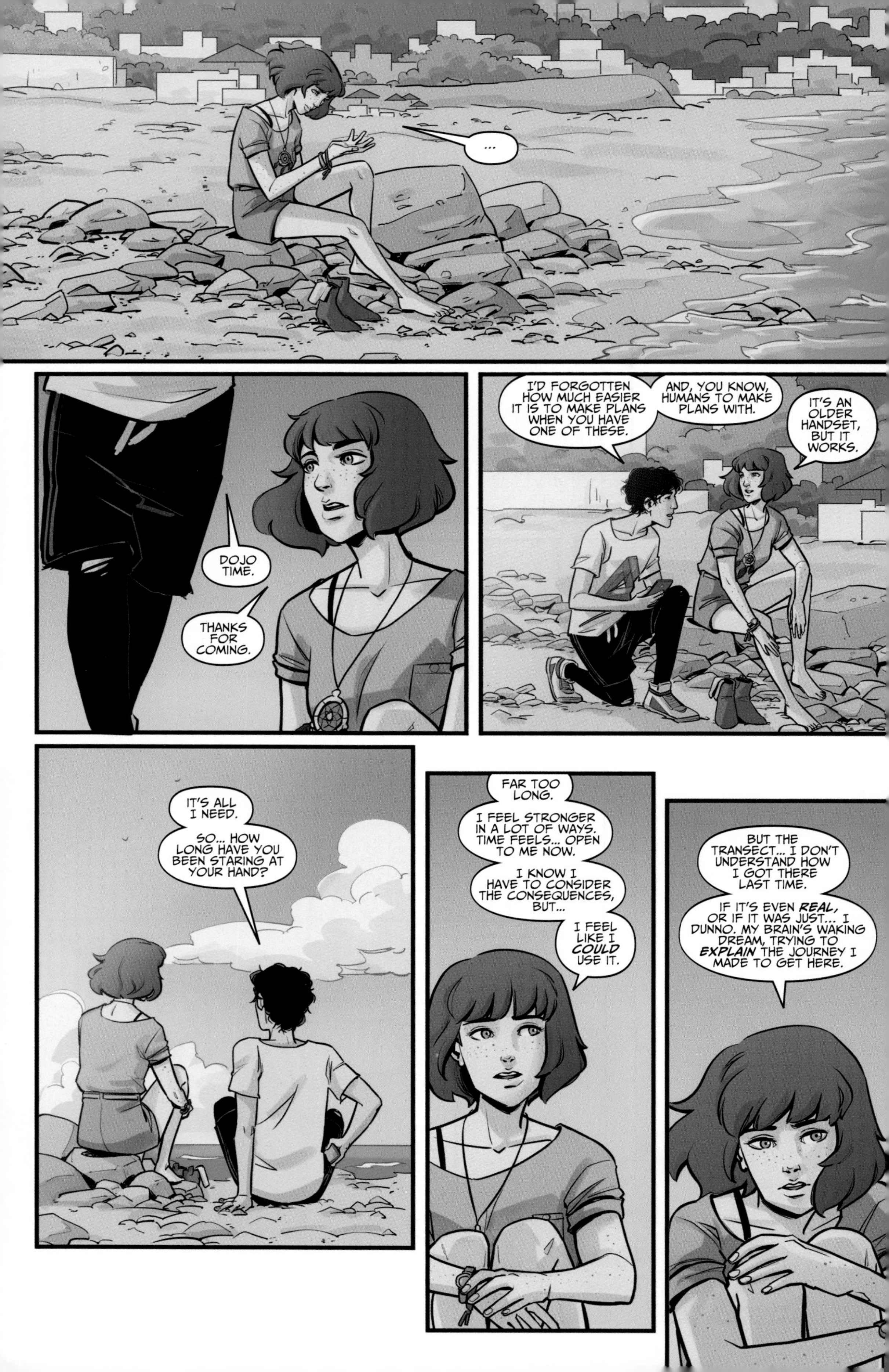
...
DOJO TIME.
THANKS FOR COMING.
I'D FORGOTTEN HOW MUCH EASIER IT IS TO MAKE PLANS WHEN YOU HAVE ONE OF THESE.
AND, YOU KNOW, HUMANS TO MAKE PLANS WITH.
IT'S AN OLDER HANDSET, BUT IT WORKS.
IT'S ALL I NEED.
SO... HOW LONG HAVE YOU BEEN STARING AT YOUR HAND?
FAR TOO LONG.
I FEEL STRONGER IN A LOT OF WAYS. TIME FEELS... OPEN TO ME NOW.
I KNOW I HAVE TO CONSIDER THE CONSEQUENCES, BUT...
I FEEL LIKE I COULD USE IT.
BUT THE TRANSECT... I DON'T UNDERSTAND HOW I GOT THERE LAST TIME.
IF IT'S EVEN REAL, OR IF IT WAS JUST... I DUNNO. MY BRAIN'S WAKING DREAM, TRYING TO EXPLAIN THE JOURNEY I MADE TO GET HERE.

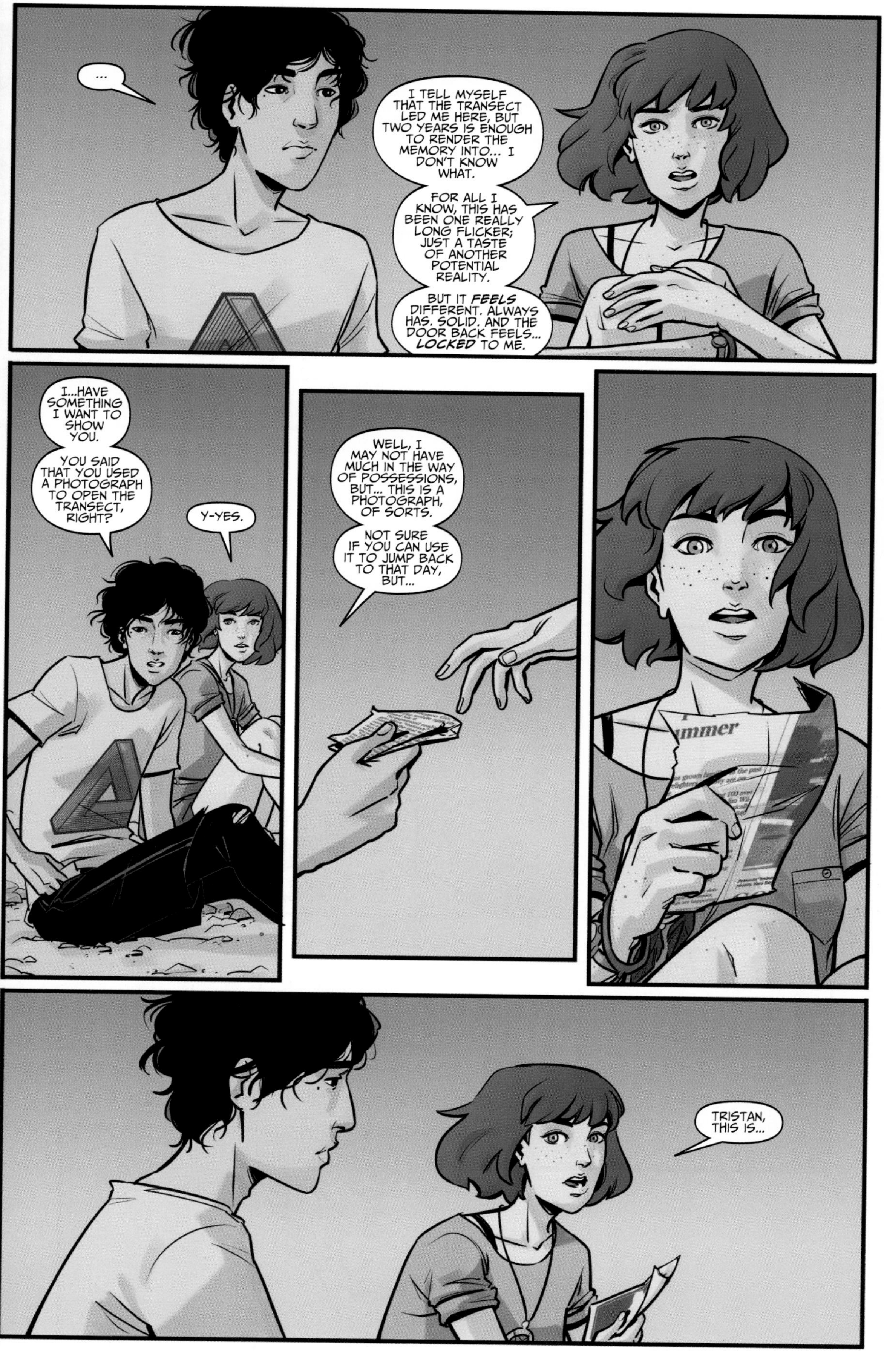
...
I TELL MYSELF THAT THE TRANSECT LED ME HERE, BUT TWO YEARS IS ENOUGH TO RENDER THE MEMORY INTO... I DON'T KNOW WHAT.
FOR ALL I KNOW, THIS HAS BEEN ONE REALLY LONG FLICKER; JUST A TASTE OF ANOTHER POTENTIAL REALITY.
BUT IT *FEELS* DIFFERENT. ALWAYS HAS. SOLID. AND THE DOOR BACK FEELS... *LOCKED* TO ME.
I...HAVE SOMETHING I WANT TO SHOW YOU.
YOU SAID THAT YOU USED A PHOTOGRAPH TO OPEN THE TRANSECT, RIGHT?
Y-YES.
WELL, I MAY NOT HAVE MUCH IN THE WAY OF POSSESSIONS, BUT... THIS IS A PHOTOGRAPH, OF SORTS.
NOT SURE IF YOU CAN USE IT TO JUMP BACK TO THAT DAY, BUT...
TRISTAN, THIS IS...

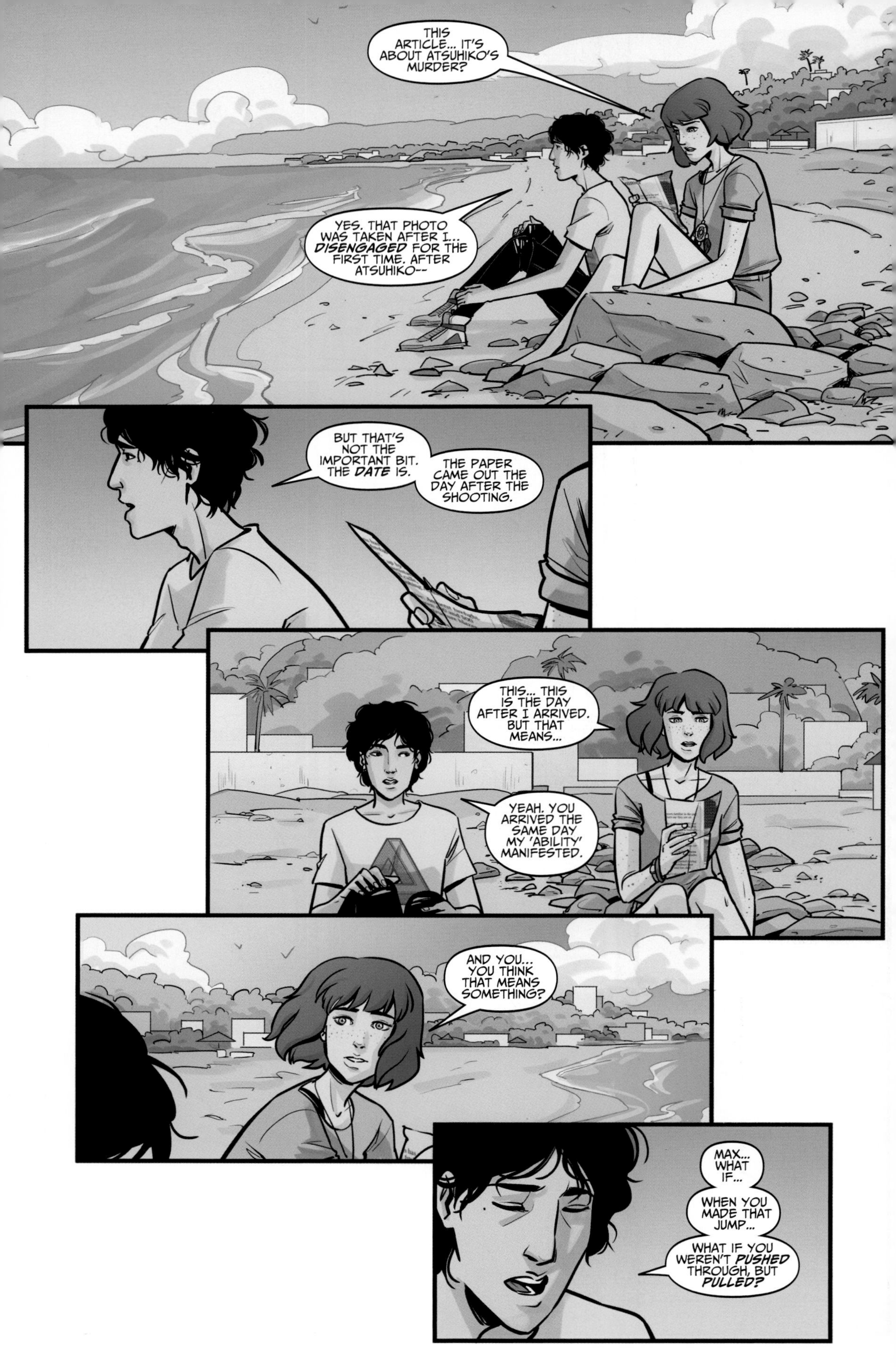
THIS ARTICLE... IT'S ABOUT ATSUHIKO'S MURDER?
YES. THAT PHOTO WAS TAKEN AFTER I... **DISENGAGED** FOR THE FIRST TIME. AFTER ATSUHIKO--
BUT THAT'S NOT THE IMPORTANT BIT. THE **DATE** IS.
THE PAPER CAME OUT THE DAY AFTER THE SHOOTING.
THIS... THIS IS THE DAY AFTER I ARRIVED. BUT THAT MEANS...
YEAH. YOU ARRIVED THE SAME DAY MY 'ABILITY' MANIFESTED.
AND YOU... YOU THINK THAT MEANS SOMETHING?
MAX... WHAT IF...
WHEN YOU MADE THAT JUMP...
WHAT IF YOU WEREN'T **PUSHED** THROUGH, BUT **PULLED?**

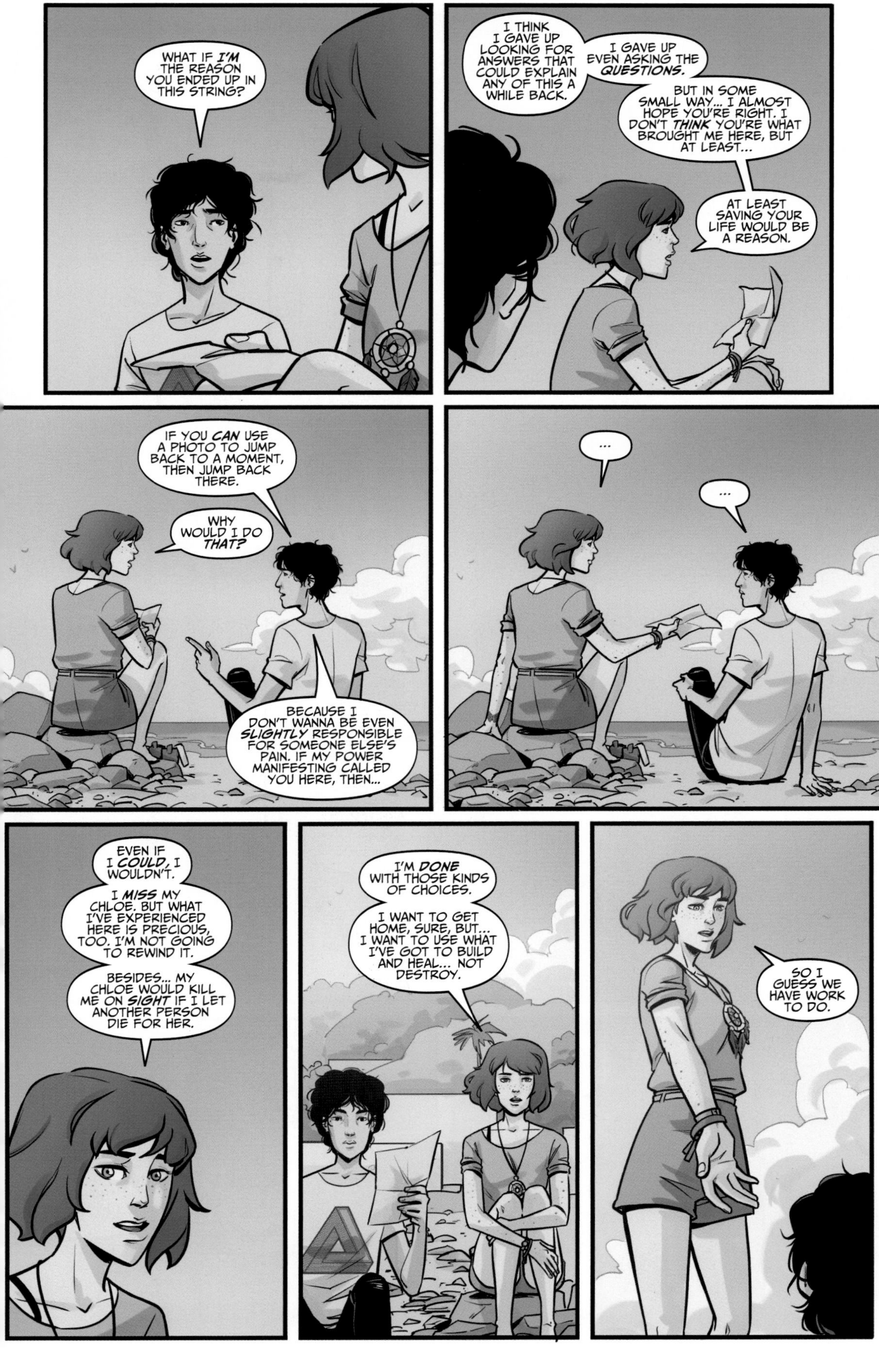
WHAT IF *I'M* THE REASON YOU ENDED UP IN THIS STRING?
I THINK I GAVE UP LOOKING FOR ANSWERS THAT COULD EXPLAIN ANY OF THIS A WHILE BACK.
I GAVE UP EVEN ASKING THE *QUESTIONS.*
BUT IN SOME SMALL WAY... I ALMOST HOPE YOU'RE RIGHT. I DON'T *THINK* YOU'RE WHAT BROUGHT ME HERE, BUT AT LEAST...
AT LEAST SAVING YOUR LIFE WOULD BE A REASON.
IF YOU *CAN* USE A PHOTO TO JUMP BACK TO A MOMENT, THEN JUMP BACK THERE.
WHY WOULD I DO *THAT?*
BECAUSE I DON'T WANNA BE EVEN *SLIGHTLY* RESPONSIBLE FOR SOMEONE ELSE'S PAIN. IF MY POWER MANIFESTING CALLED YOU HERE, THEN...
...
...
EVEN IF I *COULD,* I WOULDN'T.
I *MISS* MY CHLOE. BUT WHAT I'VE EXPERIENCED HERE IS PRECIOUS, TOO. I'M NOT GOING TO REWIND IT.
BESIDES... MY CHLOE WOULD KILL ME ON *SIGHT* IF I LET ANOTHER PERSON DIE FOR HER.
I'M *DONE* WITH THOSE KINDS OF CHOICES.
I WANT TO GET HOME, SURE, BUT... I WANT TO USE WHAT I'VE GOT TO BUILD AND HEAL... NOT DESTROY.
SO I GUESS WE HAVE WORK TO DO.

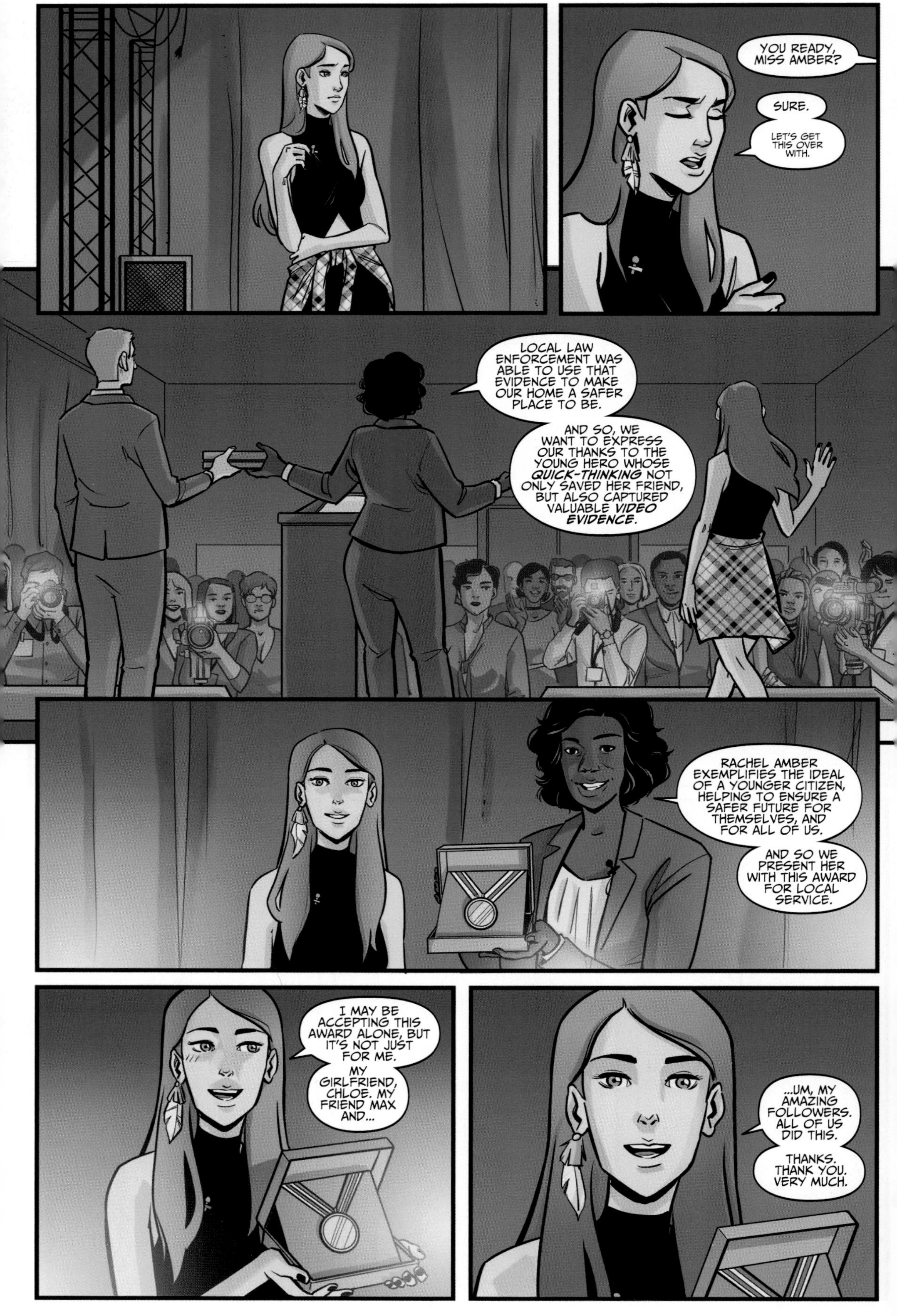
YOU READY, MISS AMBER?
SURE.
LET'S GET THIS OVER WITH.
LOCAL LAW ENFORCEMENT WAS ABLE TO USE THAT EVIDENCE TO MAKE OUR HOME A SAFER PLACE TO BE.
AND SO, WE WANT TO EXPRESS OUR THANKS TO THE YOUNG HERO WHOSE QUICK-THINKING NOT ONLY SAVED HER FRIEND, BUT ALSO CAPTURED VALUABLE VIDEO EVIDENCE.
RACHEL AMBER EXEMPLIFIES THE IDEAL OF A YOUNGER CITIZEN, HELPING TO ENSURE A SAFER FUTURE FOR THEMSELVES, AND FOR ALL OF US.
AND SO WE PRESENT HER WITH THIS AWARD FOR LOCAL SERVICE.
I MAY BE ACCEPTING THIS AWARD ALONE, BUT IT'S NOT JUST FOR ME.
MY GIRLFRIEND, CHLOE. MY FRIEND MAX AND...
...UM, MY AMAZING FOLLOWERS. ALL OF US DID THIS.
THANKS. THANK YOU. VERY MUCH.

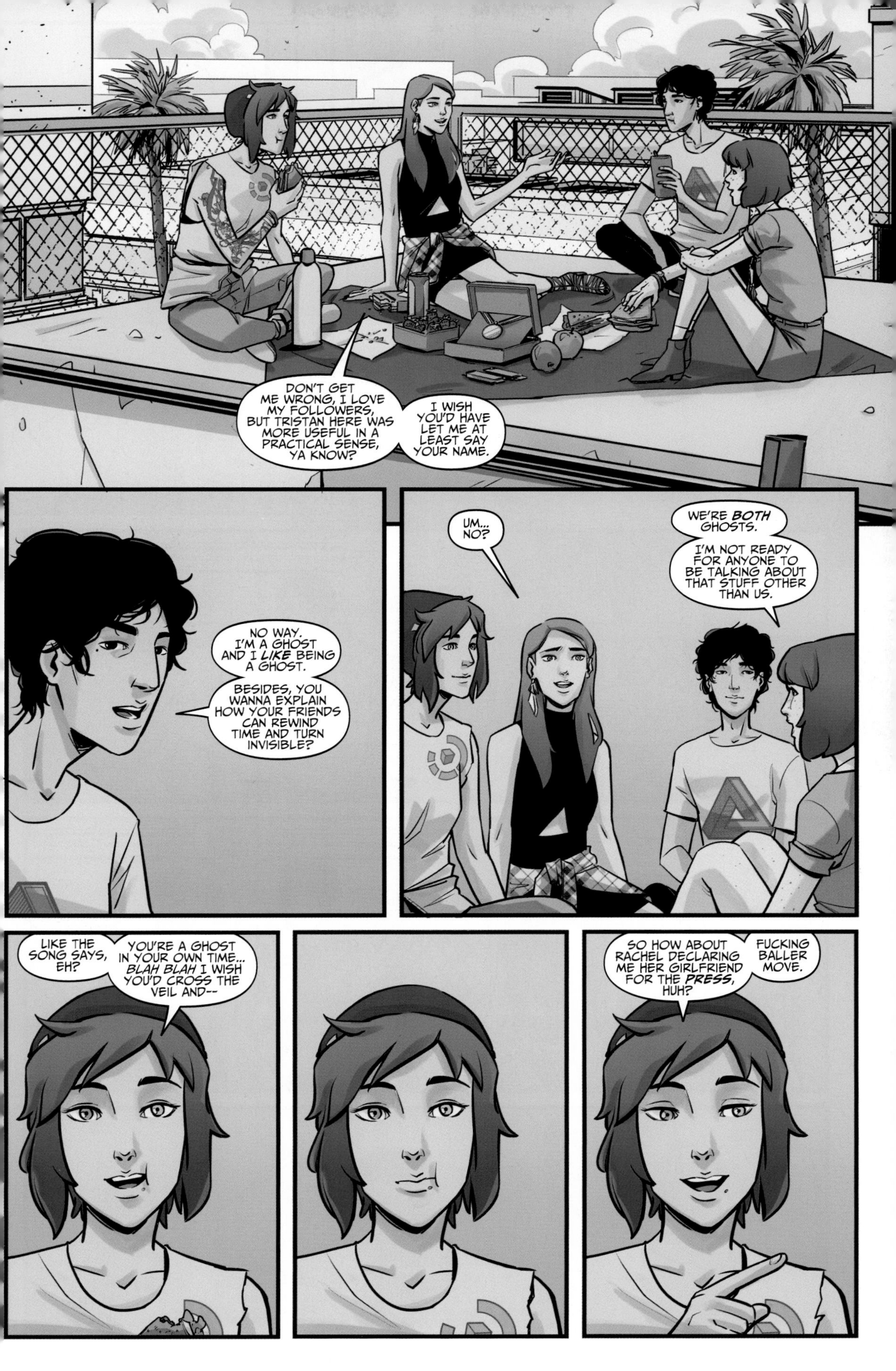
DON'T GET ME WRONG, I LOVE MY FOLLOWERS, BUT TRISTAN HERE WAS MORE USEFUL IN A PRACTICAL SENSE, YA KNOW?
I WISH YOU'D HAVE LET ME AT LEAST SAY YOUR NAME.
NO WAY. I'M A GHOST AND I *LIKE* BEING A GHOST.
BESIDES, YOU WANNA EXPLAIN HOW YOUR FRIENDS CAN REWIND TIME AND TURN INVISIBLE?
UM... NO?
WE'RE *BOTH* GHOSTS.
I'M NOT READY FOR ANYONE TO BE TALKING ABOUT THAT STUFF OTHER THAN US.
LIKE THE SONG SAYS, EH?
YOU'RE A GHOST IN YOUR OWN TIME... *BLAH BLAH* I WISH YOU'D CROSS THE VEIL AND--
SO HOW ABOUT RACHEL DECLARING ME HER GIRLFRIEND FOR THE *PRESS*, HUH?
FUCKING BALLER MOVE.

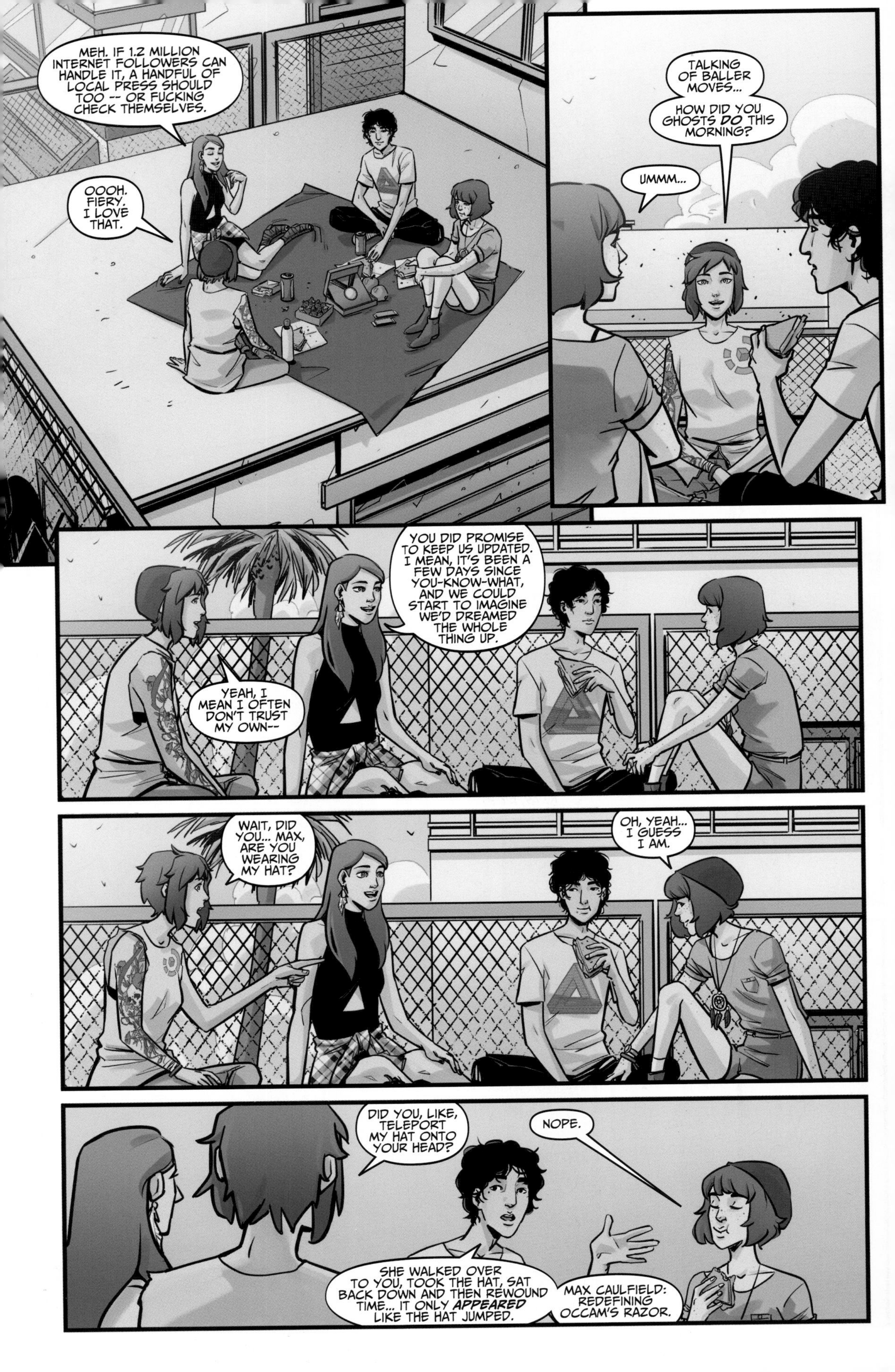
MEH. IF 1.2 MILLION INTERNET FOLLOWERS CAN HANDLE IT, A HANDFUL OF LOCAL PRESS SHOULD TOO -- OR FUCKING CHECK THEMSELVES.
OOOH. FIERY. I LOVE THAT.
TALKING OF BALLER MOVES...
HOW DID YOU GHOSTS **DO** THIS MORNING?
UMMM...
YOU DID PROMISE TO KEEP US UPDATED. I MEAN, IT'S BEEN A FEW DAYS SINCE YOU-KNOW-WHAT, AND WE COULD START TO IMAGINE WE'D DREAMED THE WHOLE THING UP.
YEAH, I MEAN I OFTEN DON'T TRUST MY OWN--
WAIT, DID YOU... MAX, ARE YOU WEARING MY HAT?
OH, YEAH... I GUESS I AM.
DID YOU, LIKE, TELEPORT MY HAT ONTO YOUR HEAD?
NOPE.
SHE WALKED OVER TO YOU, TOOK THE HAT, SAT BACK DOWN AND THEN REWOUND TIME... IT ONLY **APPEARED** LIKE THE HAT JUMPED.
MAX CAULFIELD: REDEFINING OCCAM'S RAZOR.

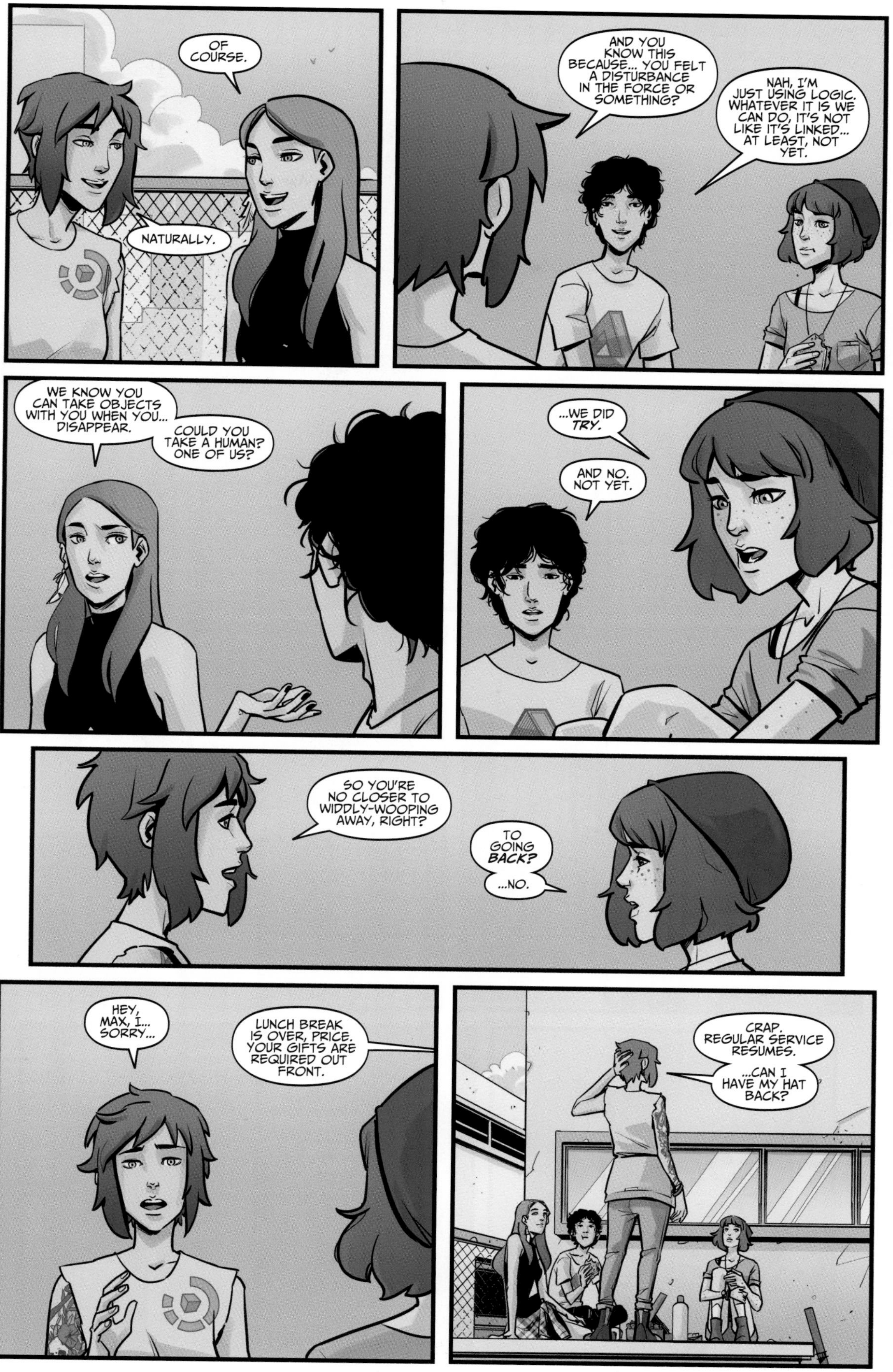
OF COURSE.
NATURALLY.
AND YOU KNOW THIS BECAUSE... YOU FELT A DISTURBANCE IN THE FORCE OR SOMETHING?
NAH, I'M JUST USING LOGIC. WHATEVER IT IS WE CAN DO, IT'S NOT LIKE IT'S LINKED... AT LEAST, NOT YET.
WE KNOW YOU CAN TAKE OBJECTS WITH YOU WHEN YOU... DISAPPEAR.
COULD YOU TAKE A HUMAN? ONE OF US?
...WE DID TRY.
AND NO. NOT YET.
SO YOU'RE NO CLOSER TO WIDDLY-WOOPING AWAY, RIGHT?
TO GOING BACK?
...NO.
HEY, MAX, I... SORRY...
LUNCH BREAK IS OVER, PRICE. YOUR GIFTS ARE REQUIRED OUT FRONT.
CRAP. REGULAR SERVICE RESUMES.
...CAN I HAVE MY HAT BACK?

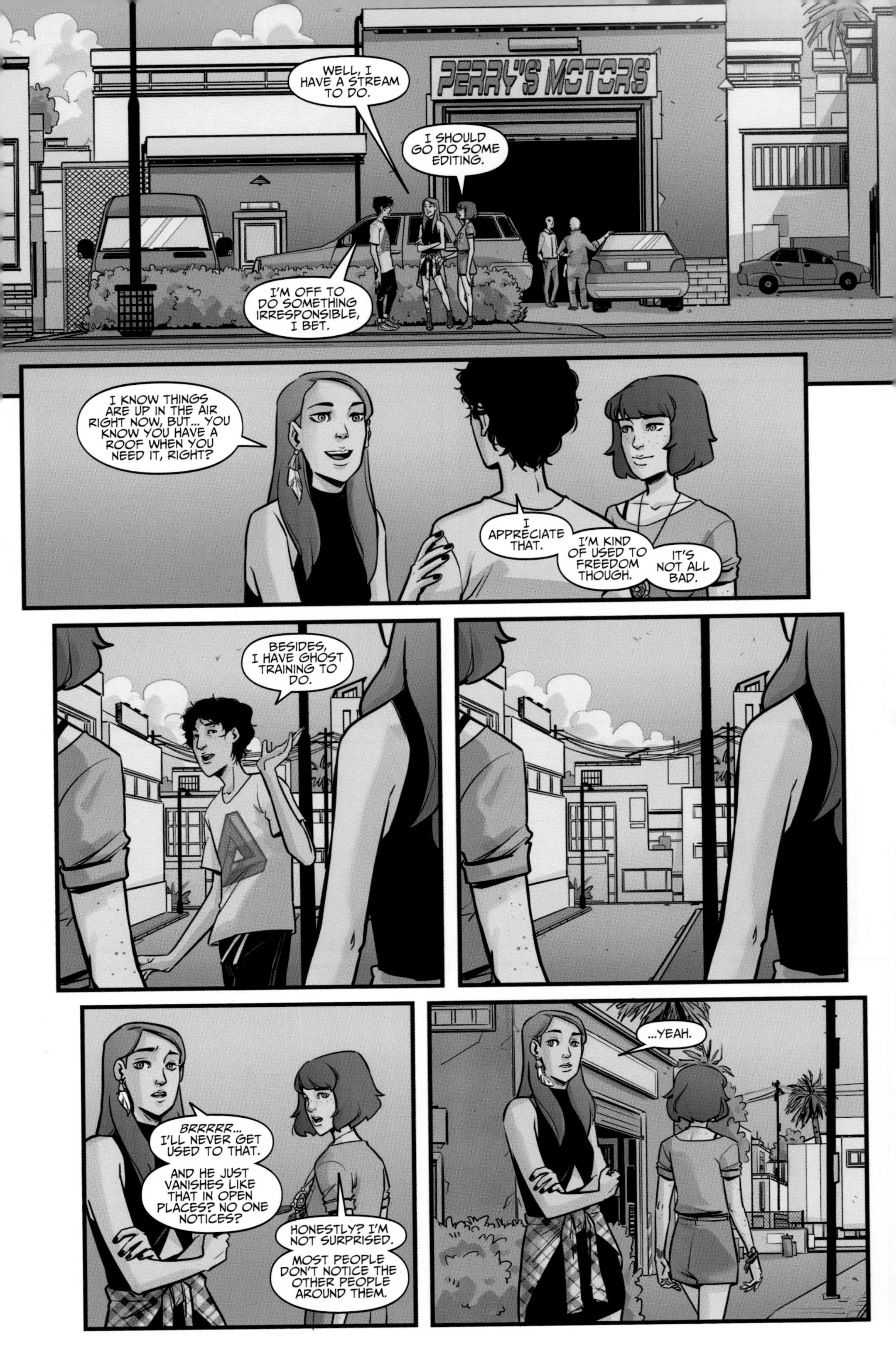
PERRY'S MOTORS
WELL, I HAVE A STREAM TO DO.
I SHOULD GO DO SOME EDITING.
I'M OFF TO DO SOMETHING IRRESPONSIBLE, I BET.
I KNOW THINGS ARE UP IN THE AIR RIGHT NOW, BUT... YOU KNOW YOU HAVE A ROOF WHEN YOU NEED IT, RIGHT?
I APPRECIATE THAT.
I'M KIND OF USED TO FREEDOM THOUGH.
IT'S NOT ALL BAD.
BESIDES, I HAVE GHOST TRAINING TO DO.
BRRRRR... I'LL NEVER GET USED TO THAT.
AND HE JUST VANISHES LIKE THAT IN OPEN PLACES? NO ONE NOTICES?
HONESTLY? I'M NOT SURPRISED.
MOST PEOPLE DON'T NOTICE THE OTHER PEOPLE AROUND THEM.
...YEAH.

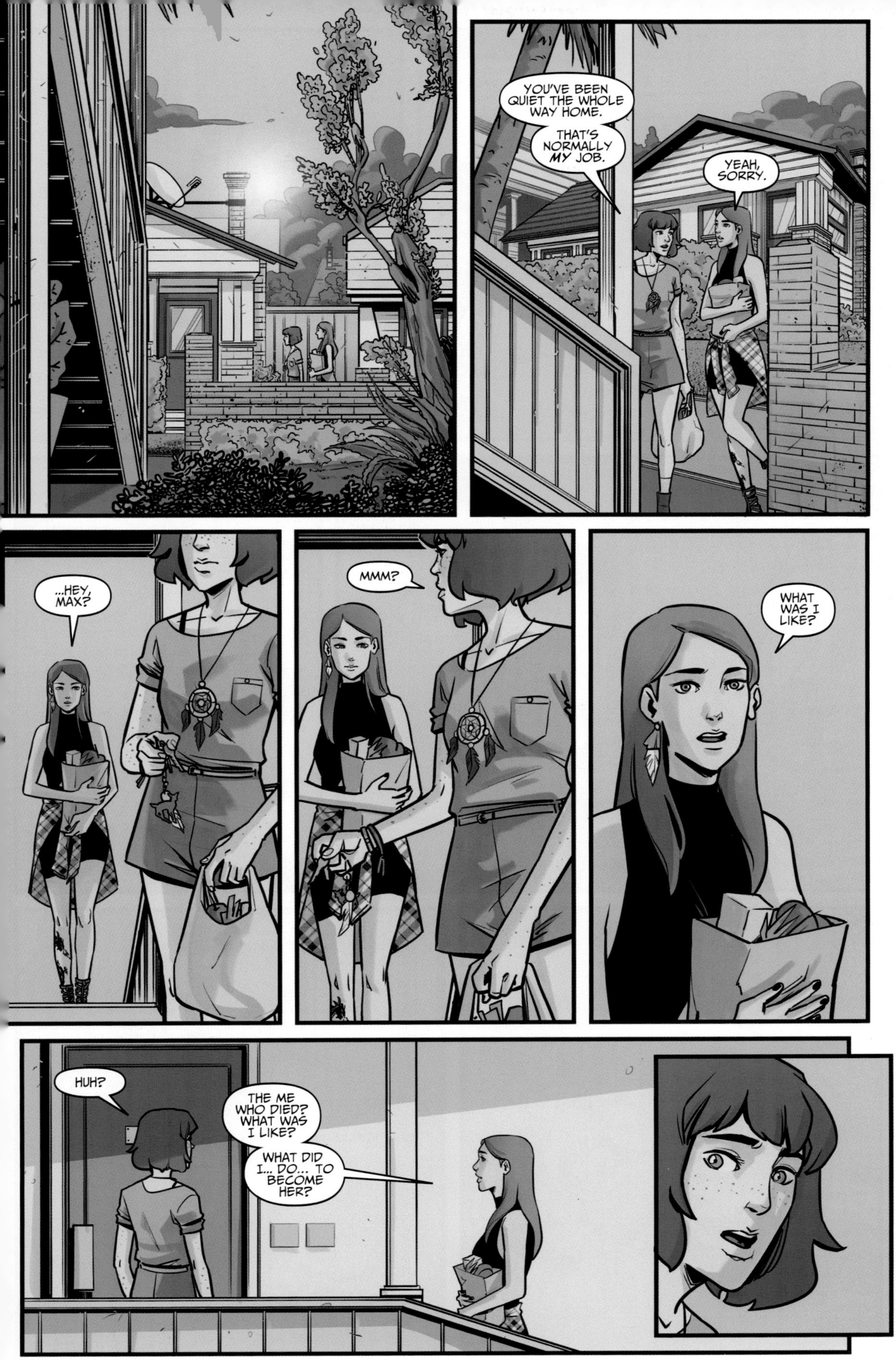
YOU'VE BEEN QUIET THE WHOLE WAY HOME.
THAT'S NORMALLY *MY* JOB.
YEAH, SORRY.
...HEY, MAX?
MMM?
WHAT WAS I LIKE?
HUH?
THE ME WHO DIED? WHAT WAS I LIKE?
WHAT DID I... DO... TO BECOME HER?

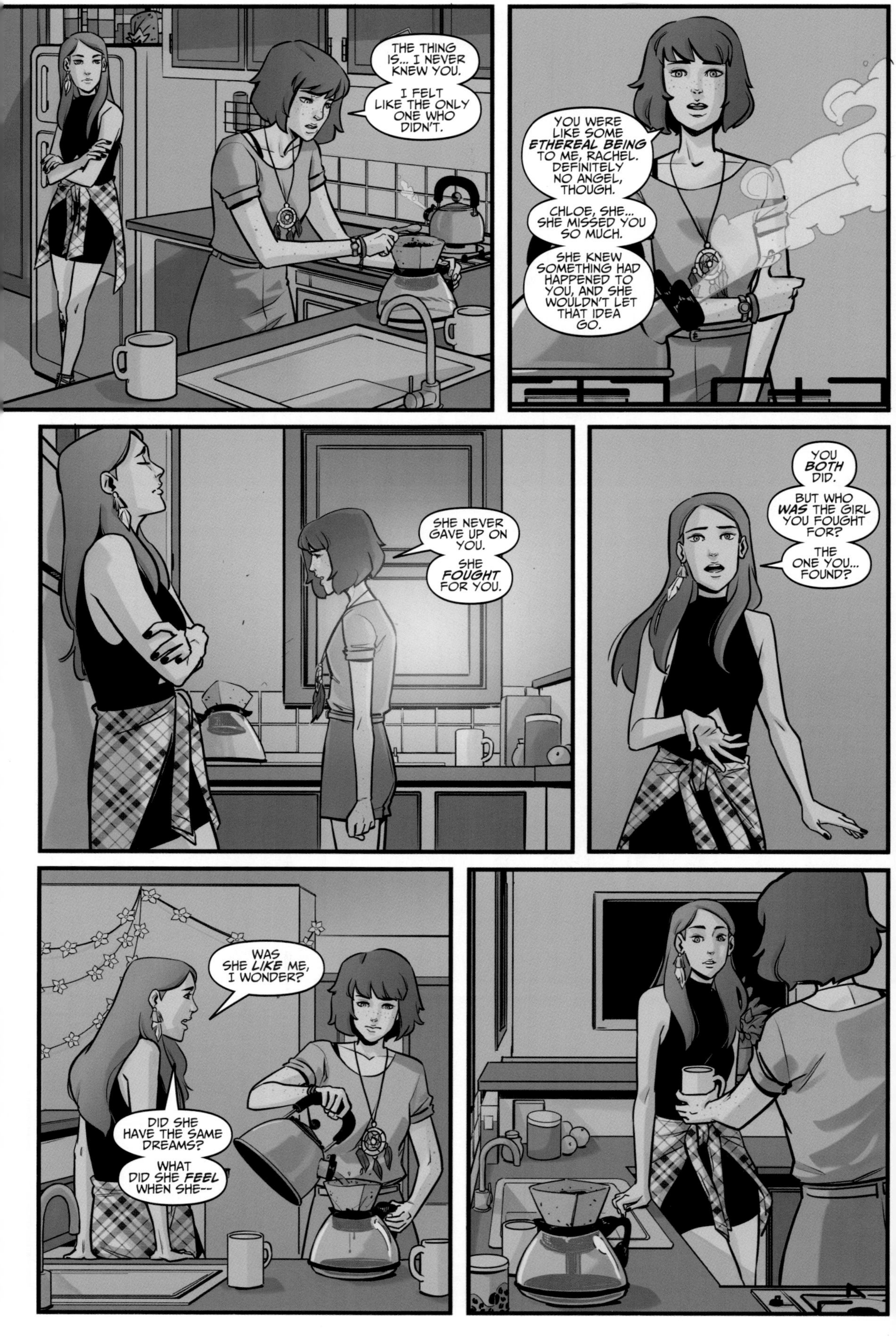
THE THING IS... I NEVER KNEW YOU.
I FELT LIKE THE ONLY ONE WHO DIDN'T.
YOU WERE LIKE SOME ETHEREAL BEING TO ME, RACHEL. DEFINITELY NO ANGEL, THOUGH.
CHLOE, SHE... SHE MISSED YOU SO MUCH.
SHE KNEW SOMETHING HAD HAPPENED TO YOU, AND SHE WOULDN'T LET THAT IDEA GO.
SHE NEVER GAVE UP ON YOU.
SHE FOUGHT FOR YOU.
YOU BOTH DID.
BUT WHO WAS THE GIRL YOU FOUGHT FOR?
THE ONE YOU... FOUND?
WAS SHE LIKE ME, I WONDER?
DID SHE HAVE THE SAME DREAMS?
WHAT DID SHE FEEL WHEN SHE--

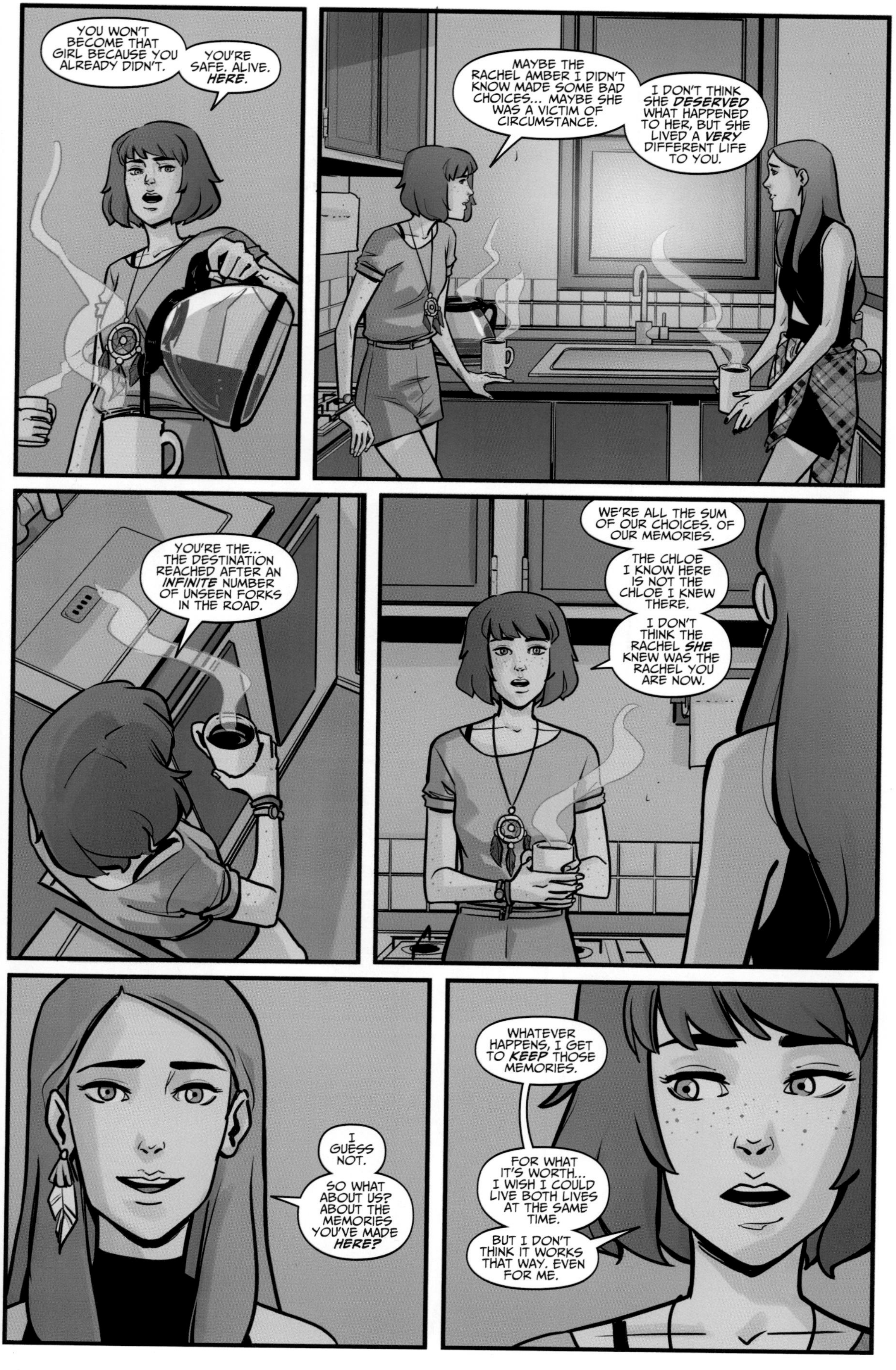

YOU WON'T BECOME THAT GIRL BECAUSE YOU ALREADY DIDN'T.
YOU'RE SAFE. ALIVE. *HERE.*
MAYBE THE RACHEL AMBER I DIDN'T KNOW MADE SOME BAD CHOICES... MAYBE SHE WAS A VICTIM OF CIRCUMSTANCE.
I DON'T THINK SHE *DESERVED* WHAT HAPPENED TO HER, BUT SHE LIVED A *VERY* DIFFERENT LIFE TO YOU.
YOU'RE THE... THE DESTINATION REACHED AFTER AN *INFINITE* NUMBER OF UNSEEN FORKS IN THE ROAD.
WE'RE ALL THE SUM OF OUR CHOICES. OF OUR MEMORIES.
THE CHLOE I KNOW HERE IS NOT THE CHLOE I KNEW THERE.
I DON'T THINK THE RACHEL *SHE* KNEW WAS THE RACHEL YOU ARE NOW.
I GUESS NOT.
SO WHAT ABOUT US? ABOUT THE MEMORIES YOU'VE MADE *HERE?*
WHATEVER HAPPENS, I GET TO *KEEP* THOSE MEMORIES.
FOR WHAT IT'S WORTH... I WISH I COULD LIVE BOTH LIVES AT THE SAME TIME.
BUT I DON'T THINK IT WORKS THAT WAY. EVEN FOR ME.

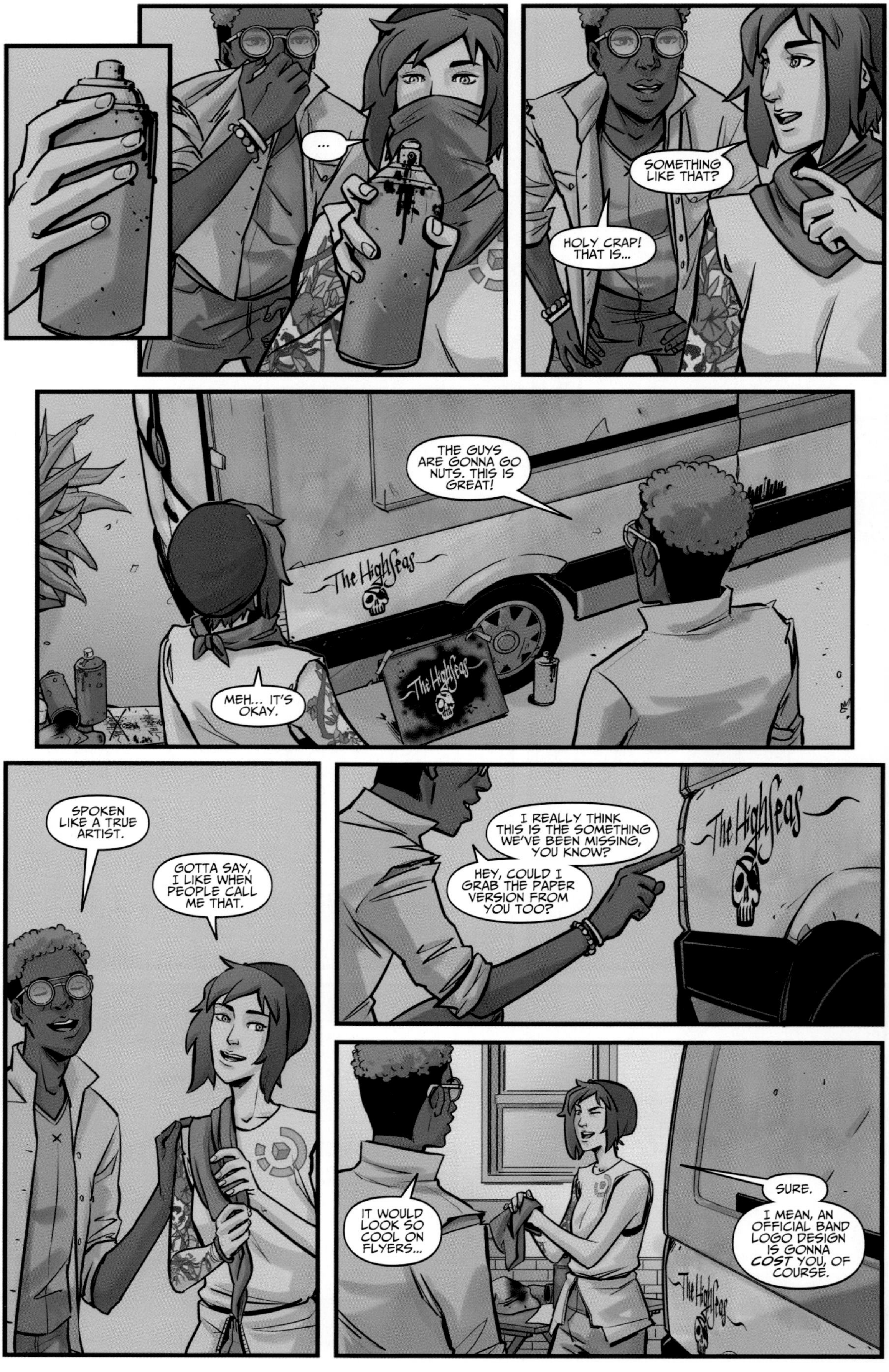
...
SOMETHING LIKE THAT?
HOLY CRAP! THAT IS...
THE GUYS ARE GONNA GO NUTS. THIS IS GREAT!
The HighSeas
MEH... IT'S OKAY.
The HighSeas
SPOKEN LIKE A TRUE ARTIST.
GOTTA SAY, I LIKE WHEN PEOPLE CALL ME THAT.
I REALLY THINK THIS IS THE SOMETHING WE'VE BEEN MISSING, YOU KNOW?
HEY, COULD I GRAB THE PAPER VERSION FROM YOU TOO?
The HighSeas
IT WOULD LOOK SO COOL ON FLYERS...
SURE.
I MEAN, AN OFFICIAL BAND LOGO DESIGN IS GONNA ***COST*** YOU, OF COURSE.
The HighSeas

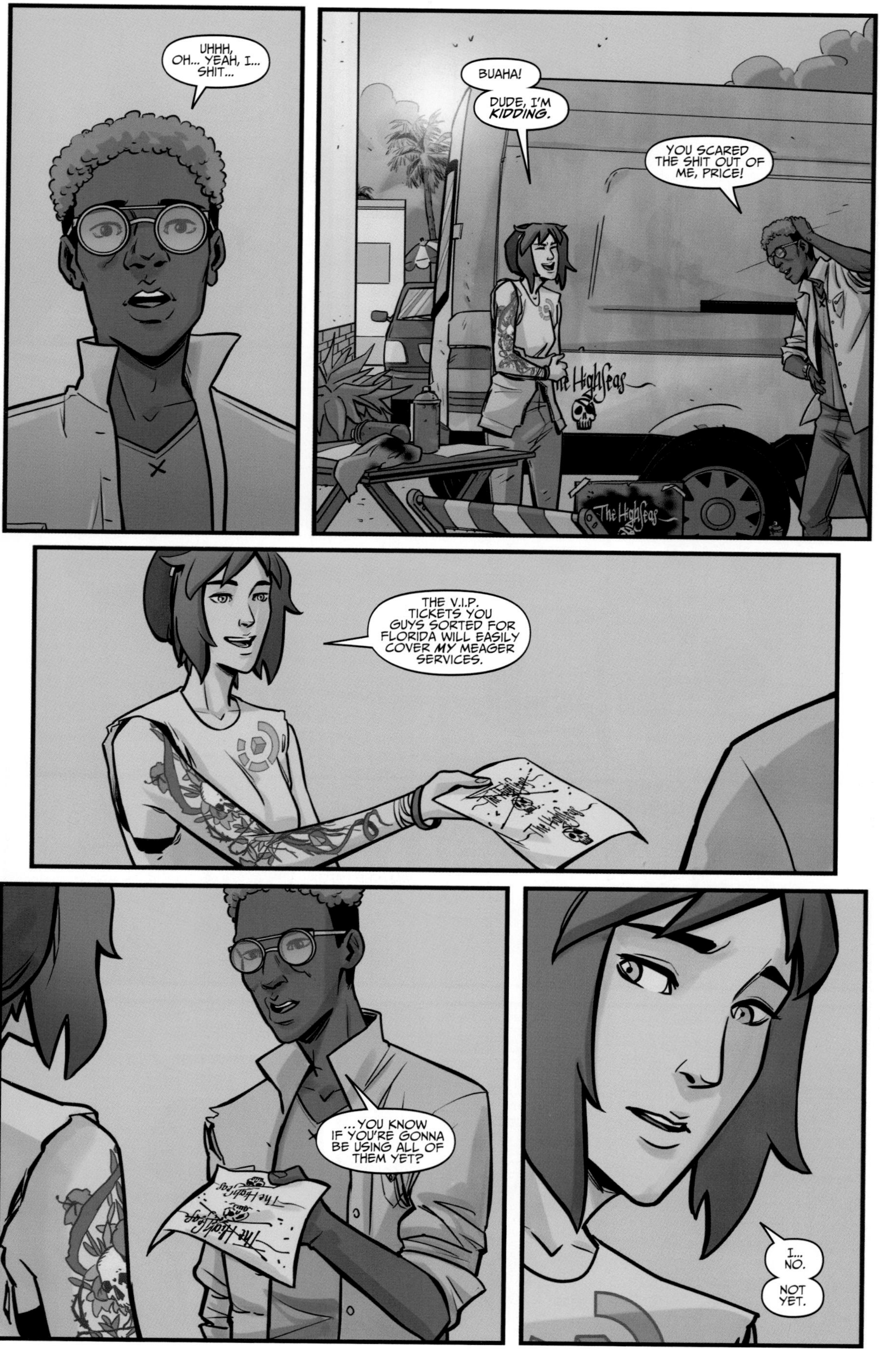
UHHH, OH... YEAH, I... SHIT...
BUAHA!
DUDE, I'M KIDDING.
YOU SCARED THE SHIT OUT OF ME, PRICE!
The HighSeas
The HighSeas
THE V.I.P. TICKETS YOU GUYS SORTED FOR FLORIDA WILL EASILY COVER MY MEAGER SERVICES.
...YOU KNOW IF YOU'RE GONNA BE USING ALL OF THEM YET?
I... NO.
NOT YET.

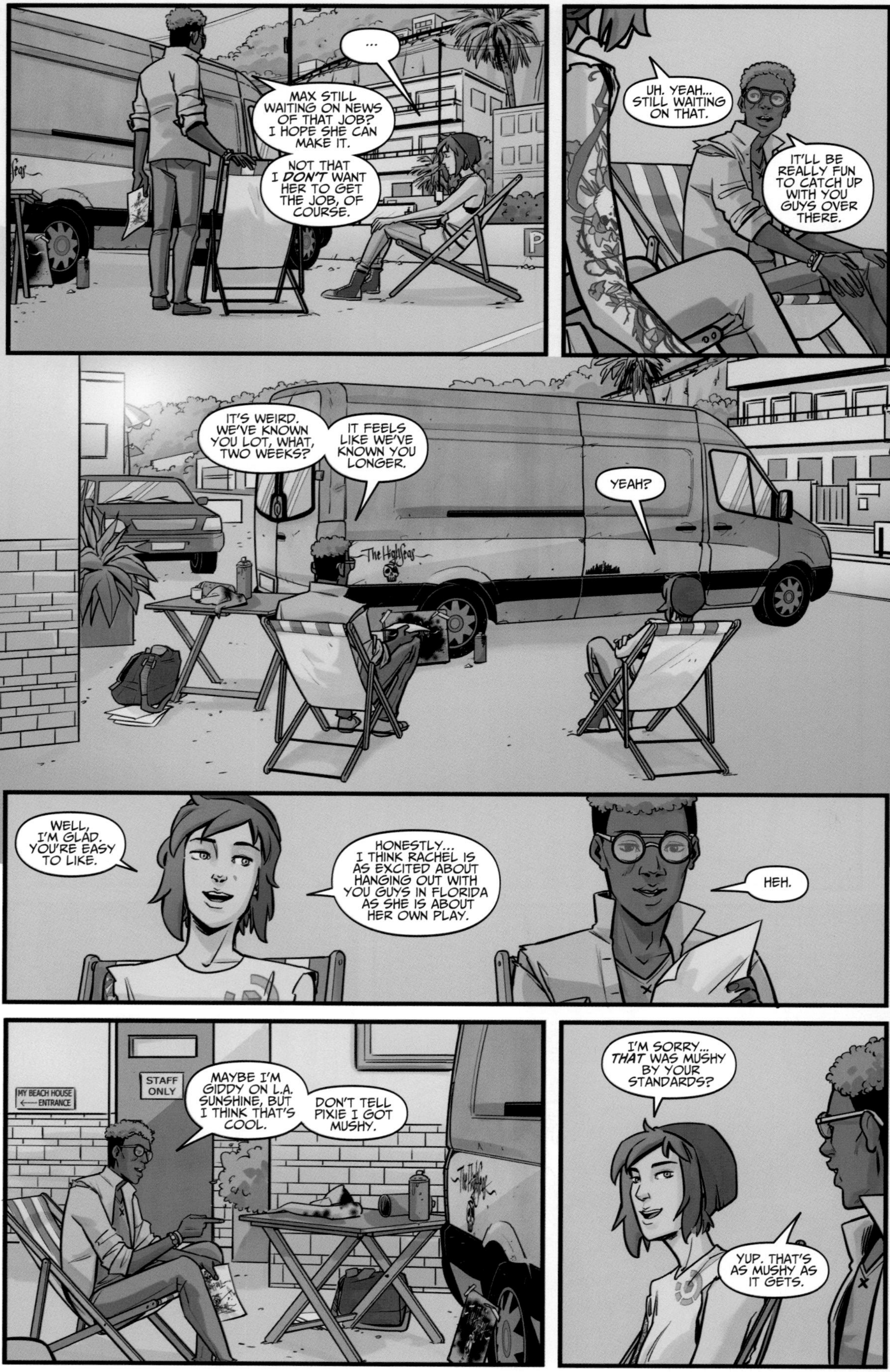
...
MAX STILL WAITING ON NEWS OF THAT JOB? I HOPE SHE CAN MAKE IT.
NOT THAT I *DON'T* WANT HER TO GET THE JOB, OF COURSE.
P
UH. YEAH... STILL WAITING ON THAT.
IT'LL BE REALLY FUN TO CATCH UP WITH YOU GUYS OVER THERE.
IT'S WEIRD. WE'VE KNOWN YOU LOT, WHAT, TWO WEEKS?
IT FEELS LIKE WE'VE KNOWN YOU LONGER.
YEAH?
The HighSeas
WELL, I'M GLAD. YOU'RE EASY TO LIKE.
HONESTLY... I THINK RACHEL IS AS EXCITED ABOUT HANGING OUT WITH YOU GUYS IN FLORIDA AS SHE IS ABOUT HER OWN PLAY.
HEH.
MY BEACH HOUSE ← ENTRANCE
STAFF ONLY
MAYBE I'M GIDDY ON L.A. SUNSHINE, BUT I THINK THAT'S COOL.
DON'T TELL PIXIE I GOT MUSHY.
I'M SORRY... *THAT* WAS MUSHY BY YOUR STANDARDS?
YUP. THAT'S AS MUSHY AS IT GETS.

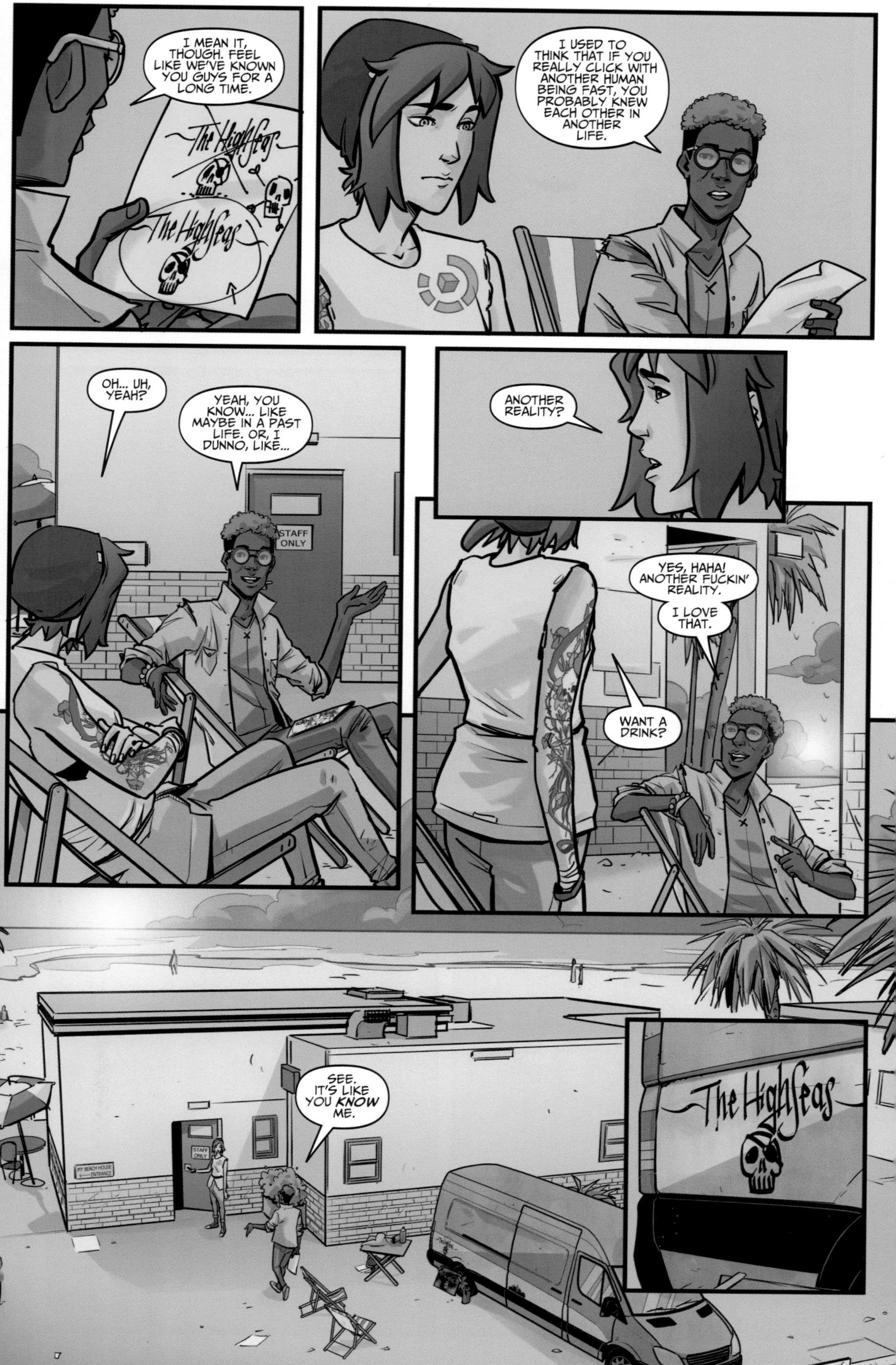
I MEAN IT, THOUGH. FEEL LIKE WE'VE KNOWN YOU GUYS FOR A LONG TIME.
The HighSeas
The HighSeas
I USED TO THINK THAT IF YOU REALLY CLICK WITH ANOTHER HUMAN BEING FAST, YOU PROBABLY KNEW EACH OTHER IN ANOTHER LIFE.
OH... UH, YEAH?
YEAH, YOU KNOW... LIKE MAYBE IN A PAST LIFE. OR, I DUNNO, LIKE...
STAFF ONLY
ANOTHER REALITY?
YES, HAHA! ANOTHER FUCKIN' REALITY.
I LOVE THAT.
WANT A DRINK?
SEE. IT'S LIKE YOU *KNOW* ME.
MY BEACH HOUSE ENTRANCE
STAFF ONLY
The HighSeas

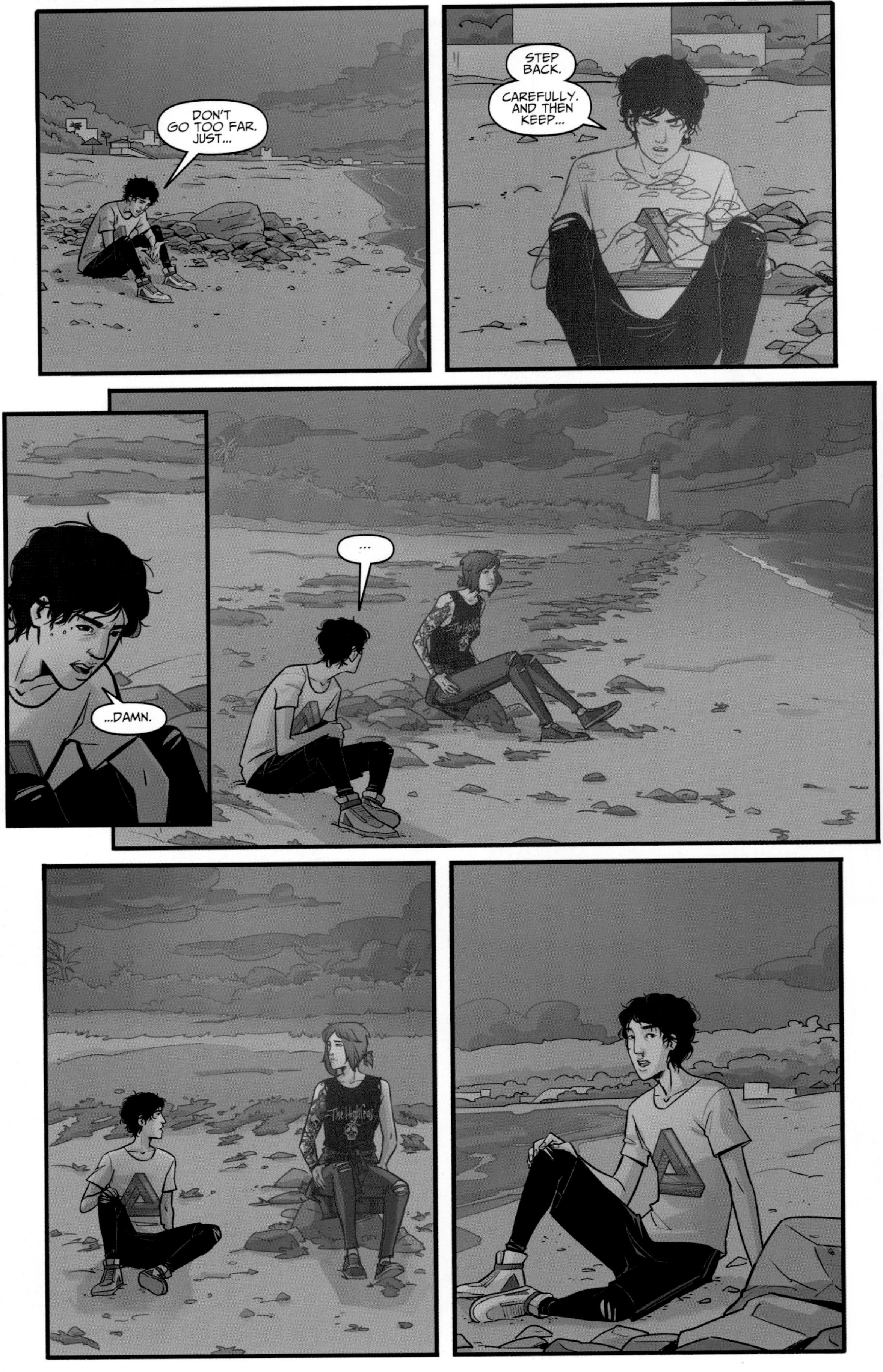
DON'T GO TOO FAR. JUST...
STEP BACK.
CAREFULLY. AND THEN KEEP...
...DAMN.
...
The Highfeys
The Highfeys

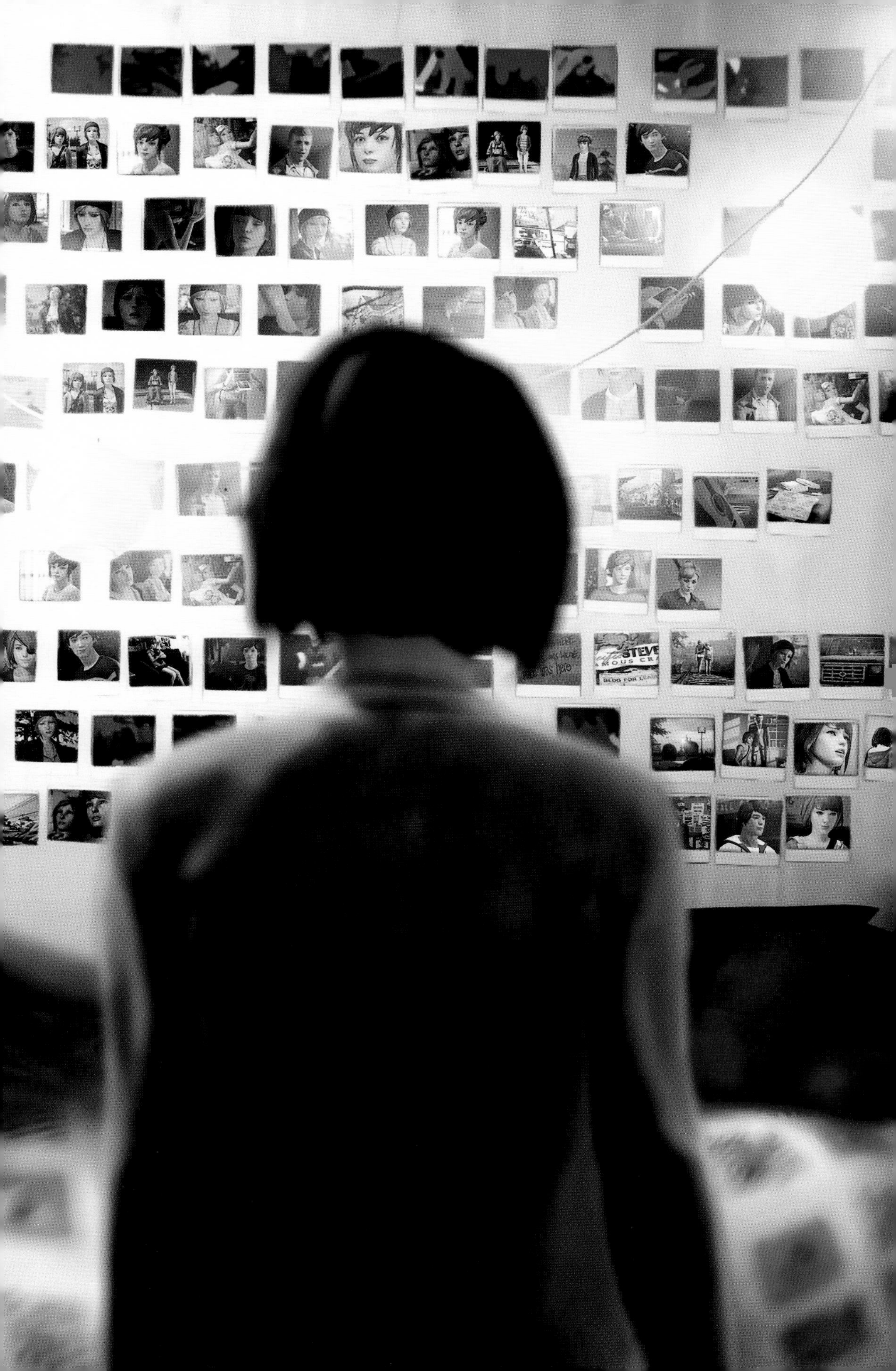
was here
BLOG FOR

CHAPTER 3

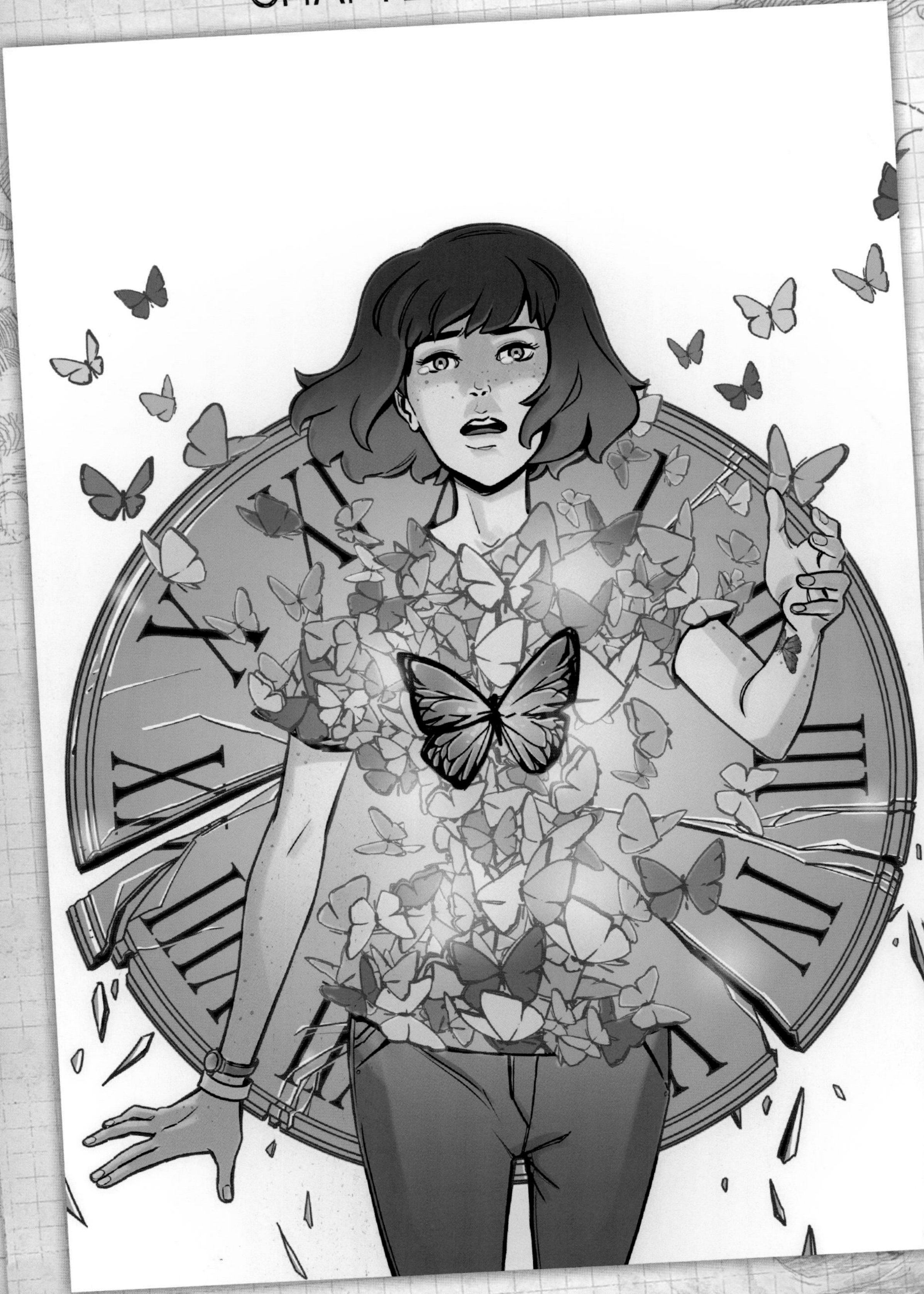

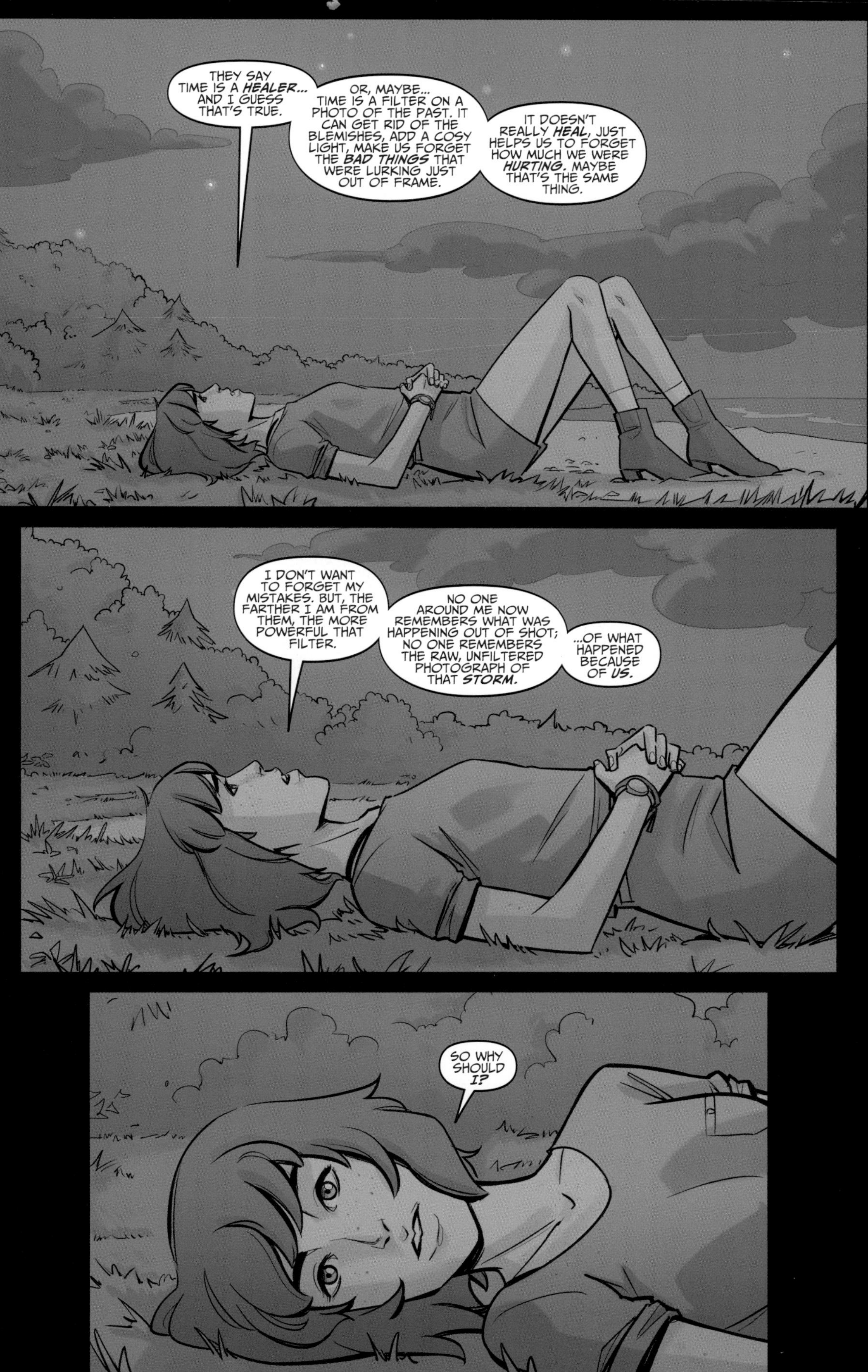
THEY SAY TIME IS A HEALER... AND I GUESS THAT'S TRUE.
OR, MAYBE... TIME IS A FILTER ON A PHOTO OF THE PAST. IT CAN GET RID OF THE BLEMISHES, ADD A COSY LIGHT, MAKE US FORGET THE BAD THINGS THAT WERE LURKING JUST OUT OF FRAME.
IT DOESN'T REALLY HEAL, JUST HELPS US TO FORGET HOW MUCH WE WERE HURTING. MAYBE THAT'S THE SAME THING.
I DON'T WANT TO FORGET MY MISTAKES. BUT, THE FARTHER I AM FROM THEM, THE MORE POWERFUL THAT FILTER.
NO ONE AROUND ME NOW REMEMBERS WHAT WAS HAPPENING OUT OF SHOT; NO ONE REMEMBERS THE RAW, UNFILTERED PHOTOGRAPH OF THAT STORM.
...OF WHAT HAPPENED BECAUSE OF US.
SO WHY SHOULD I?

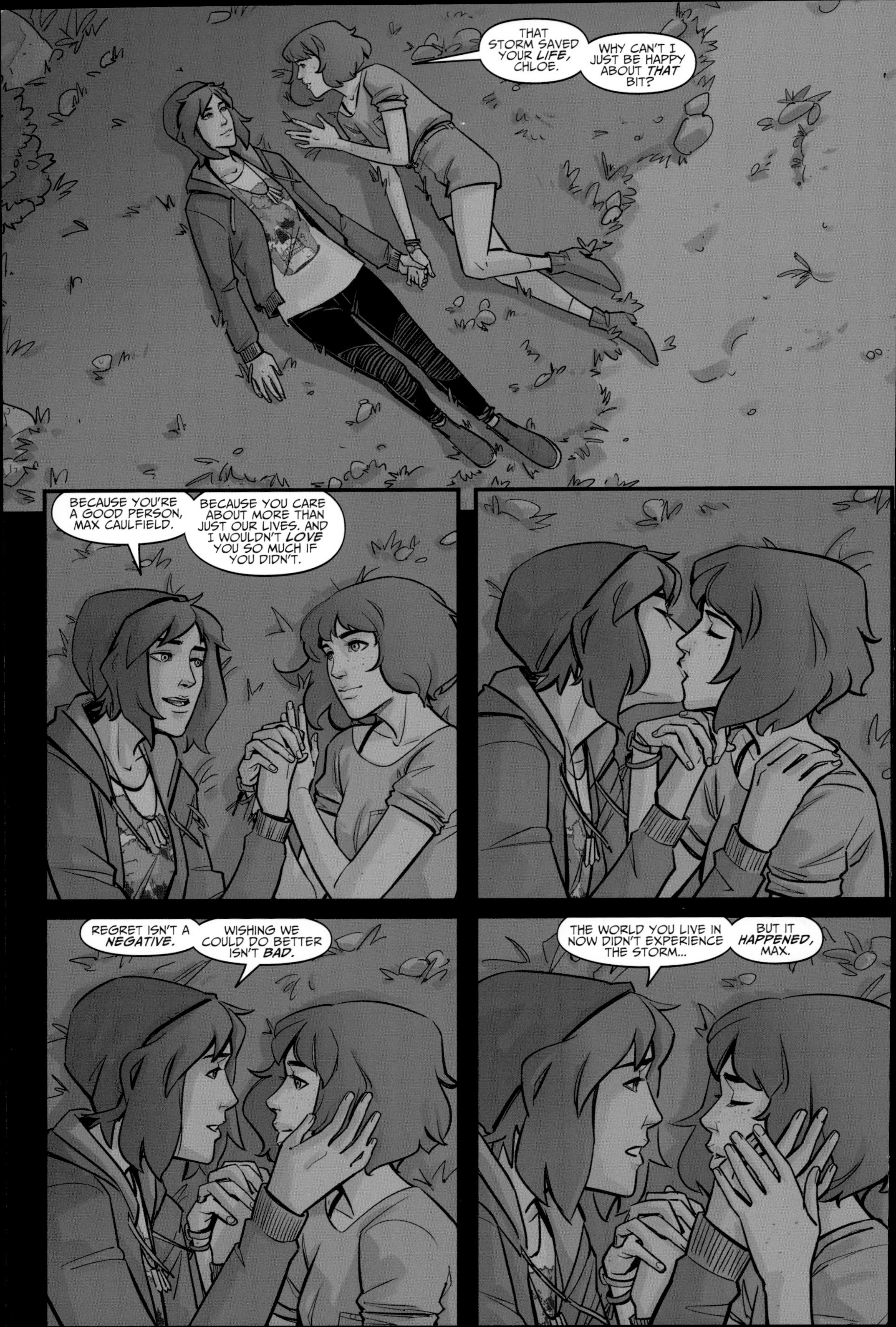
THAT STORM SAVED YOUR LIFE, CHLOE.
WHY CAN'T I JUST BE HAPPY ABOUT THAT BIT?
BECAUSE YOU'RE A GOOD PERSON, MAX CAULFIELD.
BECAUSE YOU CARE ABOUT MORE THAN JUST OUR LIVES. AND I WOULDN'T LOVE YOU SO MUCH IF YOU DIDN'T.
REGRET ISN'T A NEGATIVE.
WISHING WE COULD DO BETTER ISN'T BAD.
THE WORLD YOU LIVE IN NOW DIDN'T EXPERIENCE THE STORM...
BUT IT HAPPENED, MAX.

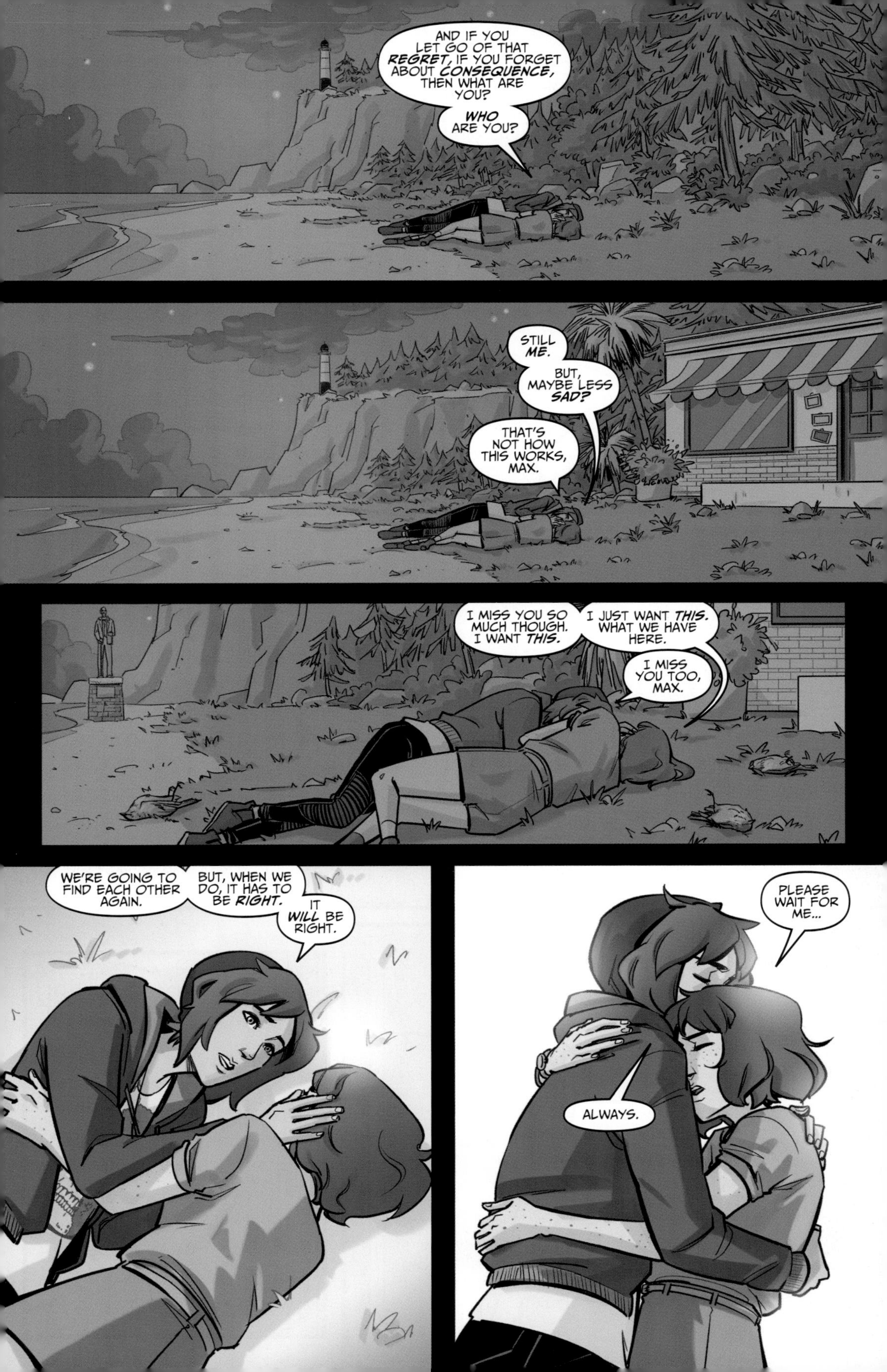
AND IF YOU LET GO OF THAT REGRET, IF YOU FORGET ABOUT CONSEQUENCE, THEN WHAT ARE YOU?
WHO ARE YOU?
STILL ME.
BUT, MAYBE LESS SAD?
THAT'S NOT HOW THIS WORKS, MAX.
I MISS YOU SO MUCH THOUGH. I WANT THIS.
I JUST WANT THIS. WHAT WE HAVE HERE.
I MISS YOU TOO, MAX.
WE'RE GOING TO FIND EACH OTHER AGAIN.
BUT, WHEN WE DO, IT HAS TO BE RIGHT.
IT WILL BE RIGHT.
PLEASE WAIT FOR ME...
ALWAYS.

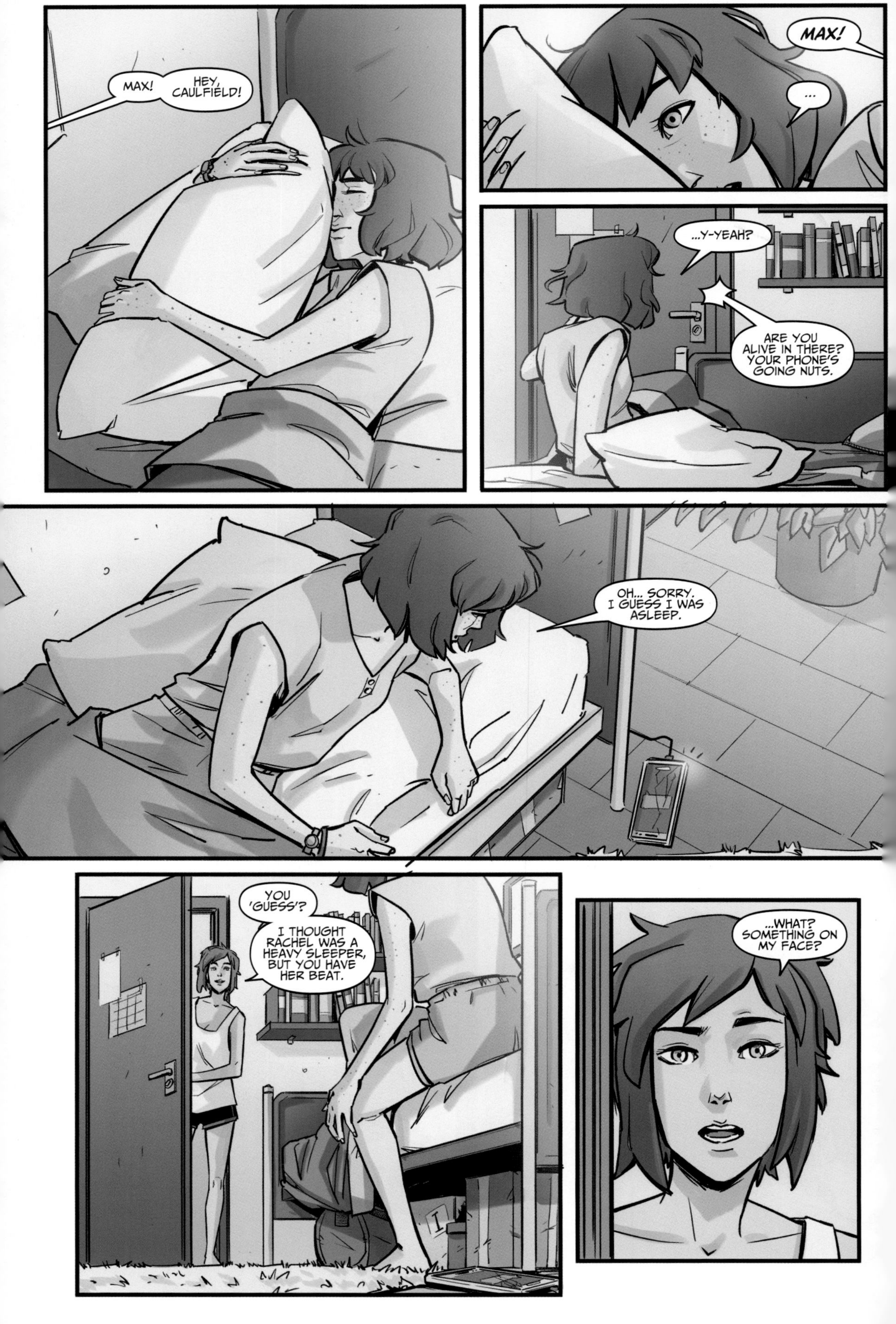
MAX!
HEY, CAULFIELD!
MAX!
...
...Y-YEAH?
ARE YOU ALIVE IN THERE? YOUR PHONE'S GOING NUTS.
OH... SORRY. I GUESS I WAS ASLEEP.
YOU 'GUESS'?
I THOUGHT RACHEL WAS A HEAVY SLEEPER, BUT YOU HAVE HER BEAT.
...WHAT? SOMETHING ON MY FACE?

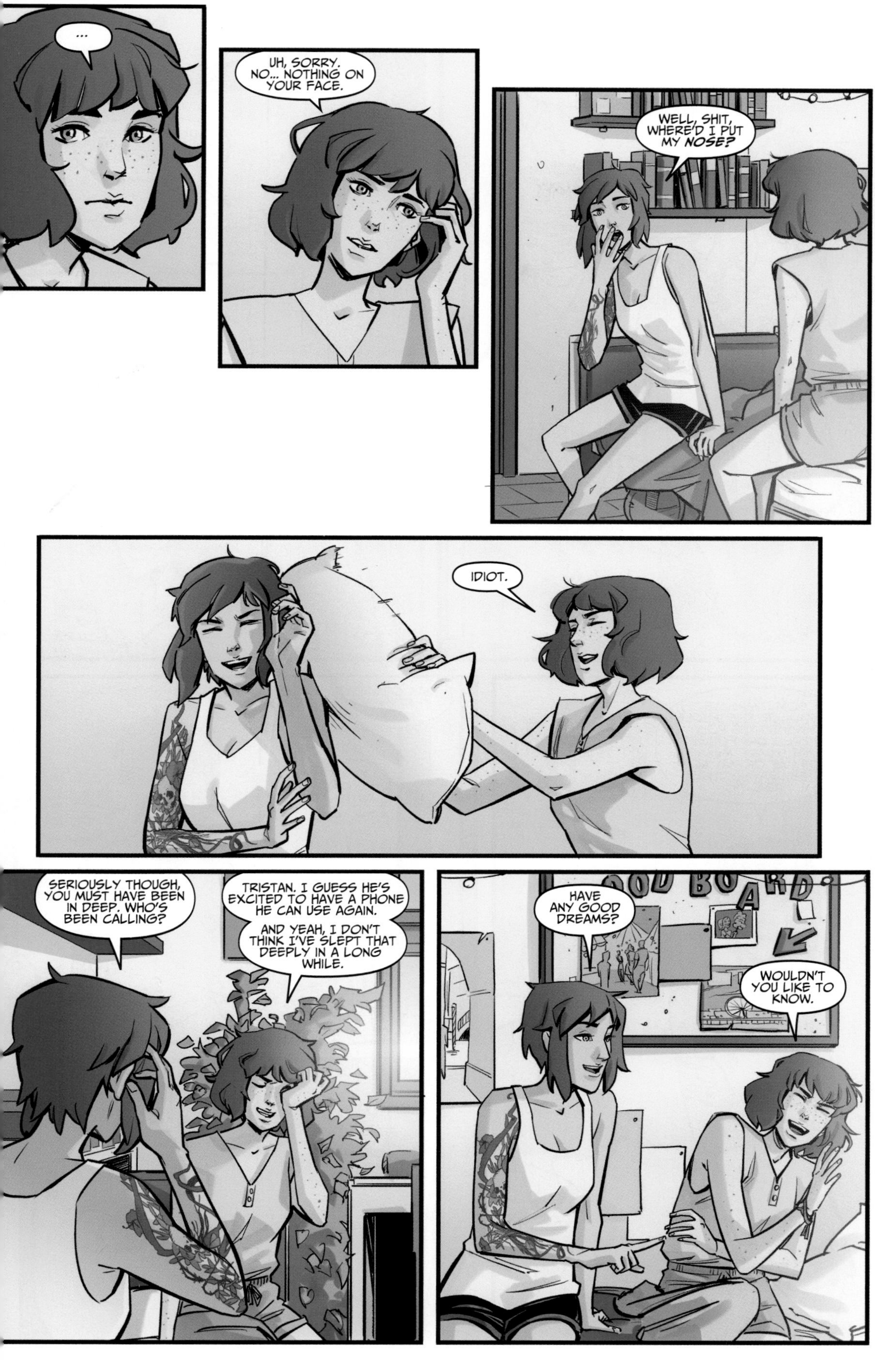
...
UH, SORRY. NO... NOTHING ON YOUR FACE.
WELL, SHIT, WHERE'D I PUT MY *NOSE?*
IDIOT.
SERIOUSLY THOUGH, YOU MUST HAVE BEEN IN DEEP. WHO'S BEEN CALLING?
TRISTAN. I GUESS HE'S EXCITED TO HAVE A PHONE HE CAN USE AGAIN.
AND YEAH, I DON'T THINK I'VE SLEPT THAT DEEPLY IN A LONG WHILE.
HAVE ANY GOOD DREAMS?
WOULDN'T YOU LIKE TO KNOW.

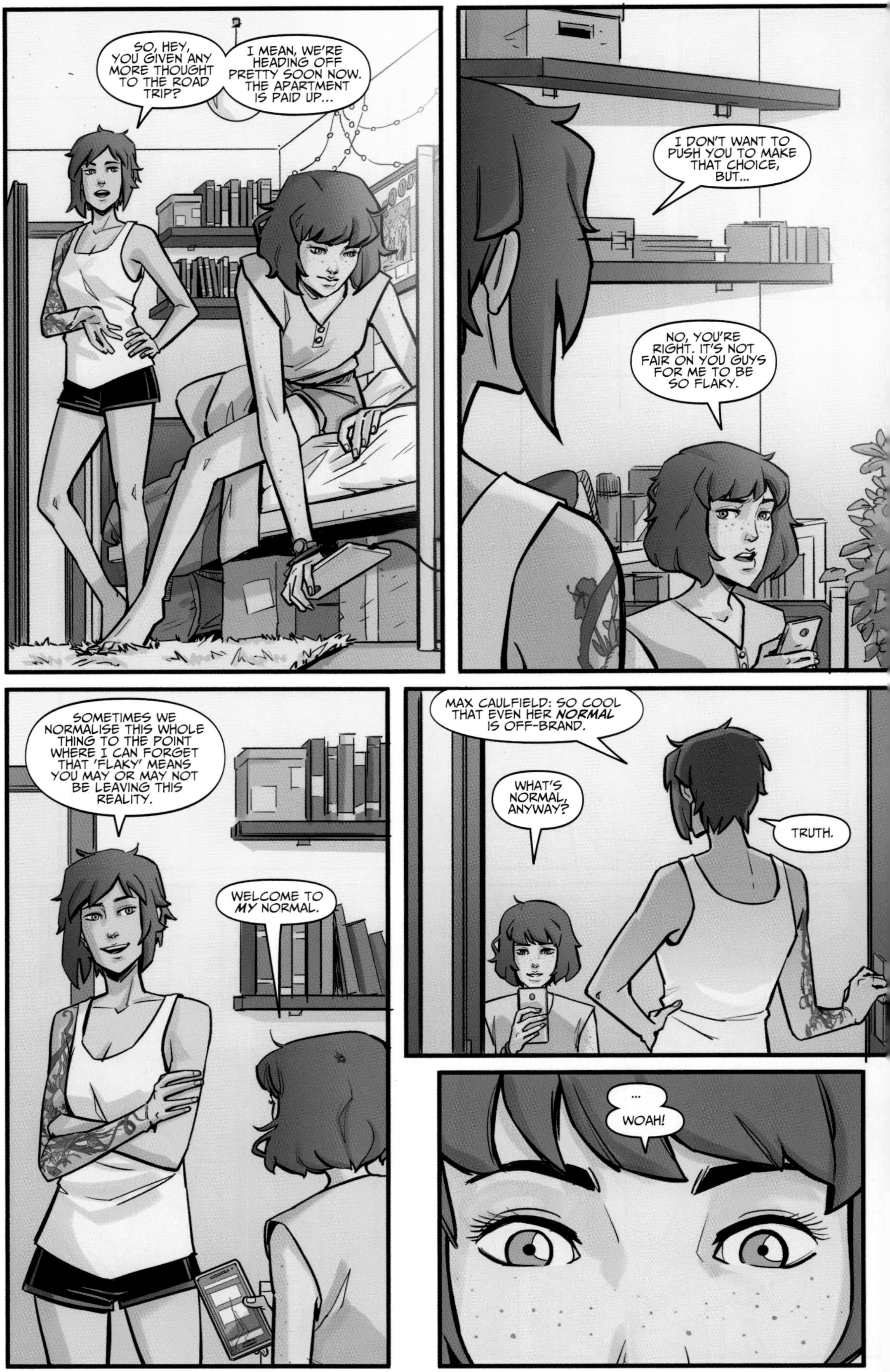
SO, HEY, YOU GIVEN ANY MORE THOUGHT TO THE ROAD TRIP?
I MEAN, WE'RE HEADING OFF PRETTY SOON NOW. THE APARTMENT IS PAID UP...
I DON'T WANT TO PUSH YOU TO MAKE THAT CHOICE, BUT...
NO, YOU'RE RIGHT. IT'S NOT FAIR ON YOU GUYS FOR ME TO BE SO FLAKY.
SOMETIMES WE NORMALISE THIS WHOLE THING TO THE POINT WHERE I CAN FORGET THAT 'FLAKY' MEANS YOU MAY OR MAY NOT BE LEAVING THIS REALITY.
WELCOME TO MY NORMAL.
MAX CAULFIELD: SO COOL THAT EVEN HER NORMAL IS OFF-BRAND.
WHAT'S NORMAL, ANYWAY?
TRUTH.
...
WOAH!

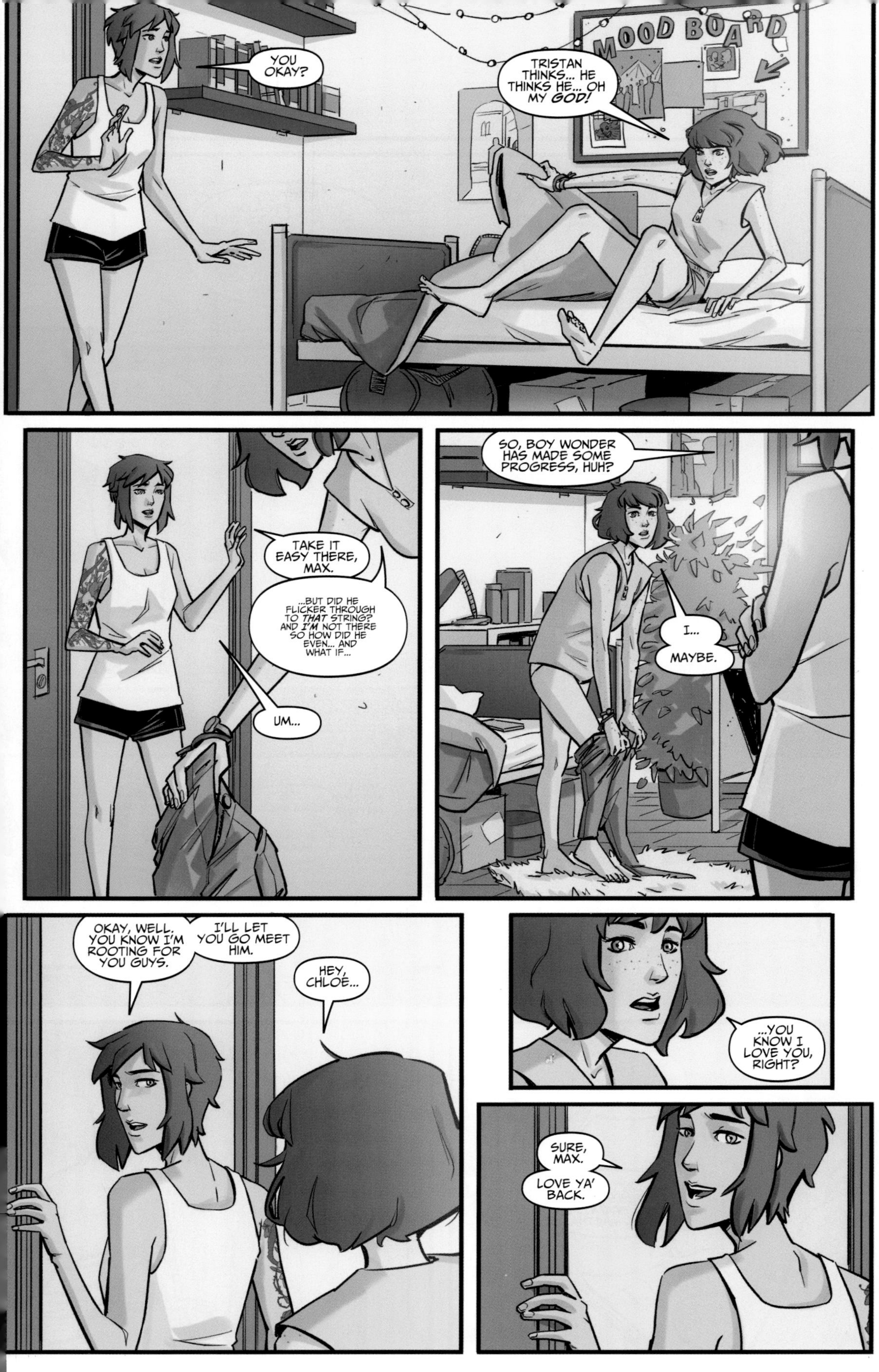
MOOD BOARD
YOU OKAY?
TRISTAN THINKS... HE THINKS HE... OH MY GOD!
TAKE IT EASY THERE, MAX.
...BUT DID HE FLICKER THROUGH TO THAT STRING? AND I'M NOT THERE SO HOW DID HE EVEN... AND WHAT IF...
UM...
SO, BOY WONDER HAS MADE SOME PROGRESS, HUH?
I...
MAYBE.
OKAY, WELL. YOU KNOW I'M ROOTING FOR YOU GUYS.
I'LL LET YOU GO MEET HIM.
HEY, CHLOE...
...YOU KNOW I LOVE YOU, RIGHT?
SURE, MAX.
LOVE YA' BACK.

DEATH IS A WONDERFUL MOTIVATOR FOR THOSE LEFT BEHIND.

HERS HAS IMPACT BECAUSE SHE WAS YOUNG AND VIBRANT... SHE HAS, IN HER DEATH, BECOME A SYMBOL OF LIFE CUT SHORT. A VICTIM OF A MIND GAME. A FLOWER PLUCKED TOO SOON.

IT CAN BE ARGUED THAT OPHELIA PLAYS A MORE PIVOTAL ROLE IN *DEATH* THAN SHE DID IN LIFE.

LIKE ANY GOOD *FRIDGE-MAIDEN,* AM I RIGHT, TERRY?

IT'S TERRANCE.

A FRIDGE MAIDEN?

YOU KNOW, SHAKESPEARE PUT HER IN A *FRIDGE?*

I DON'T THINK FRIDGES WERE EVEN *INVENTED* THEN, MARTHA.

HAYLET

Ha Ha Ha Ha Ha Ha Ha Ha Ha Ha Ha Ha Ha Ha Ha Ha Ha Ha Ha Ha Ha Ha Ha Ha Ha Ha Ha Ha Ha Ha Ha Ha Ha Ha

...

OPHELIA HAD
A LIFE, THOUGH.
SHE DIDN'T *KNOW*
SHE WAS GOING
TO DIE.

WE ONLY
SEE HER AS
TRAGIC BECAUSE
WE KNOW WHAT'S
COMING. *SHE*
DOESN'T.

OH,
VERY GOOD,
RACHEL.

THIS TOUCHES ON
SOMETHING VERY
IMPORTANT FOR ALL
OF US TO CONSIDER
BEFORE THE
DRESS-RUN.

MAKE. LIFE.
COUNT.

IT'S EASY TO
COLOR OUR VIEW BASED
ON THEIR DEATHS, BUT
WE MUSTN'T PLAY THE
TRAGEDY OF THESE
CHARACTERS.

"THE PLAY'S
THE THING." YOU
JUST LIVE THESE
LIVES AND LET
THE PLAY DO
THE WORK.

TAKE
FIVE!

I STILL DON'T
UNDERSTAND WHY
YOU'D SAY SHE'S
IN A FRIDGE.

POOR TERRY.
POP CULTURE
HAPPENS TO
OTHER PEOPLE,
DOESN'T IT.

IT'S
TERRANCE.

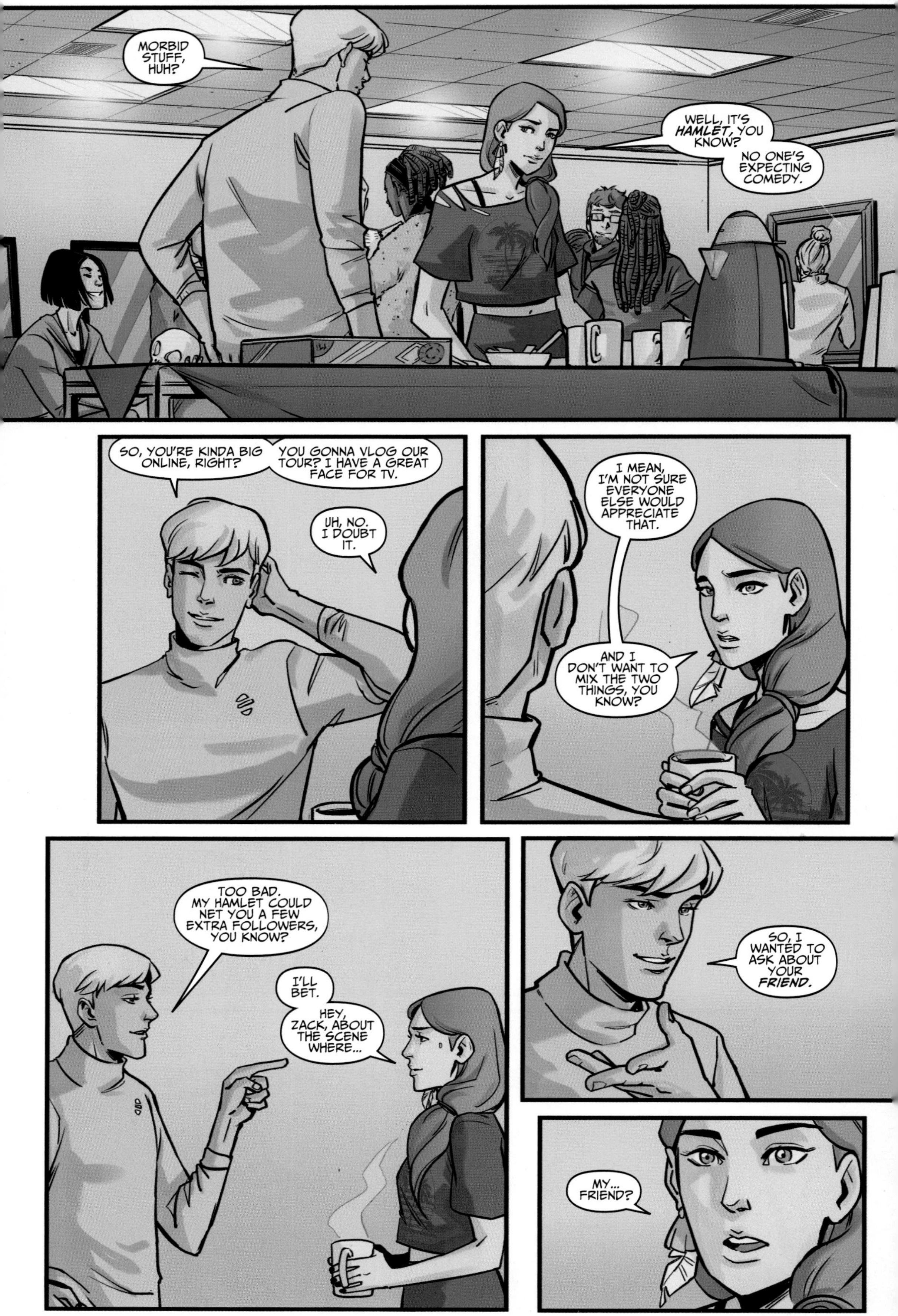
MORBID STUFF, HUH?
WELL, IT'S HAMLET, YOU KNOW?
NO ONE'S EXPECTING COMEDY.
SO, YOU'RE KINDA BIG ONLINE, RIGHT?
YOU GONNA VLOG OUR TOUR? I HAVE A GREAT FACE FOR TV.
UH, NO. I DOUBT IT.
I MEAN, I'M NOT SURE EVERYONE ELSE WOULD APPRECIATE THAT.
AND I DON'T WANT TO MIX THE TWO THINGS, YOU KNOW?
TOO BAD. MY HAMLET COULD NET YOU A FEW EXTRA FOLLOWERS, YOU KNOW?
I'LL BET.
HEY, ZACK, ABOUT THE SCENE WHERE...
SO, I WANTED TO ASK ABOUT YOUR FRIEND.
MY... FRIEND?

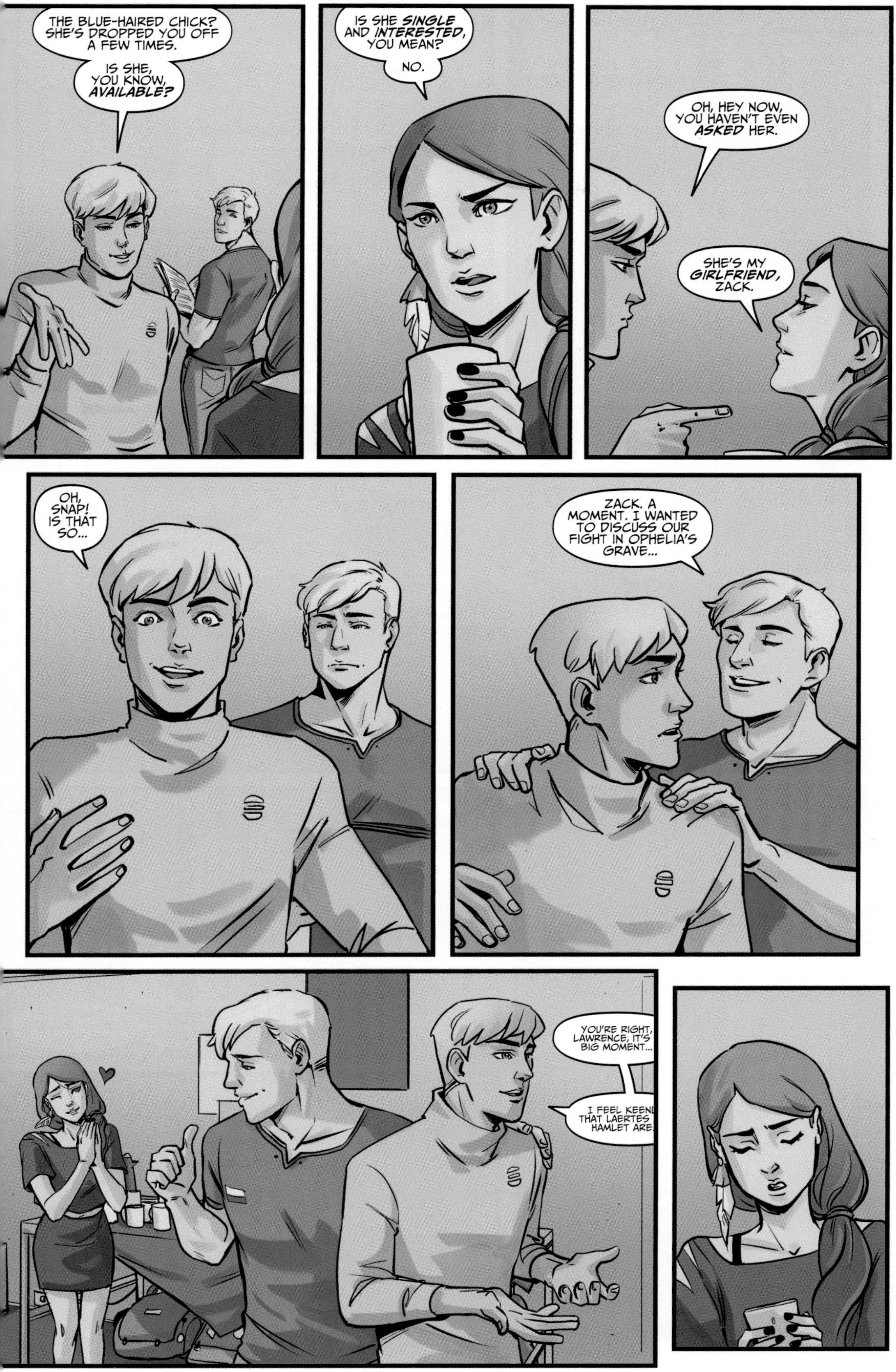
THE BLUE-HAIRED CHICK? SHE'S DROPPED YOU OFF A FEW TIMES.
IS SHE, YOU KNOW, AVAILABLE?
IS SHE SINGLE AND INTERESTED, YOU MEAN?
NO.
OH, HEY NOW, YOU HAVEN'T EVEN ASKED HER.
SHE'S MY GIRLFRIEND, ZACK.
OH, SNAP! IS THAT SO...
ZACK. A MOMENT. I WANTED TO DISCUSS OUR FIGHT IN OPHELIA'S GRAVE...
YOU'RE RIGHT, LAWRENCE, IT'S BIG MOMENT...
I FEEL KEENL THAT LAERTES HAMLET ARE

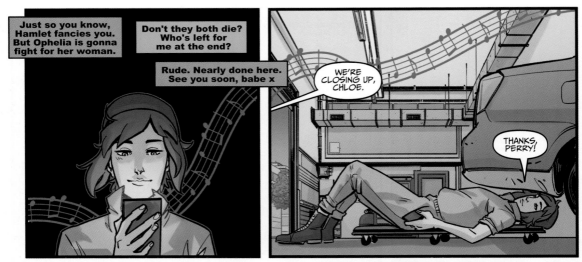

Just so you know, Hamlet fancies you. But Ophelia is gonna fight for her woman.

Don't they both die? Who's left for me at the end?

Rude. Nearly done here. See you soon, babe x

WE'RE CLOSING UP, CHLOE.

THANKS, PERRY!

IT'S SURE GONNA FEEL *QUIET* AROUND HERE WHEN YOU GO.

YOU DID AN *AMAZING* JOB ON THAT OLD CAMPER, BY THE WAY.

GLADYS? *THANKS!*

AND DEAL'S A DEAL... SHE'S YOURS TO SELL WHEN WE GET BACK.

CLICK

YOU'LL GET A CUT, AFTER ALL YOU'VE DONE TO THAT OLD THING.

I'M NOT GOING TO SAY NO TO THAT.

AH, SORRY! I WONDERED IF CHLOE PRICE WAS HERE?

YOU CUT IT FINE. WE'RE JUST ABOUT TO *CLOSE UP.*

WELL, *TIMING* IS KINDA MY FORTE.

SORRY TO BUG YOU *HERE*, BUT PAUL SAID I MIGHT FIND YOU.

HEY, NO WORRIES! IGNORE PERRY.

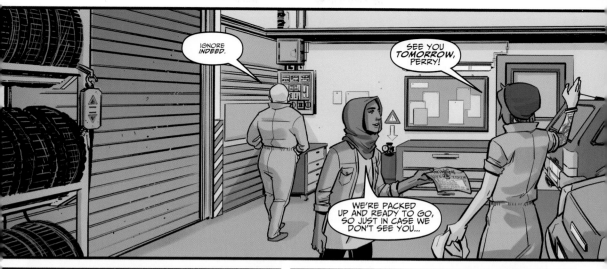

IGNORE *INDEED.*

SEE YOU *TOMORROW,* PERRY!

WE'RE PACKED UP AND READY TO GO, SO JUST IN CASE WE DON'T SEE YOU...

OH, COOL! *TOUR DATES!*

DAMN, I STILL CAN'T GET USED TO SEEING MY ART BEING USED LIKE *THIS.*

WELL, YOU SHOULD. YOU'RE *AMAZING.*

DID MAX HEAR ABOUT HER JOB YET?

...NAH.

OUCH. THERE'S NOT MUCH *TIME* LEFT...

YEAH.

YOU'RE NOT WRONG.

STILL, IT'S JUST ONE TRIP.

AND THIS JOB SOUNDS LIKE SOMETHING PRETTY *LIFE-CHANGING.*

IT... YEAH, IT'S A PRETTY BIG DEAL.

HEY... YOU *OKAY?*

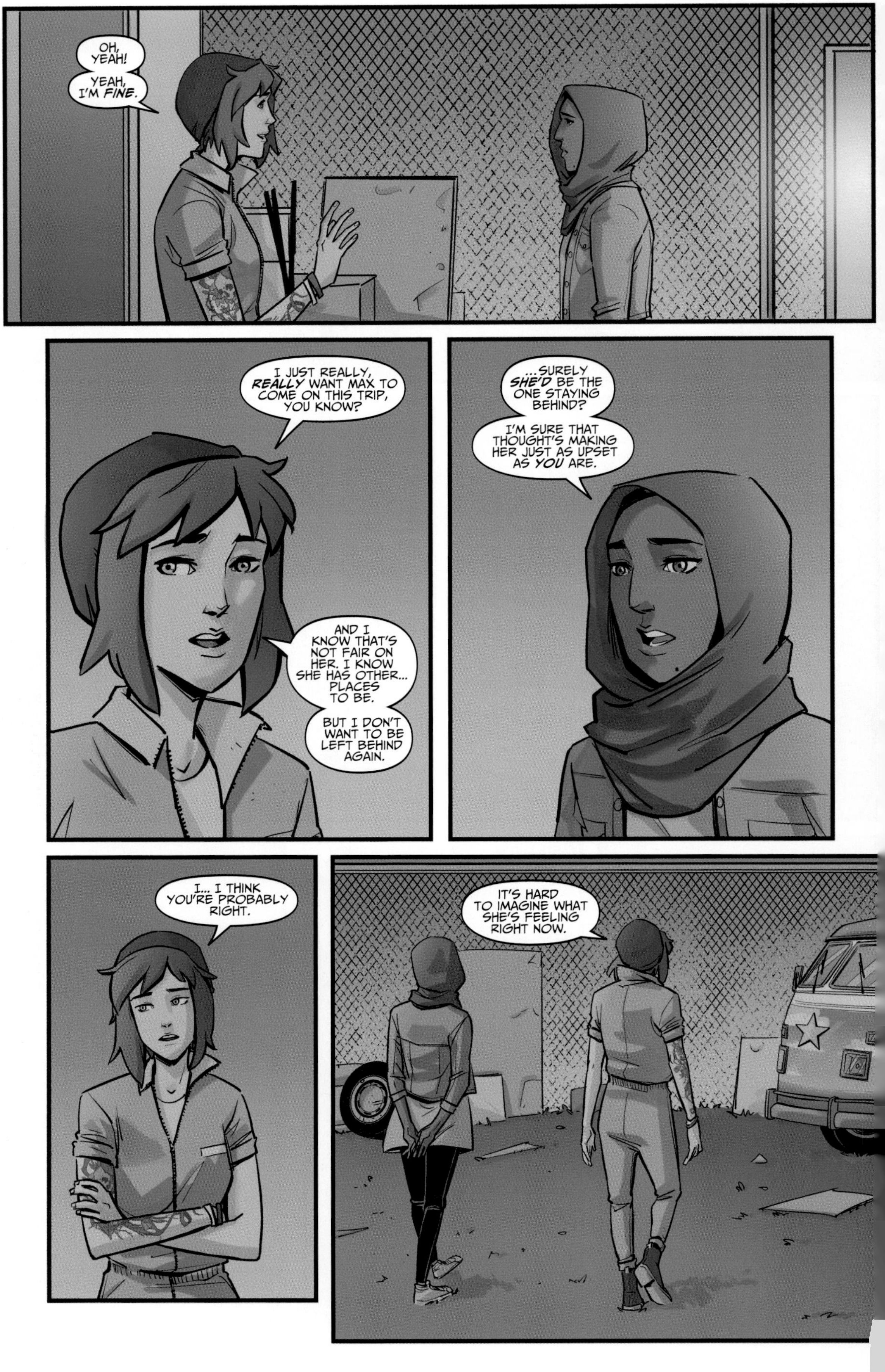
OH, YEAH!
YEAH, I'M *FINE*.
I JUST REALLY, ***REALLY*** WANT MAX TO COME ON THIS TRIP, YOU KNOW?
AND I KNOW THAT'S NOT FAIR ON HER. I KNOW SHE HAS OTHER... PLACES TO BE.
BUT I DON'T WANT TO BE LEFT BEHIND AGAIN.
...SURELY ***SHE'D*** BE THE ONE STAYING BEHIND?
I'M SURE THAT THOUGHT'S MAKING HER JUST AS UPSET AS *YOU* ARE.
I... I THINK YOU'RE PROBABLY RIGHT.
IT'S HARD TO IMAGINE WHAT SHE'S FEELING RIGHT NOW.

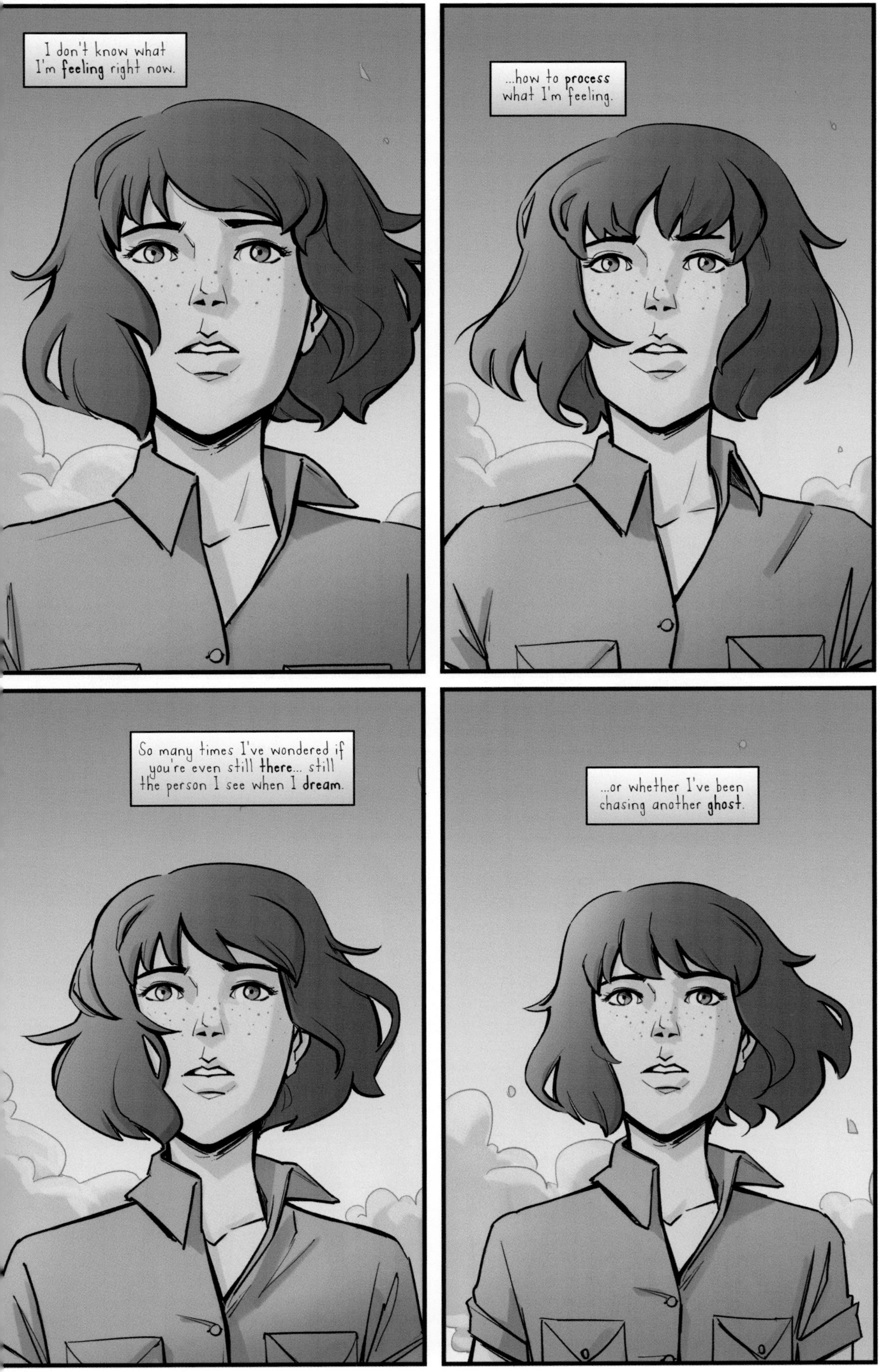
I don't know what I'm **feeling** right now.
...how to **process** what I'm feeling.
So many times I've wondered if you're even still **there**... still the person I see when I **dream**.
...or whether I've been chasing another **ghost**.

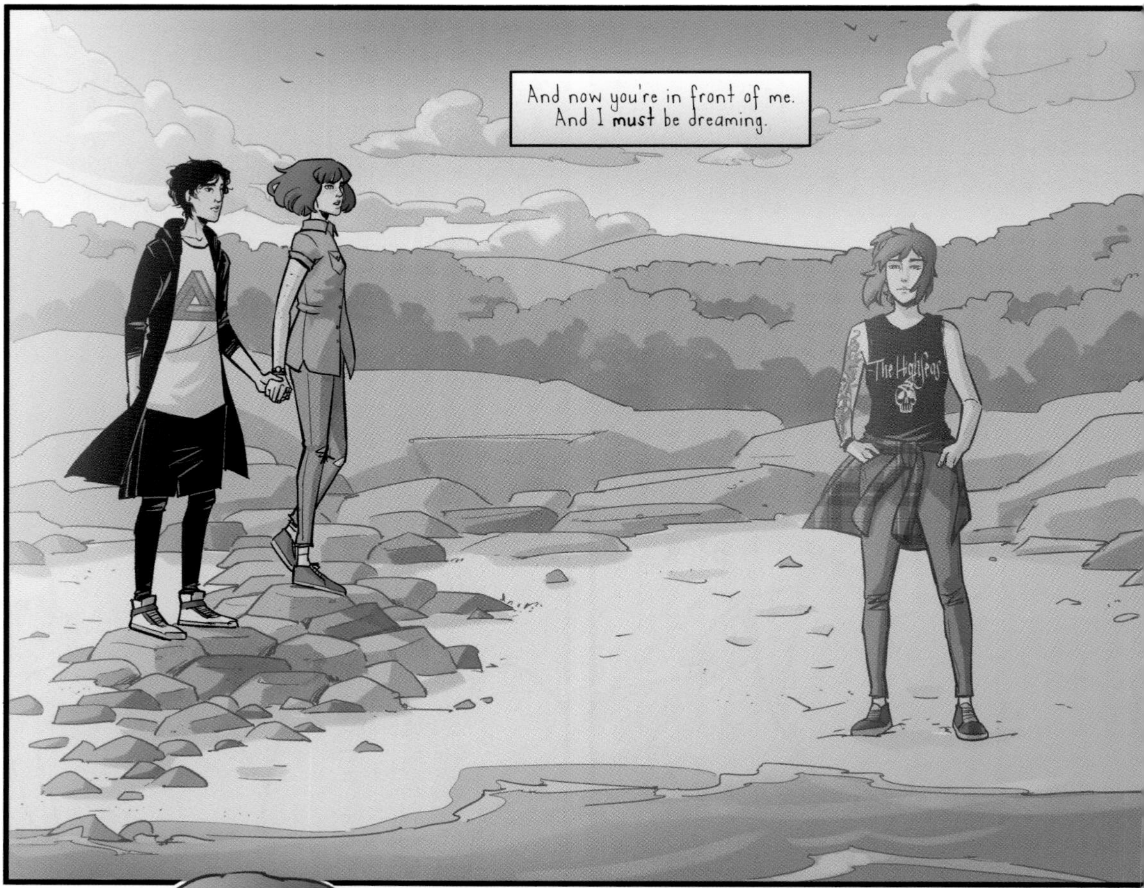
And now you're in front of me.
And I **must** be dreaming.
The HighSeas

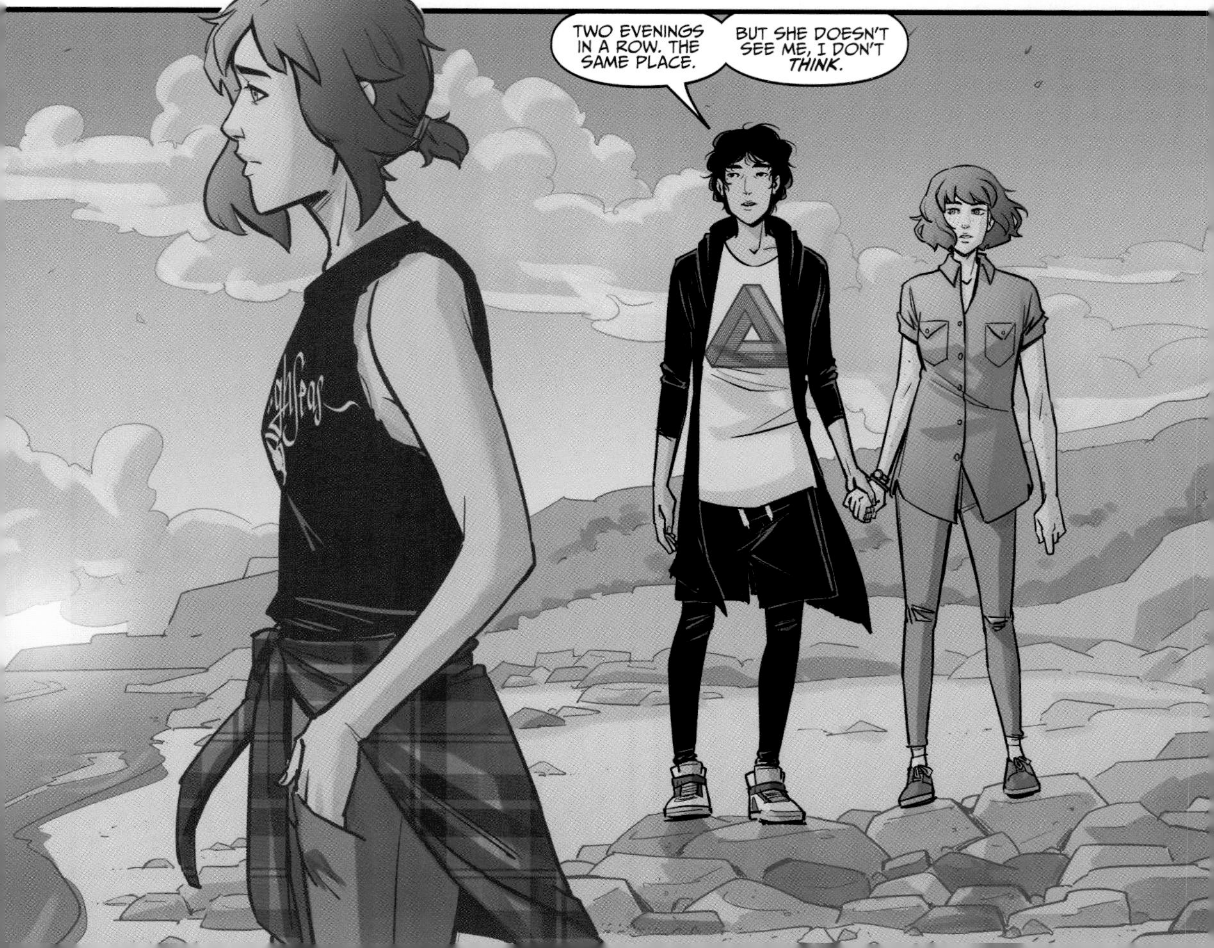
TWO EVENINGS IN A ROW. THE SAME PLACE.
BUT SHE DOESN'T SEE ME, I DON'T *THINK*.

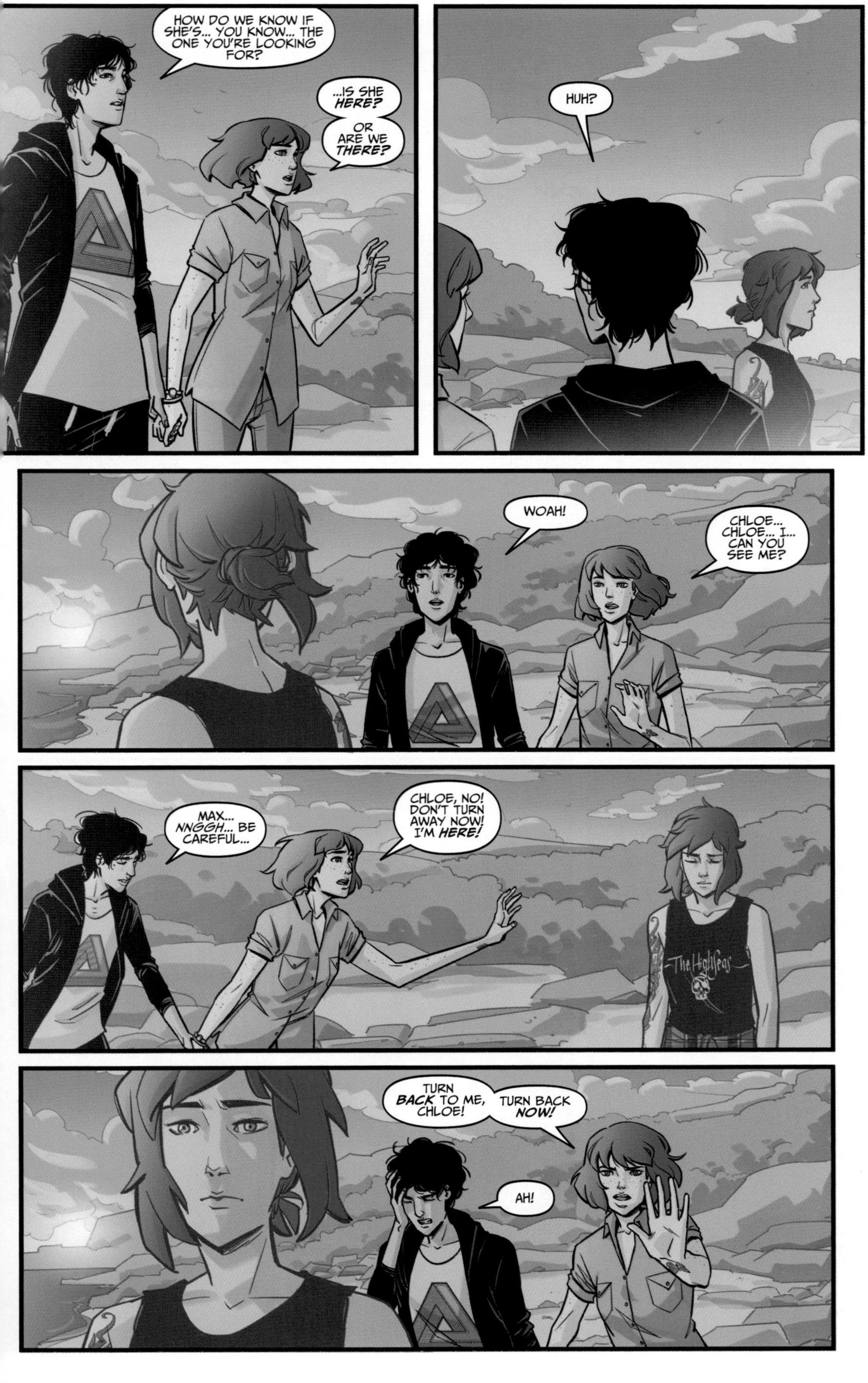
HOW DO WE KNOW IF SHE'S... YOU KNOW... THE ONE YOU'RE LOOKING FOR?
...IS SHE *HERE?*
OR ARE WE *THERE?*
HUH?
WOAH!
CHLOE... CHLOE... I... CAN YOU SEE ME?
MAX... *NNGGH*... BE CAREFUL...
CHLOE, NO! DON'T TURN AWAY NOW! I'M *HERE!*
The HighSeas
TURN *BACK* TO ME, CHLOE!
TURN BACK *NOW!*
AH!

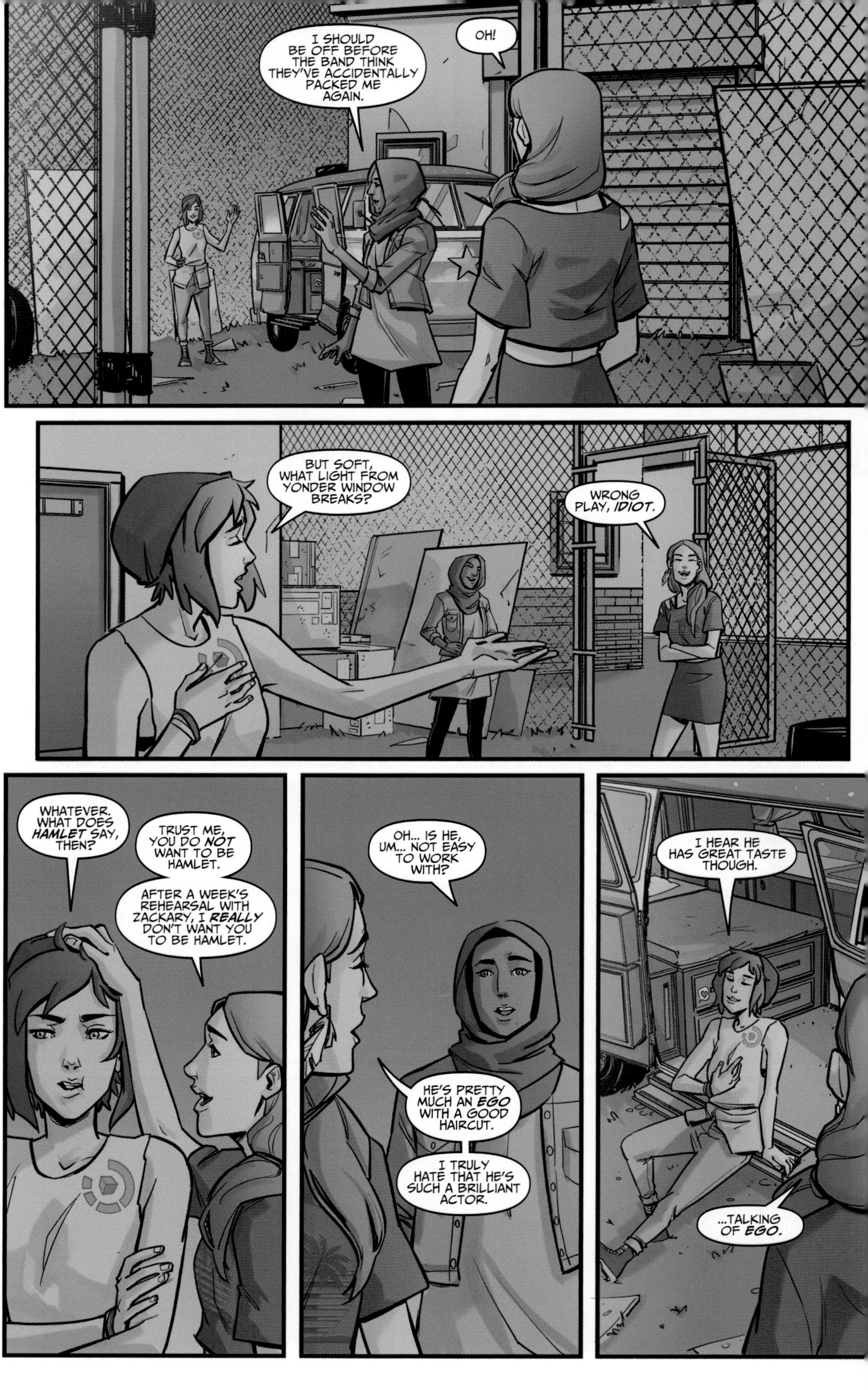
I SHOULD BE OFF BEFORE THE BAND THINK THEY'VE ACCIDENTALLY PACKED ME AGAIN.
OH!
BUT SOFT, WHAT LIGHT FROM YONDER WINDOW BREAKS?
WRONG PLAY, IDIOT.
WHATEVER. WHAT DOES HAMLET SAY, THEN?
TRUST ME, YOU DO NOT WANT TO BE HAMLET.
AFTER A WEEK'S REHEARSAL WITH ZACKARY, I REALLY DON'T WANT YOU TO BE HAMLET.
OH... IS HE, UM... NOT EASY TO WORK WITH?
HE'S PRETTY MUCH AN EGO WITH A GOOD HAIRCUT.
I TRULY HATE THAT HE'S SUCH A BRILLIANT ACTOR.
I HEAR HE HAS GREAT TASTE THOUGH.
...TALKING OF EGO.

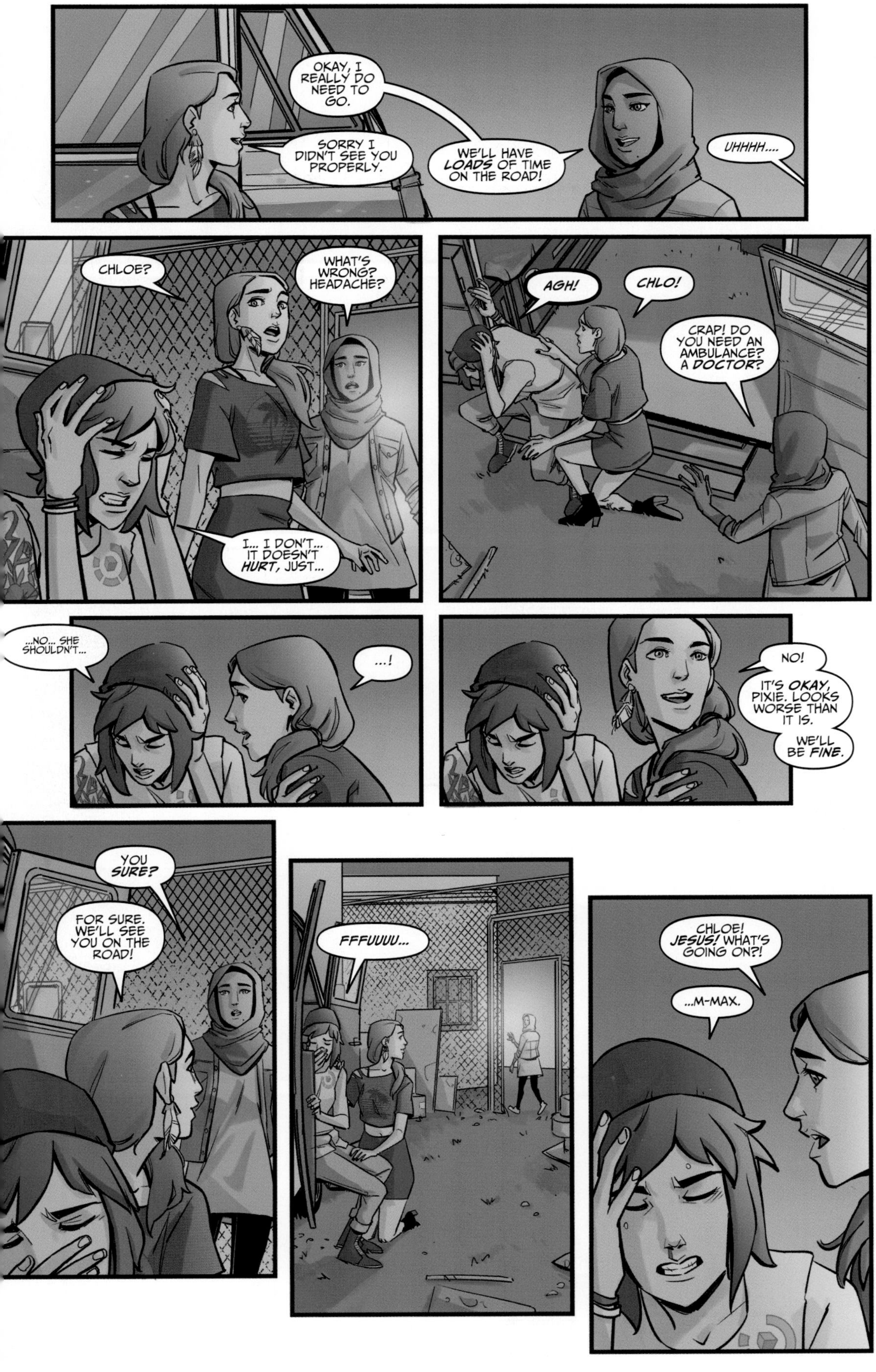
OKAY, I REALLY DO NEED TO GO.
SORRY I DIDN'T SEE YOU PROPERLY.
WE'LL HAVE *LOADS* OF TIME ON THE ROAD!
UHHHH....
CHLOE?
WHAT'S WRONG? HEADACHE?
I... I DON'T... IT DOESN'T *HURT*, JUST...
AGH!
CHLO!
CRAP! DO YOU NEED AN AMBULANCE? A *DOCTOR*?
...NO... SHE SHOULDN'T...
...!
NO!
IT'S *OKAY*, PIXIE. LOOKS WORSE THAN IT IS.
WE'LL BE *FINE*.
YOU *SURE?*
FOR SURE. WE'LL SEE YOU ON THE ROAD!
FFFUUUU...
CHLOE! *JESUS!* WHAT'S GOING ON?!
...M-MAX.

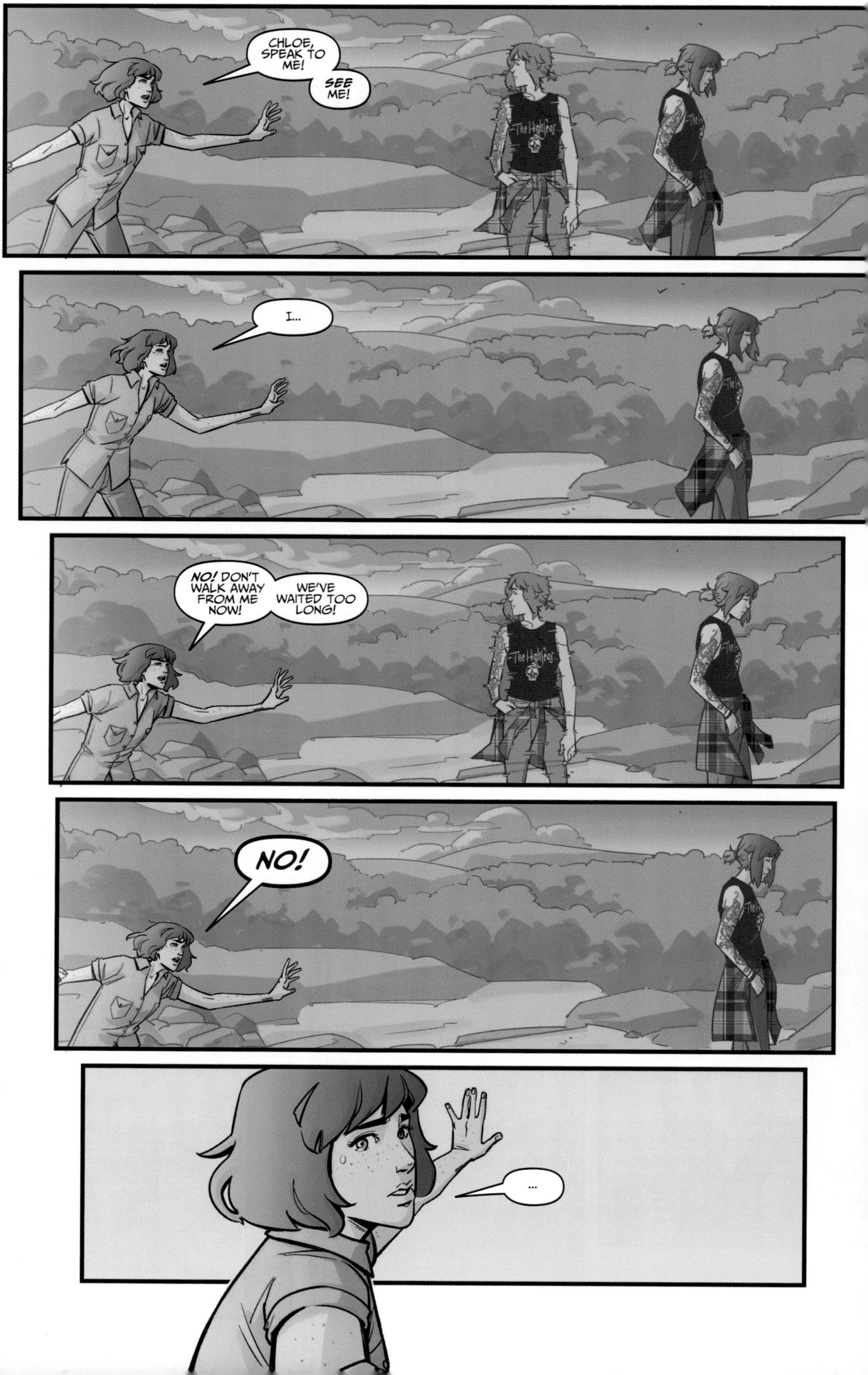

CHLOE, SPEAK TO ME!
SEE ME!
I...
NO! DON'T WALK AWAY FROM ME NOW!
WE'VE WAITED TOO LONG!
NO!
...

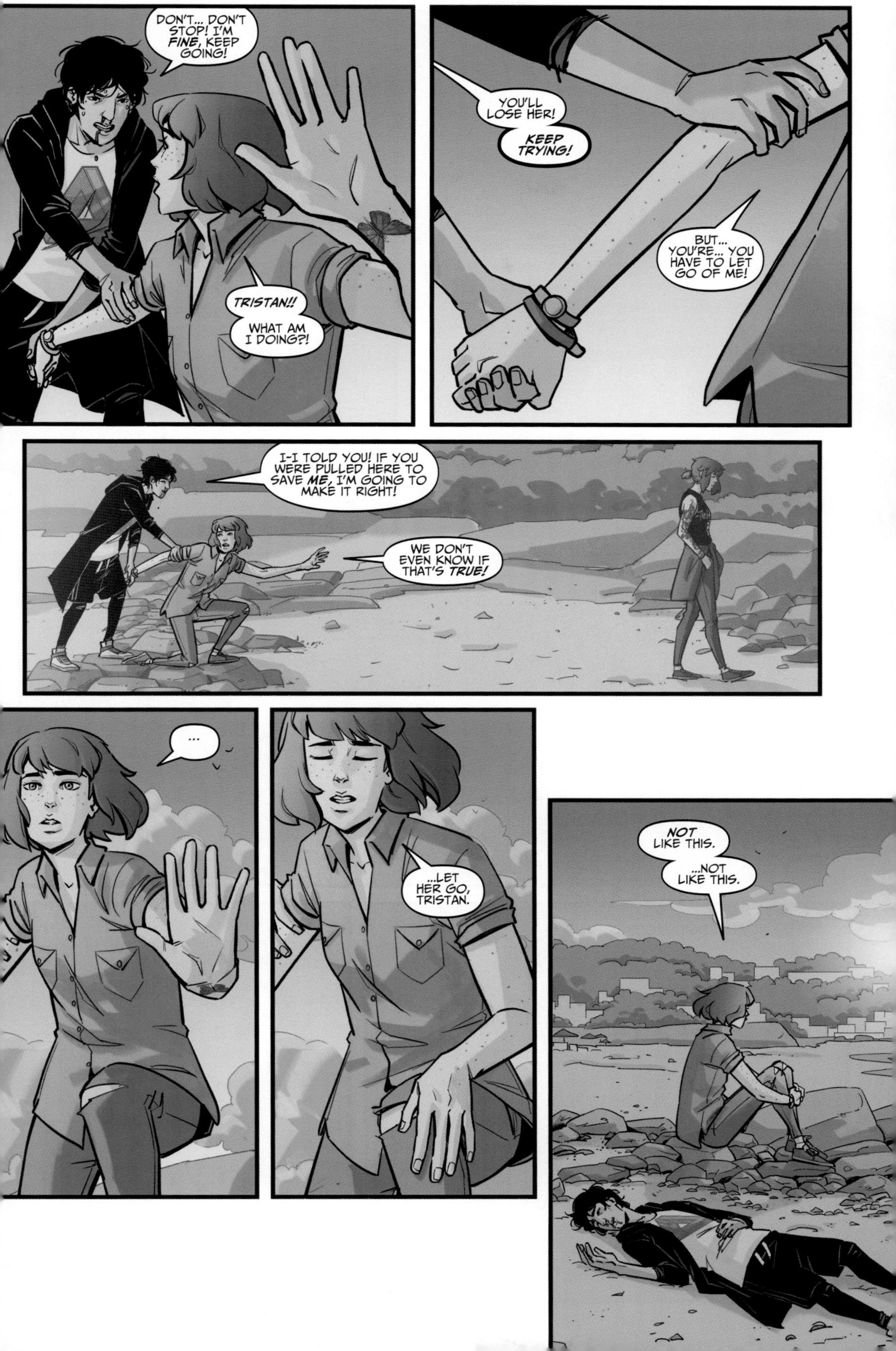
DON'T... DON'T STOP! I'M FINE, KEEP GOING!
TRISTAN!!
WHAT AM I DOING?!
YOU'LL LOSE HER!
KEEP TRYING!
BUT... YOU'RE... YOU HAVE TO LET GO OF ME!
I-I TOLD YOU! IF YOU WERE PULLED HERE TO SAVE ME, I'M GOING TO MAKE IT RIGHT!
WE DON'T EVEN KNOW IF THAT'S TRUE!
...
...LET HER GO, TRISTAN.
NOT LIKE THIS.
...NOT LIKE THIS.

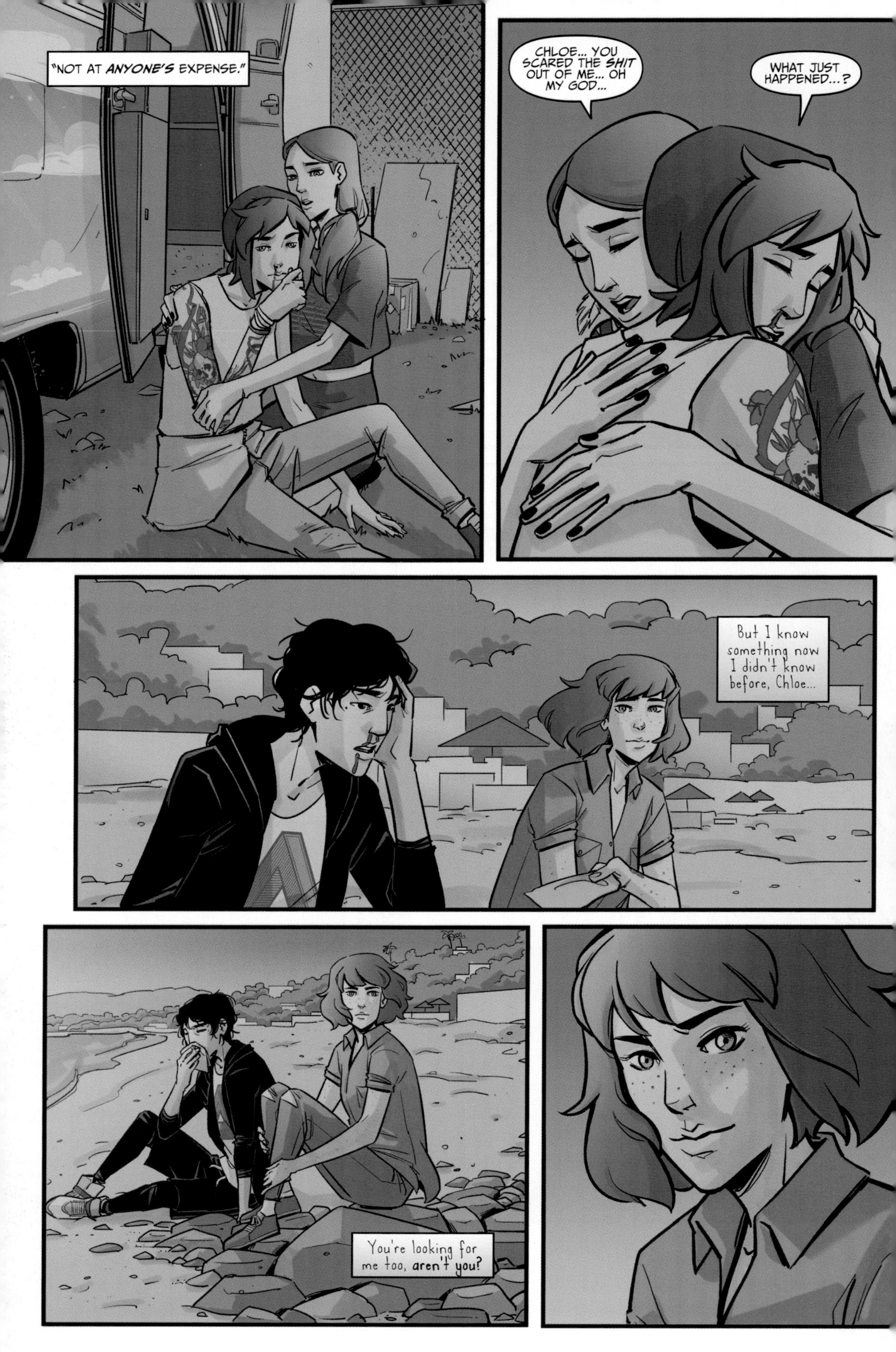
"NOT AT ANYONE'S EXPENSE."
CHLOE... YOU SCARED THE SHIT OUT OF ME... OH MY GOD...
WHAT JUST HAPPENED...?
But I know something now I didn't know before, Chloe...
You're looking for me too, aren't you?

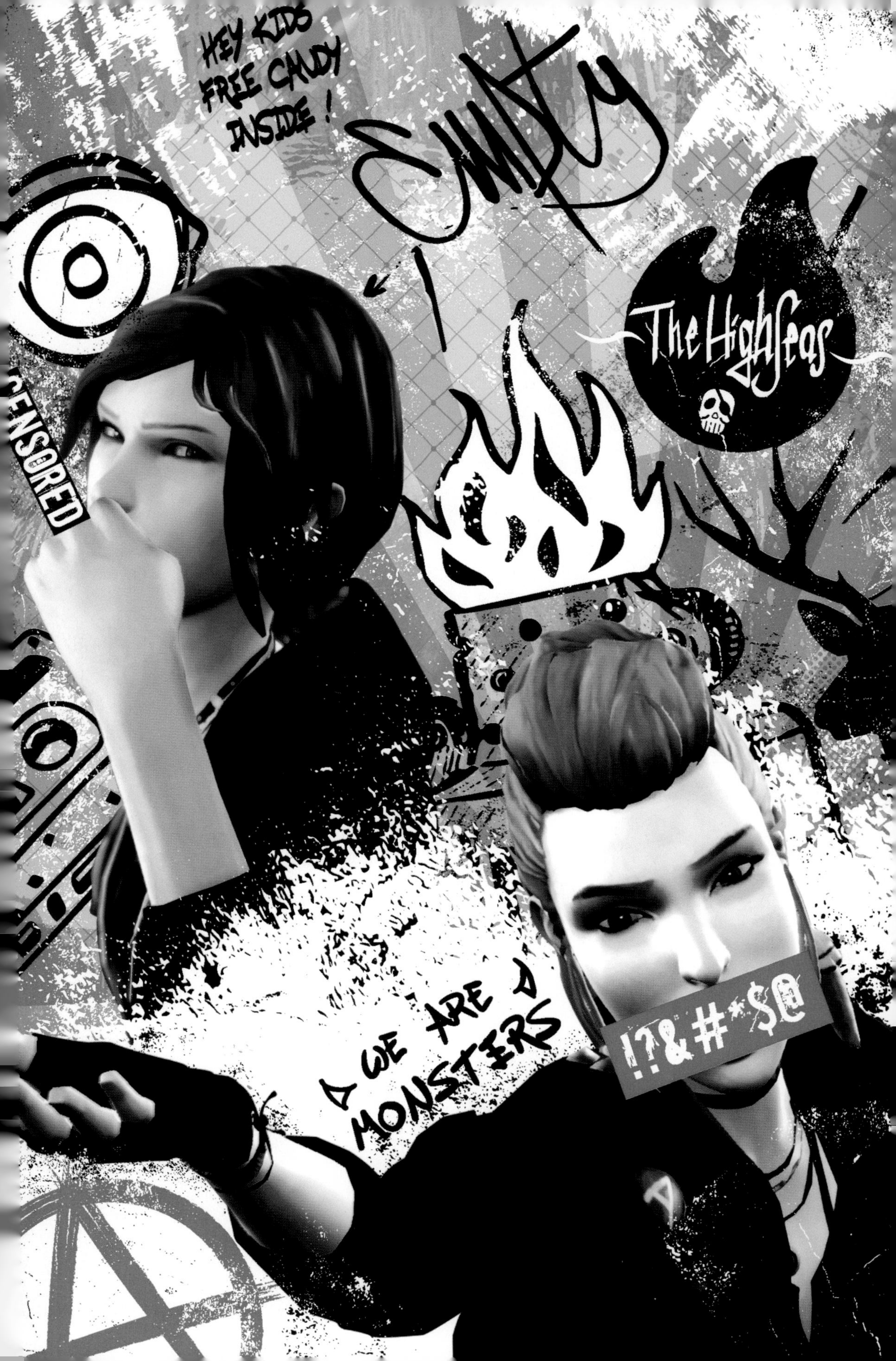
HEY KIDS
FREE CANDY
INSIDE!
CENSORED
The HighSeas
WE ARE
MONSTERS
!?&#*$@

CHAPTER 4

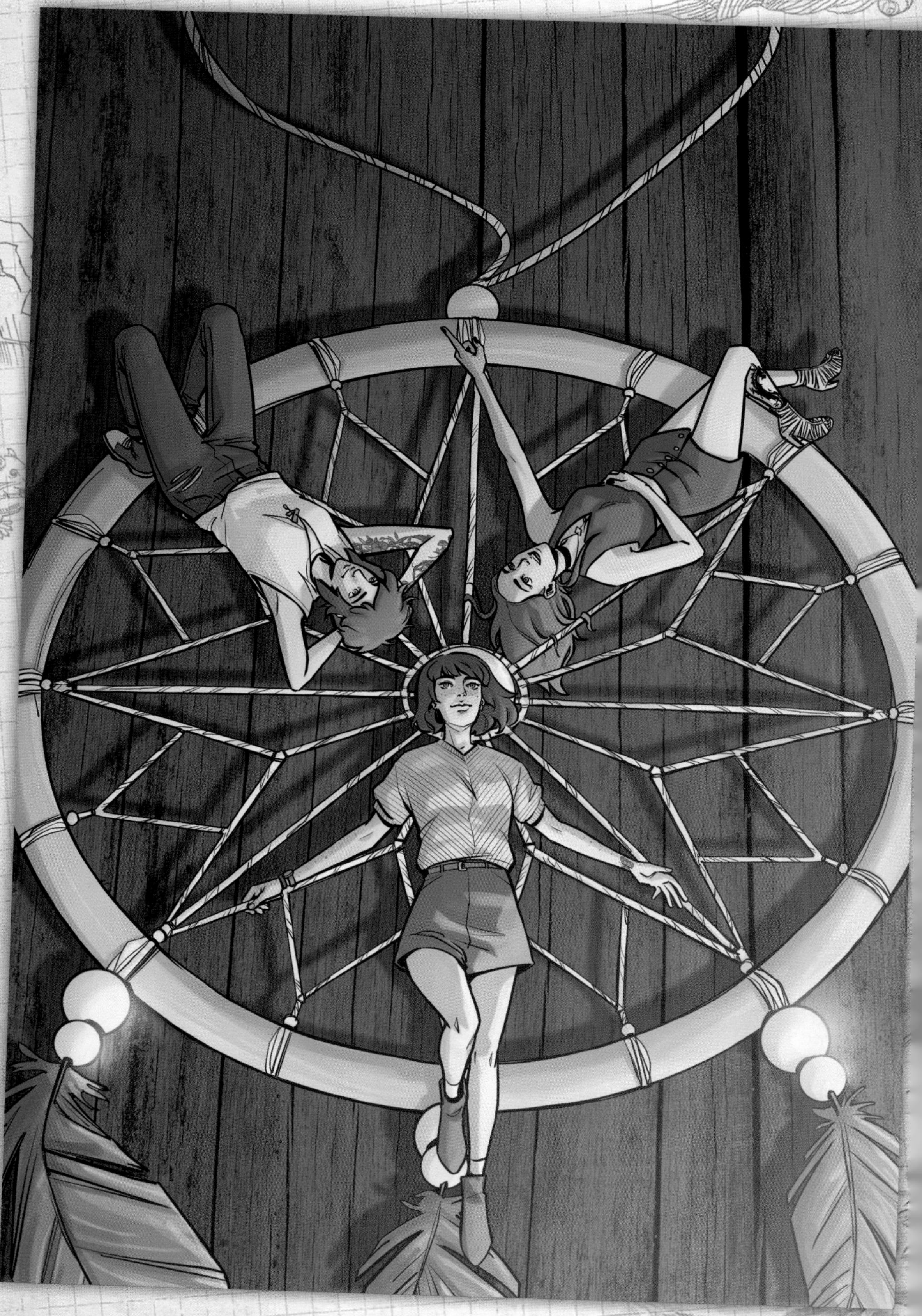

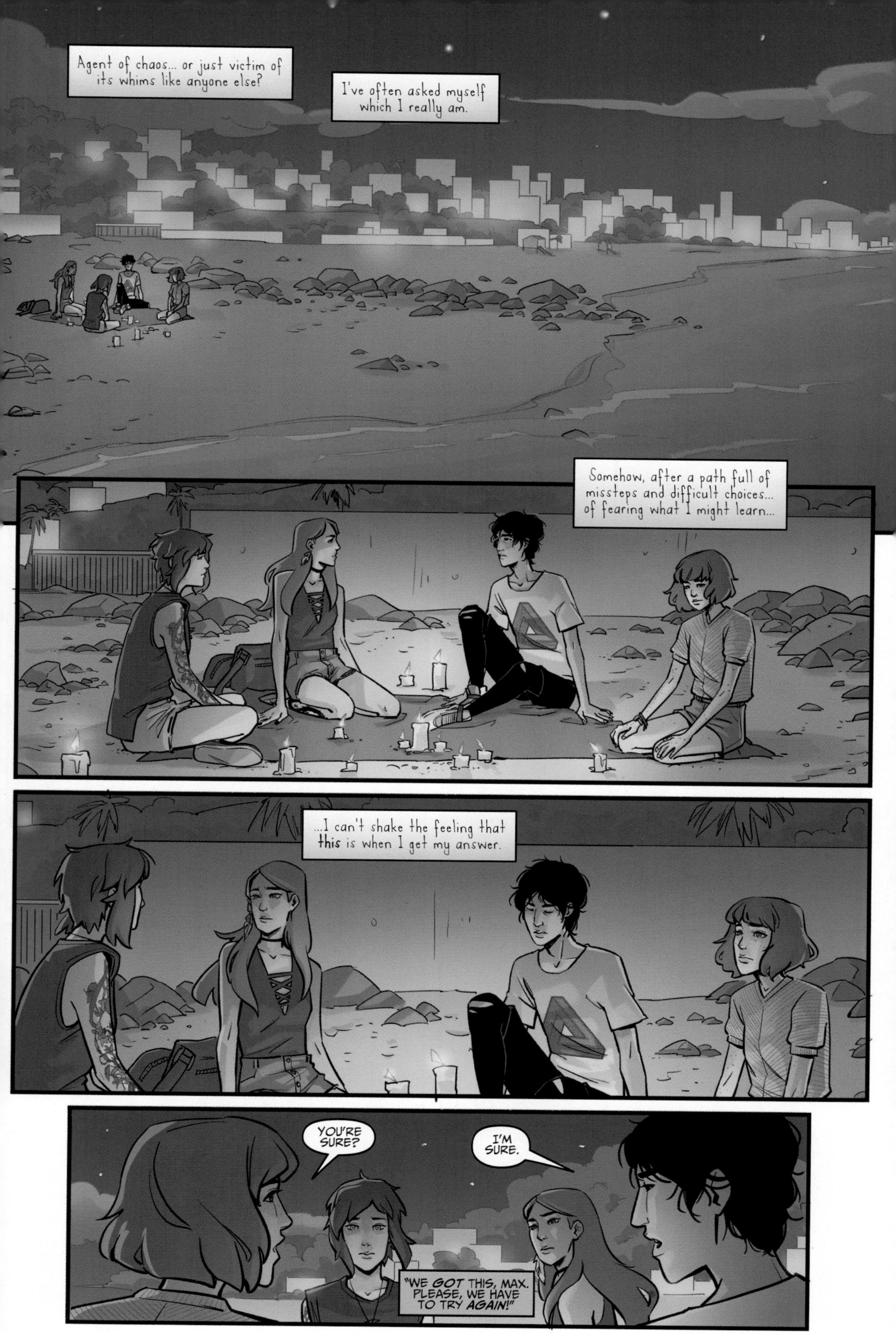
Agent of chaos... or just victim of its whims like anyone else?
I've often asked myself which I really am.
Somehow, after a path full of missteps and difficult choices... of fearing what I might learn...
...I can't shake the feeling that this is when I get my answer.
YOU'RE SURE?
I'M SURE.
"WE GOT THIS, MAX. PLEASE, WE HAVE TO TRY AGAIN!"

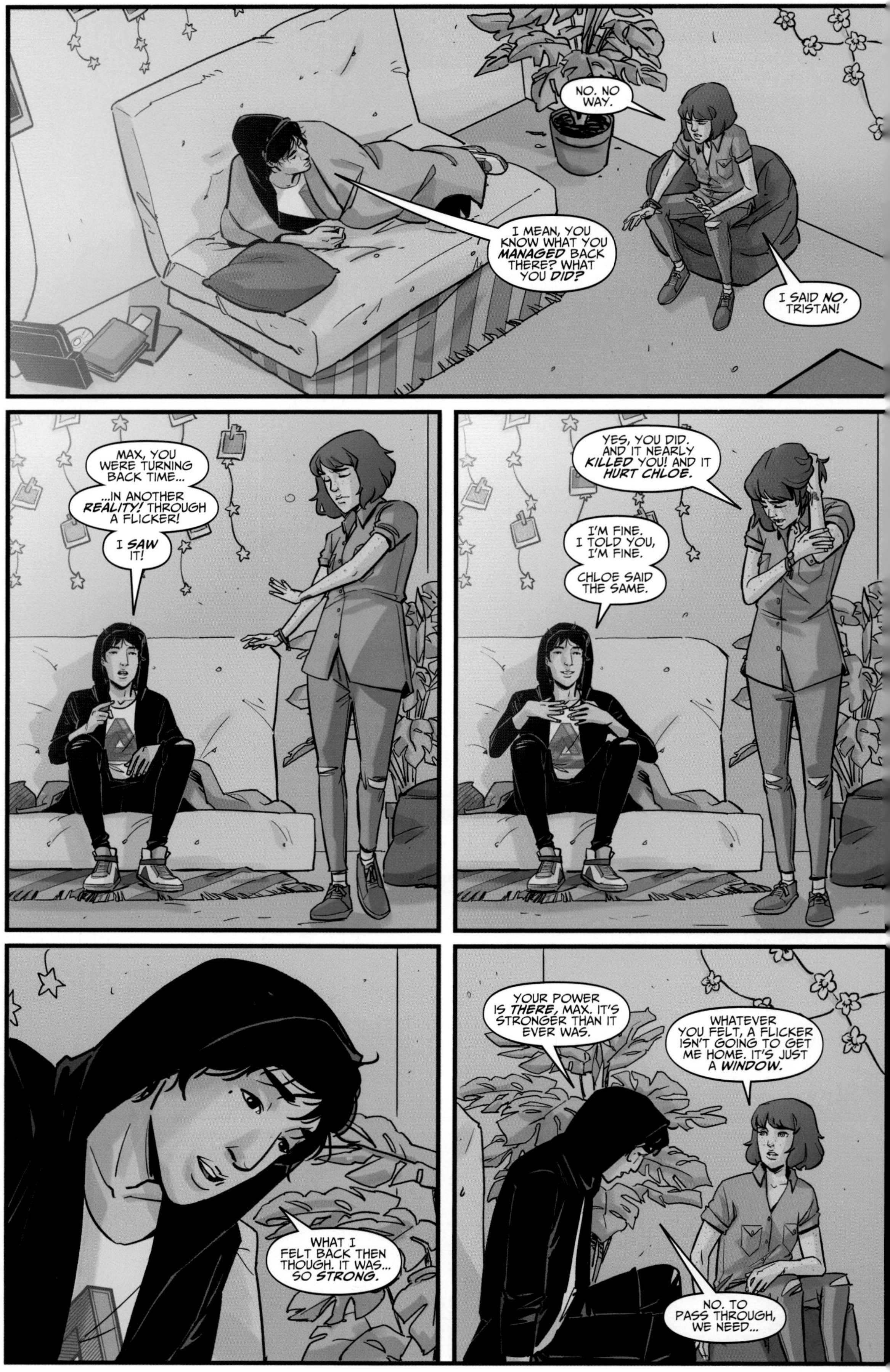
NO. NO WAY.
I MEAN, YOU KNOW WHAT YOU MANAGED BACK THERE? WHAT YOU DID?
I SAID NO, TRISTAN!
MAX, YOU WERE TURNING BACK TIME...
...IN ANOTHER REALITY! THROUGH A FLICKER!
I SAW IT!
YES, YOU DID. AND IT NEARLY KILLED YOU! AND IT HURT CHLOE.
I'M FINE. I TOLD YOU, I'M FINE.
CHLOE SAID THE SAME.
WHAT I FELT BACK THEN THOUGH. IT WAS... SO STRONG.
YOUR POWER IS THERE, MAX. IT'S STRONGER THAN IT EVER WAS.
WHATEVER YOU FELT, A FLICKER ISN'T GOING TO GET ME HOME. IT'S JUST A WINDOW.
NO. TO PASS THROUGH, WE NEED...

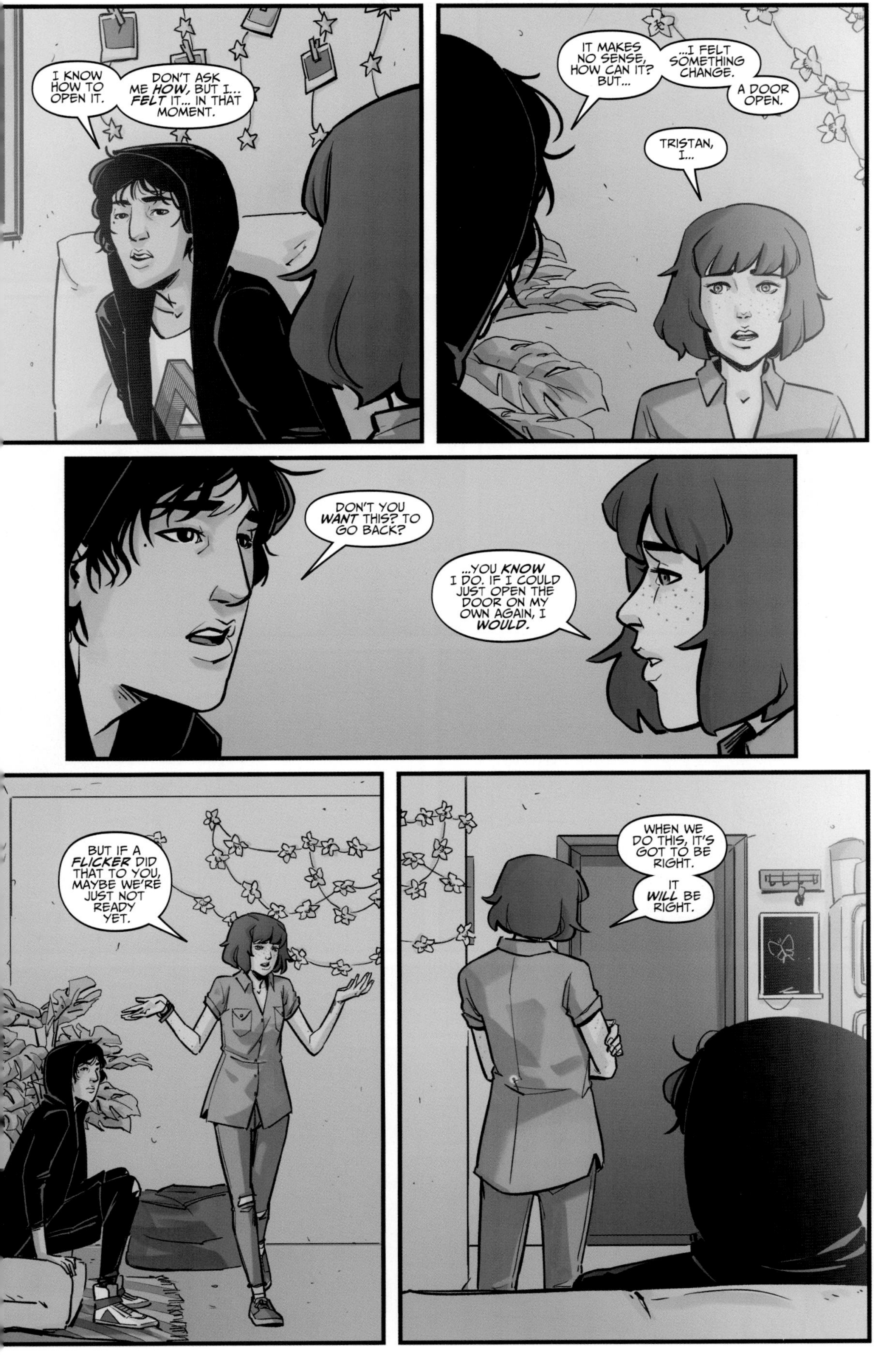
I KNOW HOW TO OPEN IT.
DON'T ASK ME HOW, BUT I... FELT IT... IN THAT MOMENT.
IT MAKES NO SENSE, HOW CAN IT? BUT...
...I FELT SOMETHING CHANGE.
A DOOR OPEN.
TRISTAN, I...
DON'T YOU WANT THIS? TO GO BACK?
...YOU KNOW I DO. IF I COULD JUST OPEN THE DOOR ON MY OWN AGAIN, I WOULD.
BUT IF A FLICKER DID THAT TO YOU, MAYBE WE'RE JUST NOT READY YET.
WHEN WE DO THIS, IT'S GOT TO BE RIGHT.
IT WILL BE RIGHT.

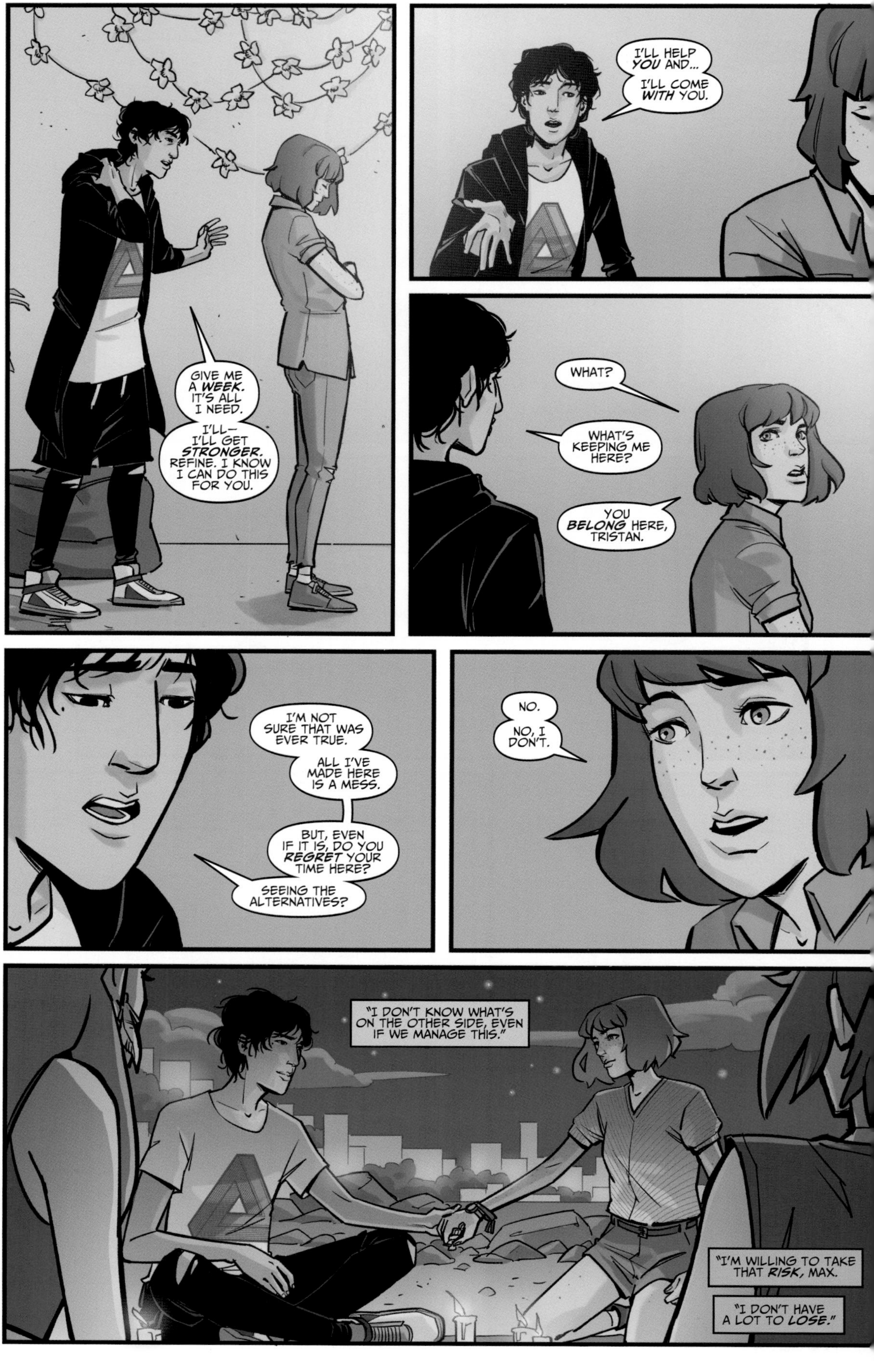
GIVE ME A WEEK. IT'S ALL I NEED.
I'LL— I'LL GET STRONGER. REFINE. I KNOW I CAN DO THIS FOR YOU.
I'LL HELP YOU AND...
I'LL COME WITH YOU.
WHAT?
WHAT'S KEEPING ME HERE?
YOU BELONG HERE, TRISTAN.
I'M NOT SURE THAT WAS EVER TRUE.
ALL I'VE MADE HERE IS A MESS.
BUT, EVEN IF IT IS, DO YOU REGRET YOUR TIME HERE?
SEEING THE ALTERNATIVES?
NO.
NO, I DON'T.
"I DON'T KNOW WHAT'S ON THE OTHER SIDE, EVEN IF WE MANAGE THIS."
"I'M WILLING TO TAKE THAT RISK, MAX.
"I DON'T HAVE A LOT TO LOSE."

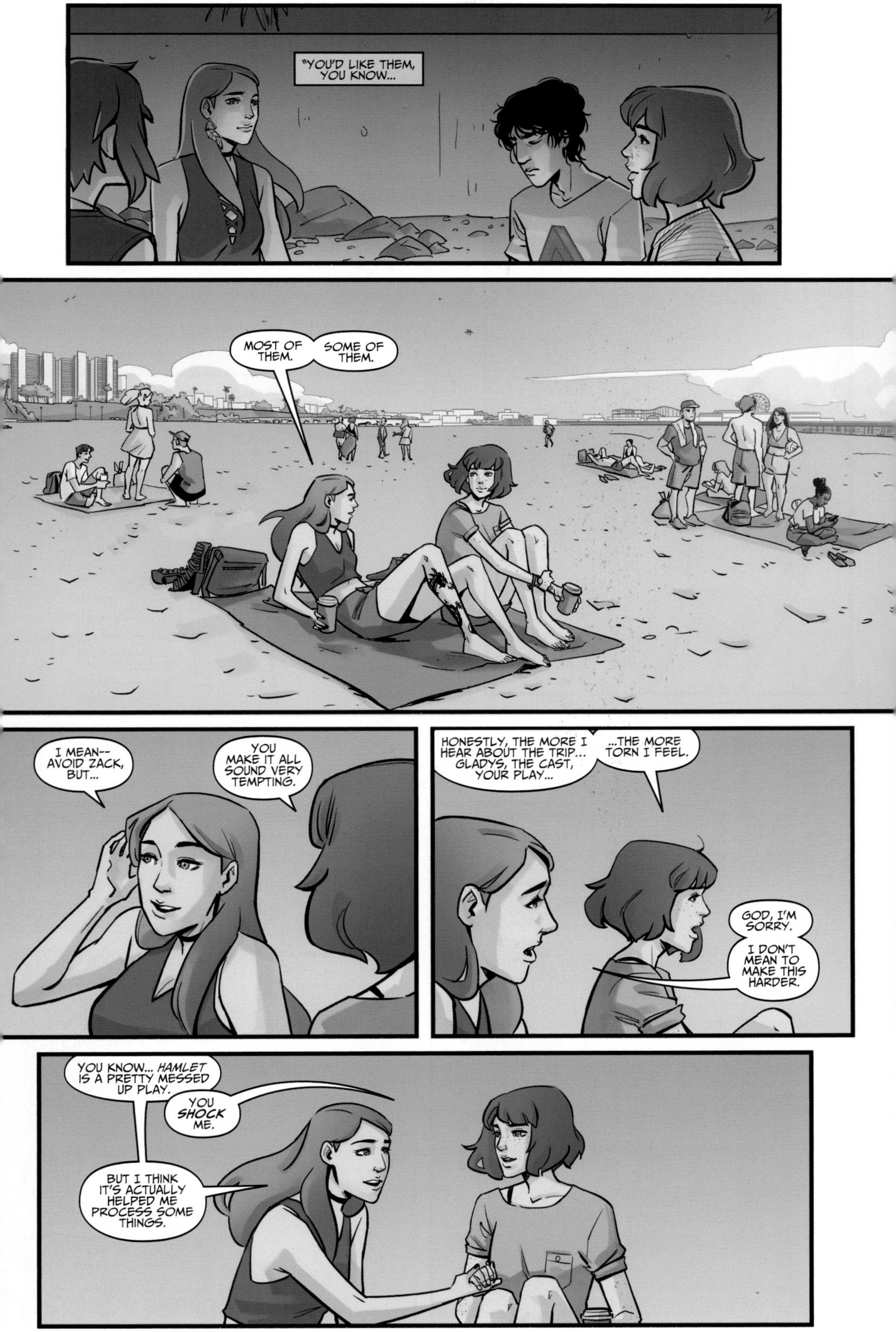
"YOU'D LIKE THEM, YOU KNOW...
MOST OF THEM.
SOME OF THEM.
I MEAN-- AVOID ZACK, BUT...
YOU MAKE IT ALL SOUND VERY TEMPTING.
HONESTLY, THE MORE I HEAR ABOUT THE TRIP... GLADYS, THE CAST, YOUR PLAY...
...THE MORE TORN I FEEL.
GOD, I'M SORRY.
I DON'T MEAN TO MAKE THIS HARDER.
YOU KNOW... *HAMLET* IS A PRETTY MESSED UP PLAY.
YOU ***SHOCK*** ME.
BUT I THINK IT'S ACTUALLY HELPED ME PROCESS SOME THINGS.

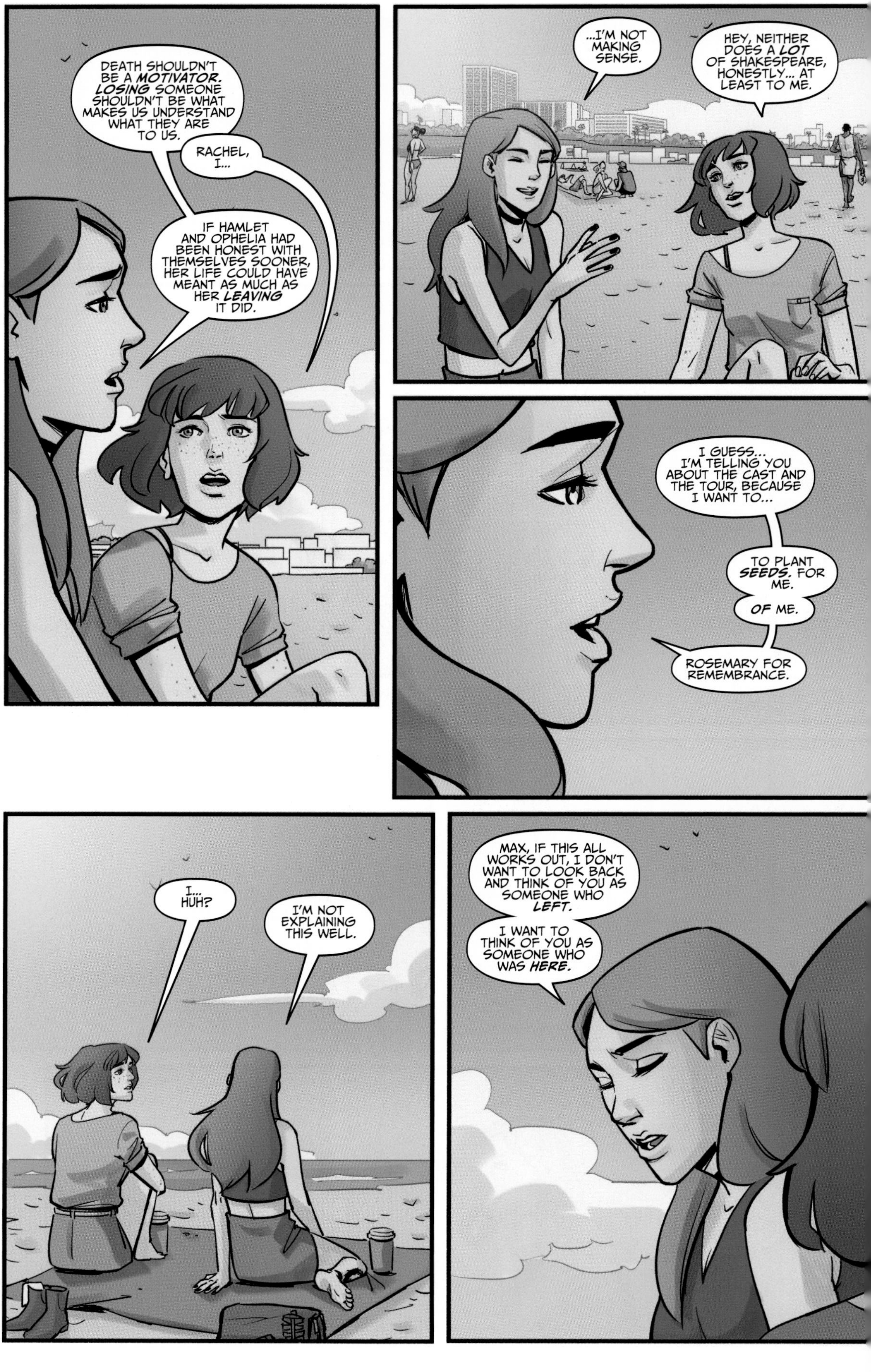
DEATH SHOULDN'T BE A MOTIVATOR. LOSING SOMEONE SHOULDN'T BE WHAT MAKES US UNDERSTAND WHAT THEY ARE TO US.
RACHEL, I...
IF HAMLET AND OPHELIA HAD BEEN HONEST WITH THEMSELVES SOONER, HER LIFE COULD HAVE MEANT AS MUCH AS HER LEAVING IT DID.
...I'M NOT MAKING SENSE.
HEY, NEITHER DOES A LOT OF SHAKESPEARE, HONESTLY... AT LEAST TO ME.
I GUESS... I'M TELLING YOU ABOUT THE CAST AND THE TOUR, BECAUSE I WANT TO...
TO PLANT SEEDS. FOR ME.
OF ME.
ROSEMARY FOR REMEMBRANCE.
I... HUH?
I'M NOT EXPLAINING THIS WELL.
MAX, IF THIS ALL WORKS OUT, I DON'T WANT TO LOOK BACK AND THINK OF YOU AS SOMEONE WHO LEFT.
I WANT TO THINK OF YOU AS SOMEONE WHO WAS HERE.

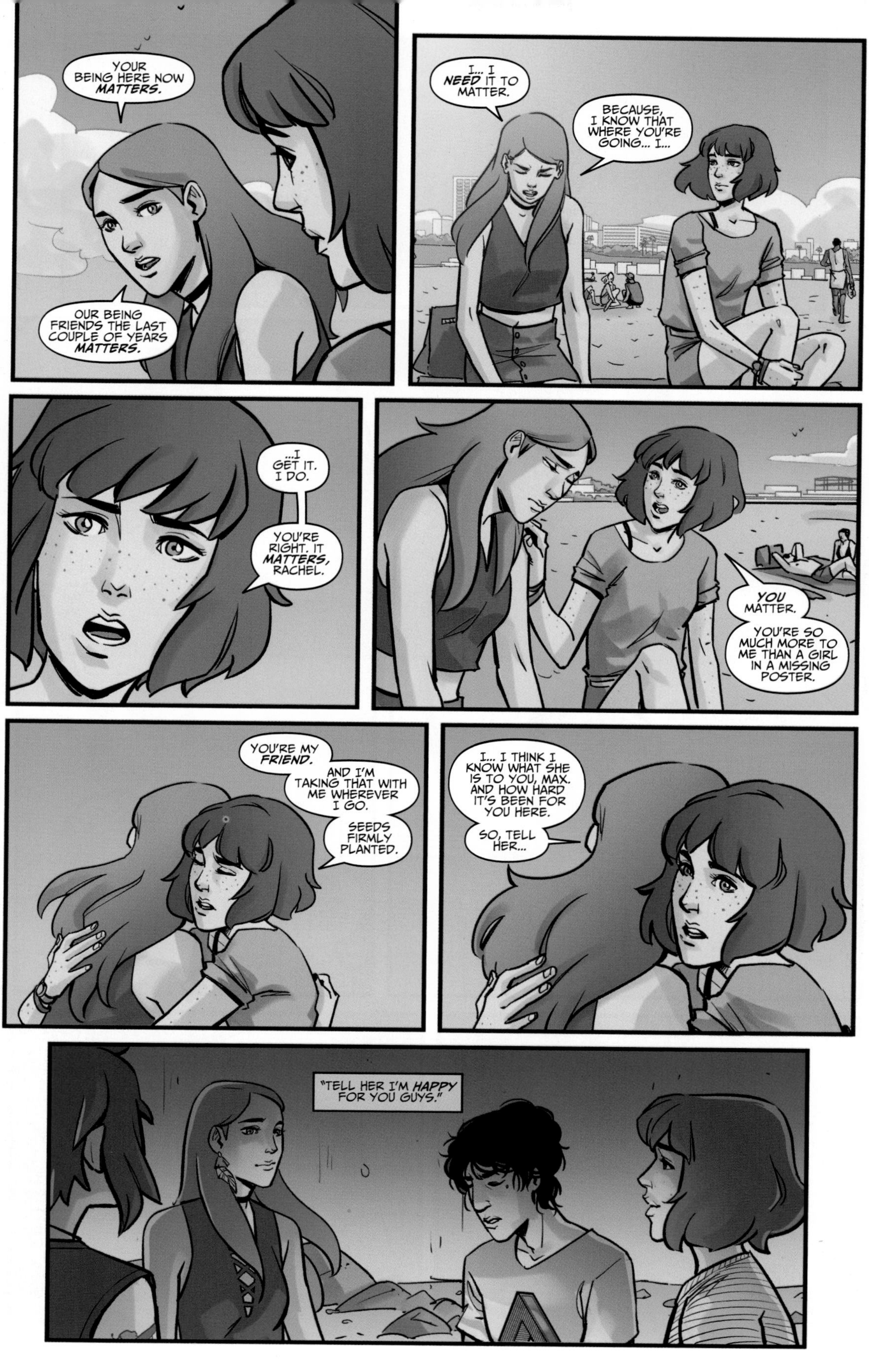
YOUR BEING HERE NOW MATTERS.
OUR BEING FRIENDS THE LAST COUPLE OF YEARS MATTERS.
I... I NEED IT TO MATTER.
BECAUSE, I KNOW THAT WHERE YOU'RE GOING... I...
...I GET IT. I DO.
YOU'RE RIGHT. IT MATTERS, RACHEL.
YOU MATTER.
YOU'RE SO MUCH MORE TO ME THAN A GIRL IN A MISSING POSTER.
YOU'RE MY FRIEND.
AND I'M TAKING THAT WITH ME WHEREVER I GO.
SEEDS FIRMLY PLANTED.
I... I THINK I KNOW WHAT SHE IS TO YOU, MAX. AND HOW HARD IT'S BEEN FOR YOU HERE.
SO, TELL HER...
"TELL HER I'M HAPPY FOR YOU GUYS."

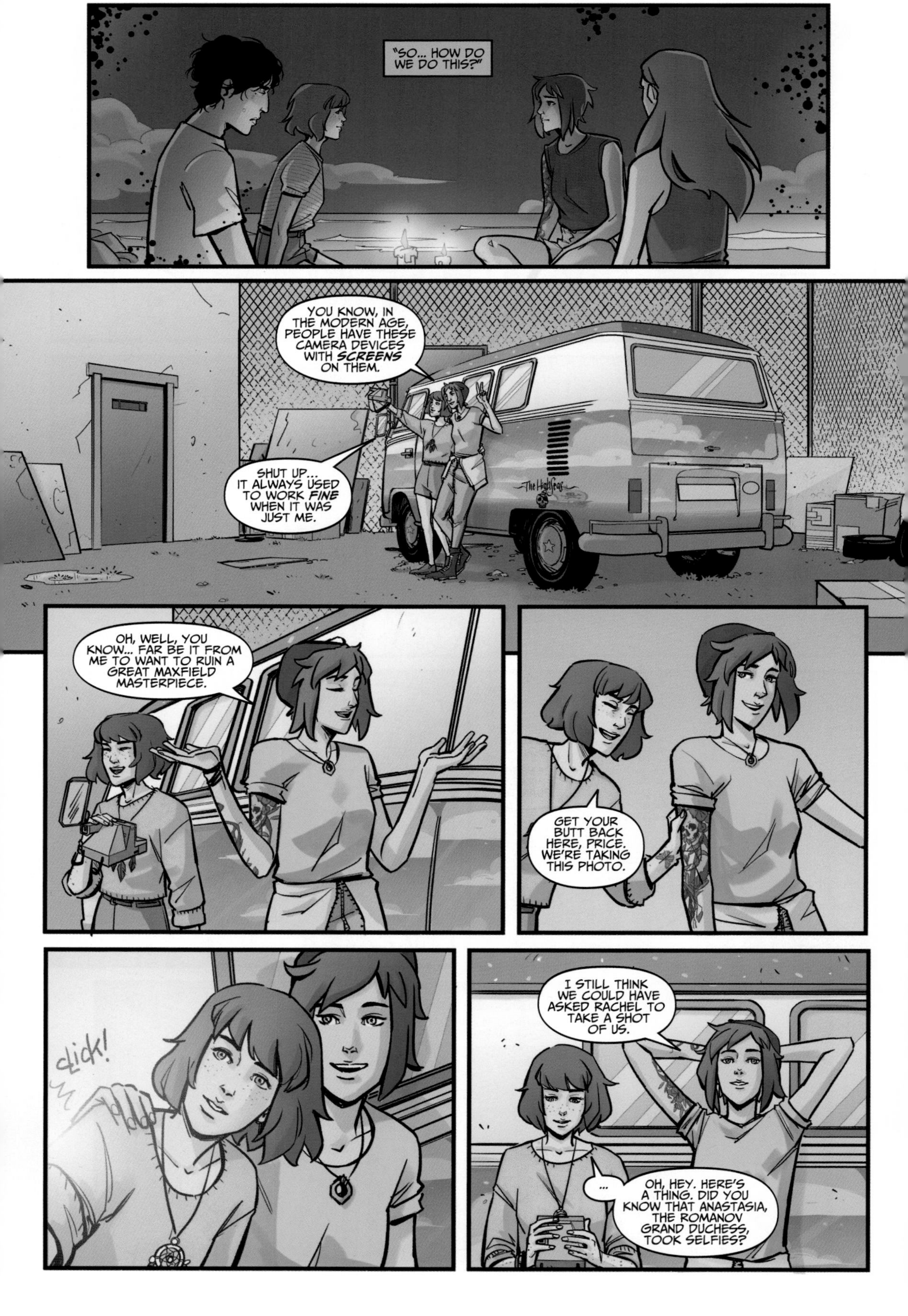
"SO... HOW DO WE DO THIS?"
YOU KNOW, IN THE MODERN AGE, PEOPLE HAVE THESE CAMERA DEVICES WITH SCREENS ON THEM.
SHUT UP... IT ALWAYS USED TO WORK FINE WHEN IT WAS JUST ME.
The HighSeas
OH, WELL, YOU KNOW... FAR BE IT FROM ME TO WANT TO RUIN A GREAT MAXFIELD MASTERPIECE.
GET YOUR BUTT BACK HERE, PRICE. WE'RE TAKING THIS PHOTO.
CLICK!
I STILL THINK WE COULD HAVE ASKED RACHEL TO TAKE A SHOT OF US.
...
OH, HEY. HERE'S A THING. DID YOU KNOW THAT ANASTASIA, THE ROMANOV GRAND DUCHESS, TOOK SELFIES?

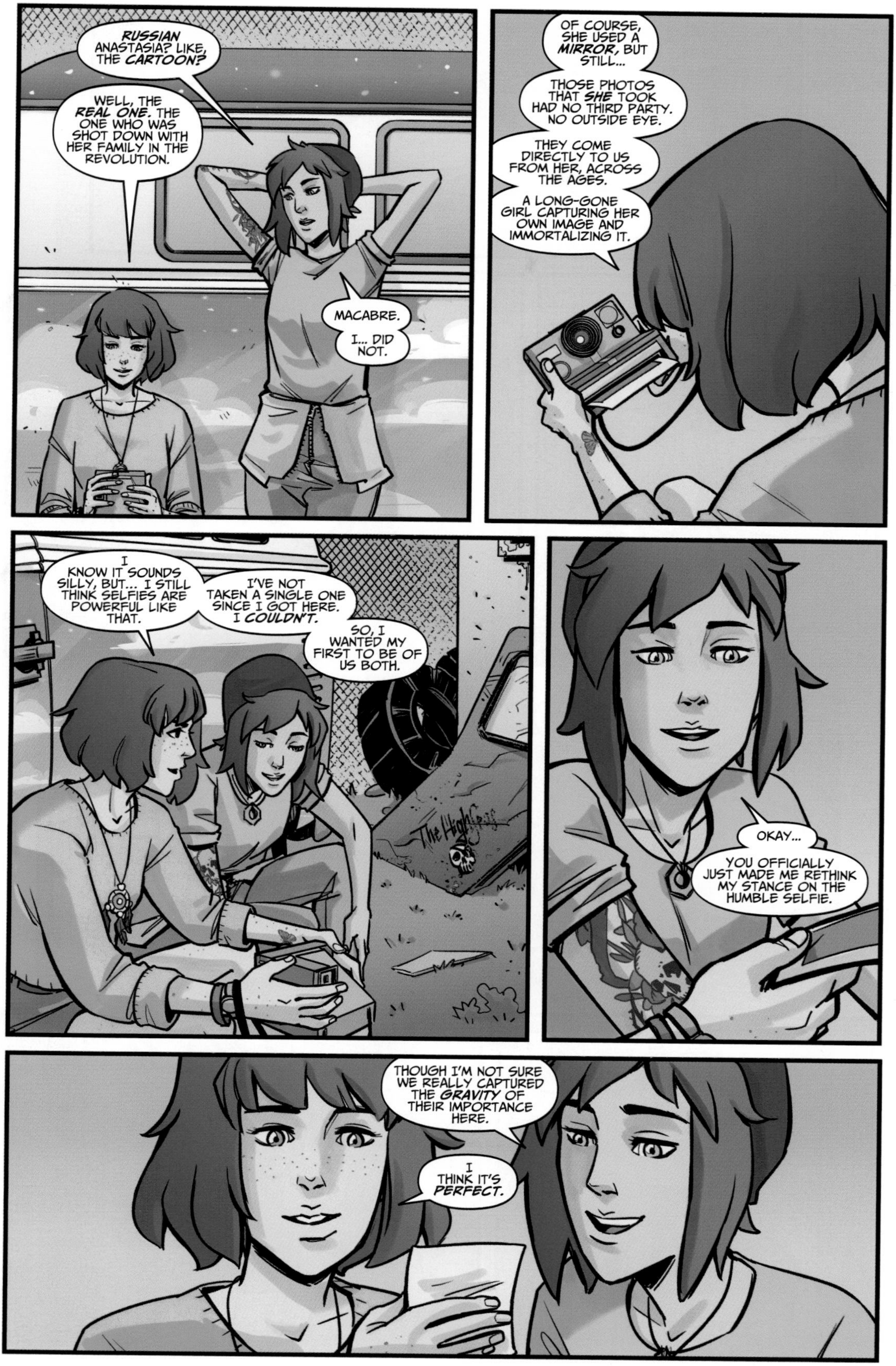
RUSSIAN ANASTASIA? LIKE, THE CARTOON?
WELL, THE REAL ONE. THE ONE WHO WAS SHOT DOWN WITH HER FAMILY IN THE REVOLUTION.
MACABRE.
I... DID NOT.
OF COURSE, SHE USED A MIRROR, BUT STILL...
THOSE PHOTOS THAT SHE TOOK HAD NO THIRD PARTY. NO OUTSIDE EYE.
THEY COME DIRECTLY TO US FROM HER, ACROSS THE AGES.
A LONG-GONE GIRL CAPTURING HER OWN IMAGE AND IMMORTALIZING IT.
I KNOW IT SOUNDS SILLY, BUT... I STILL THINK SELFIES ARE POWERFUL LIKE THAT.
I'VE NOT TAKEN A SINGLE ONE SINCE I GOT HERE. I COULDN'T.
SO, I WANTED MY FIRST TO BE OF US BOTH.
OKAY...
YOU OFFICIALLY JUST MADE ME RETHINK MY STANCE ON THE HUMBLE SELFIE.
THOUGH I'M NOT SURE WE REALLY CAPTURED THE GRAVITY OF THEIR IMPORTANCE HERE.
I THINK IT'S PERFECT.

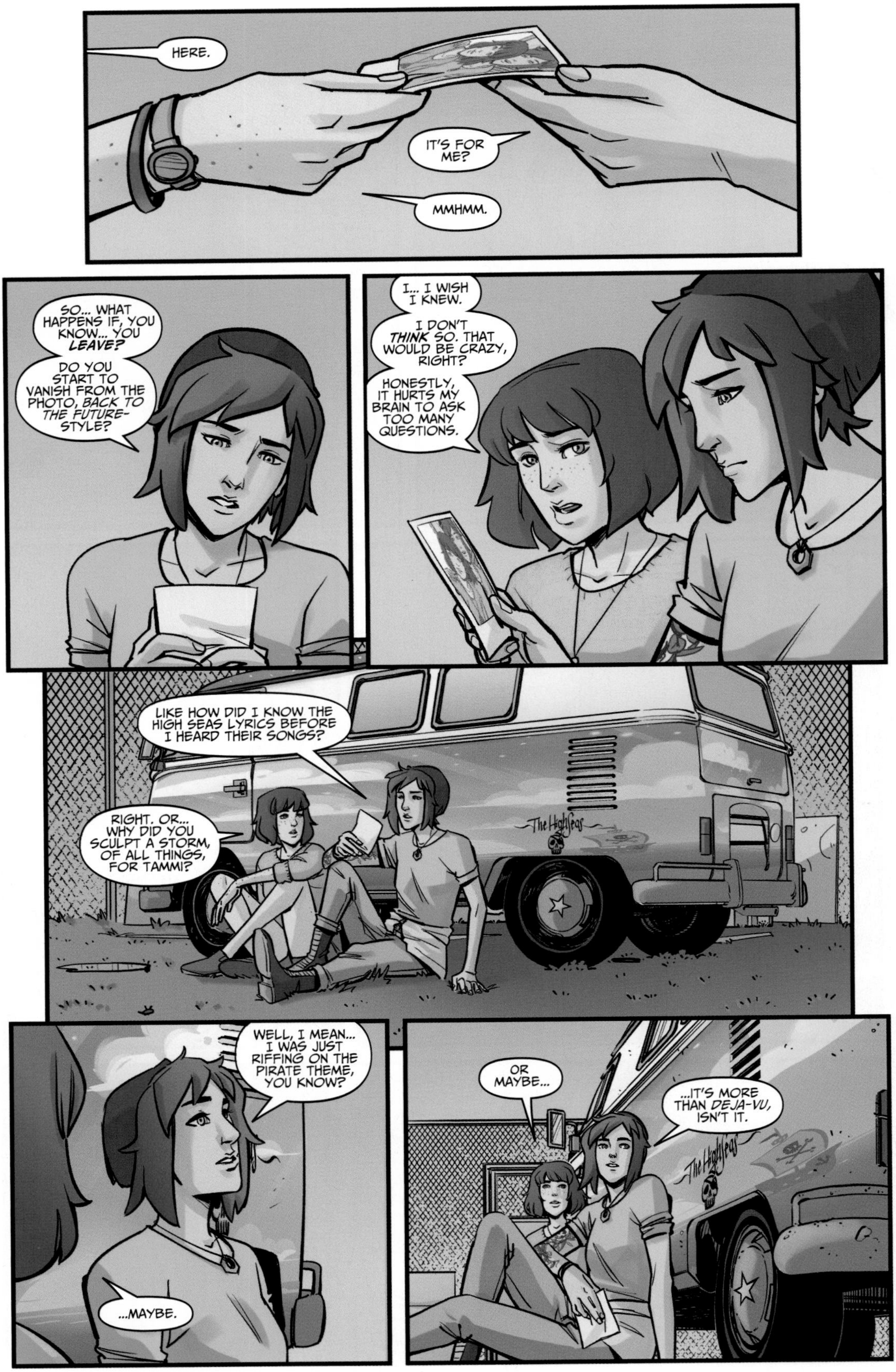
HERE.
IT'S FOR ME?
MMHMM.
SO... WHAT HAPPENS IF, YOU KNOW... YOU *LEAVE?*
DO YOU START TO VANISH FROM THE PHOTO, *BACK TO THE FUTURE*-STYLE?
I... I WISH I KNEW.
I DON'T *THINK* SO. THAT WOULD BE CRAZY, RIGHT?
HONESTLY, IT HURTS MY BRAIN TO ASK TOO MANY QUESTIONS.
LIKE HOW DID I KNOW THE HIGH SEAS LYRICS BEFORE I HEARD THEIR SONGS?
RIGHT. OR... WHY DID YOU SCULPT A STORM, OF ALL THINGS, FOR TAMMI?
The High Seas
WELL, I MEAN... I WAS JUST RIFFING ON THE PIRATE THEME, YOU KNOW?
...MAYBE.
OR MAYBE...
...IT'S MORE THAN *DEJA-VU*, ISN'T IT.
The High Seas

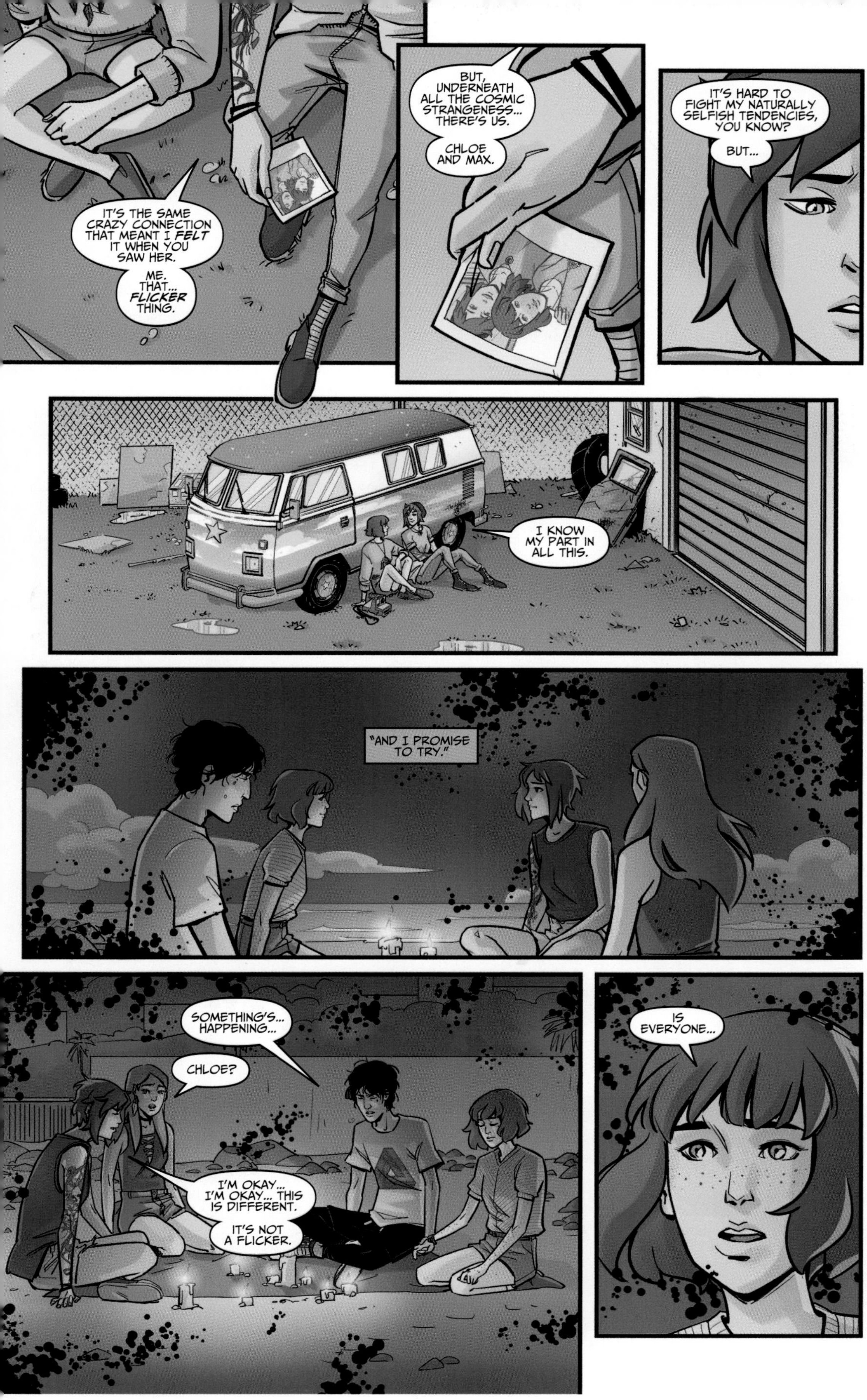
IT'S THE SAME CRAZY CONNECTION THAT MEANT I FELT IT WHEN YOU SAW HER.
ME. THAT... FLICKER THING.
BUT, UNDERNEATH ALL THE COSMIC STRANGENESS... THERE'S US.
CHLOE AND MAX.
IT'S HARD TO FIGHT MY NATURALLY SELFISH TENDENCIES, YOU KNOW?
BUT...
I KNOW MY PART IN ALL THIS.
"AND I PROMISE TO TRY."
SOMETHING'S... HAPPENING...
CHLOE?
I'M OKAY... I'M OKAY... THIS IS DIFFERENT.
IT'S NOT A FLICKER.
IS EVERYONE...

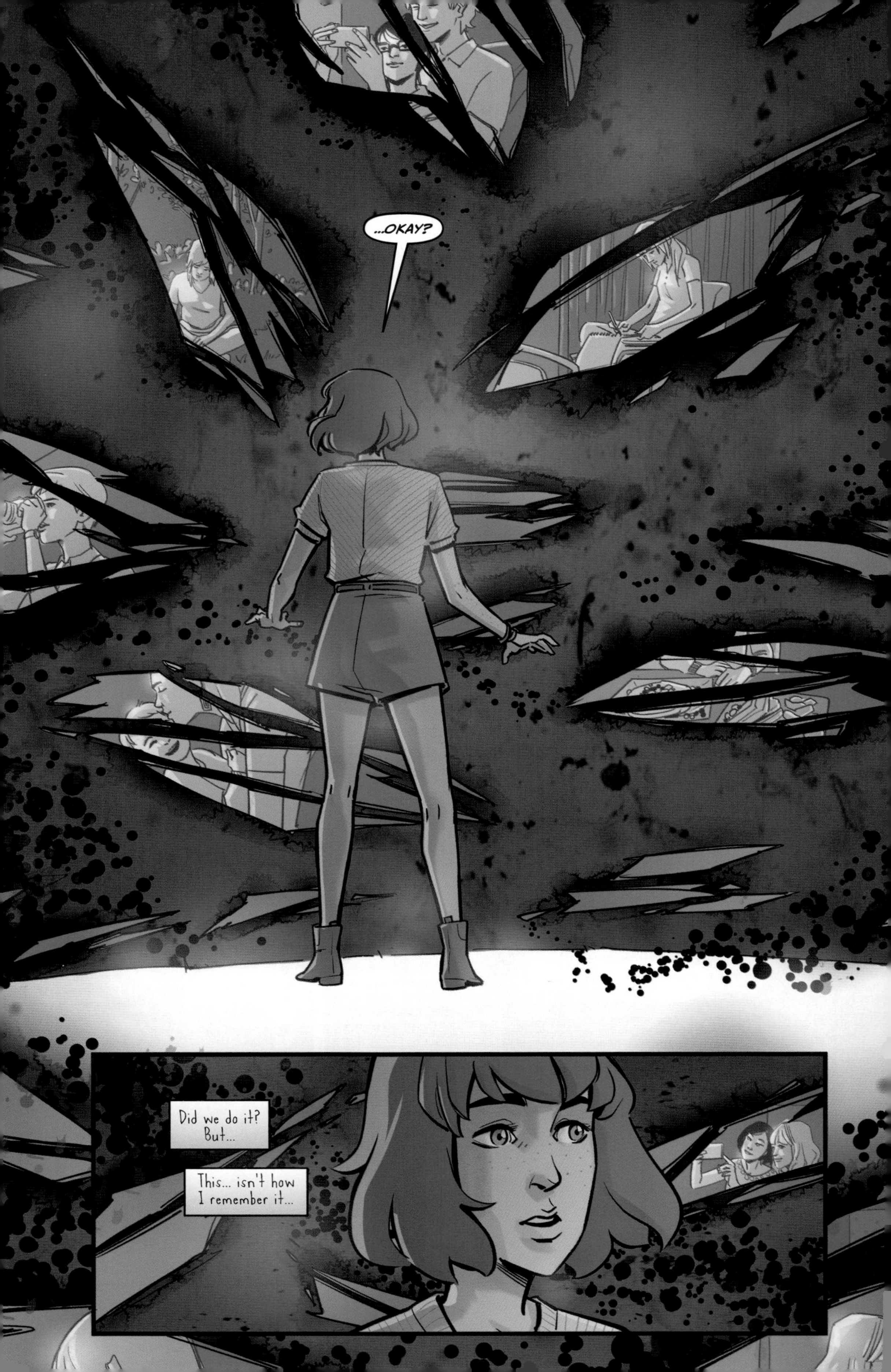
...OKAY?
Did we do it? But...
This... isn't how I remember it...

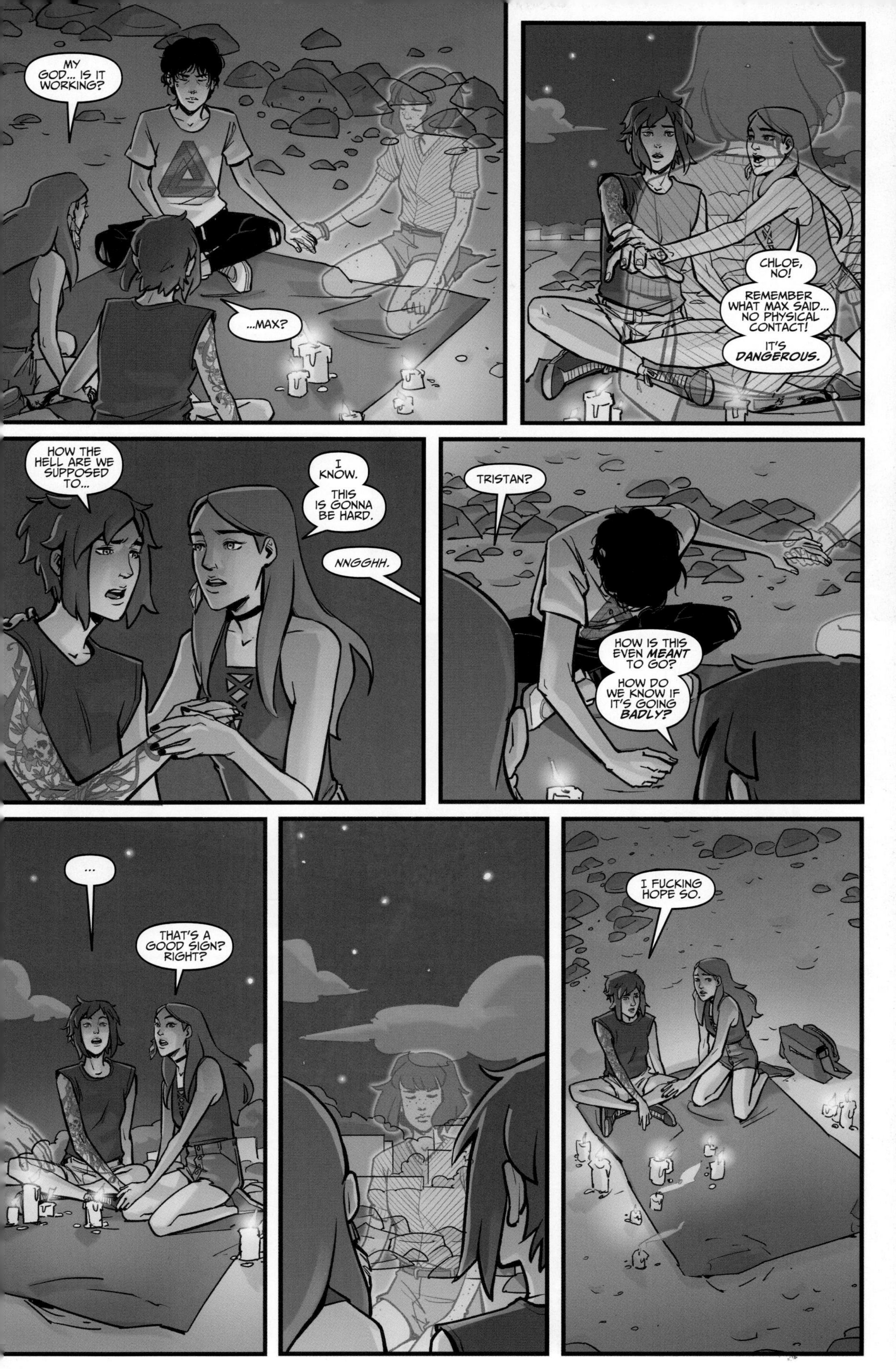
MY GOD... IS IT WORKING?
...MAX?
CHLOE, NO!
REMEMBER WHAT MAX SAID... NO PHYSICAL CONTACT!
IT'S DANGEROUS.
HOW THE HELL ARE WE SUPPOSED TO...
I KNOW.
THIS IS GONNA BE HARD.
NNGGHH.
TRISTAN?
HOW IS THIS EVEN MEANT TO GO?
HOW DO WE KNOW IF IT'S GOING BADLY?
...
THAT'S A GOOD SIGN? RIGHT?
I FUCKING HOPE SO.

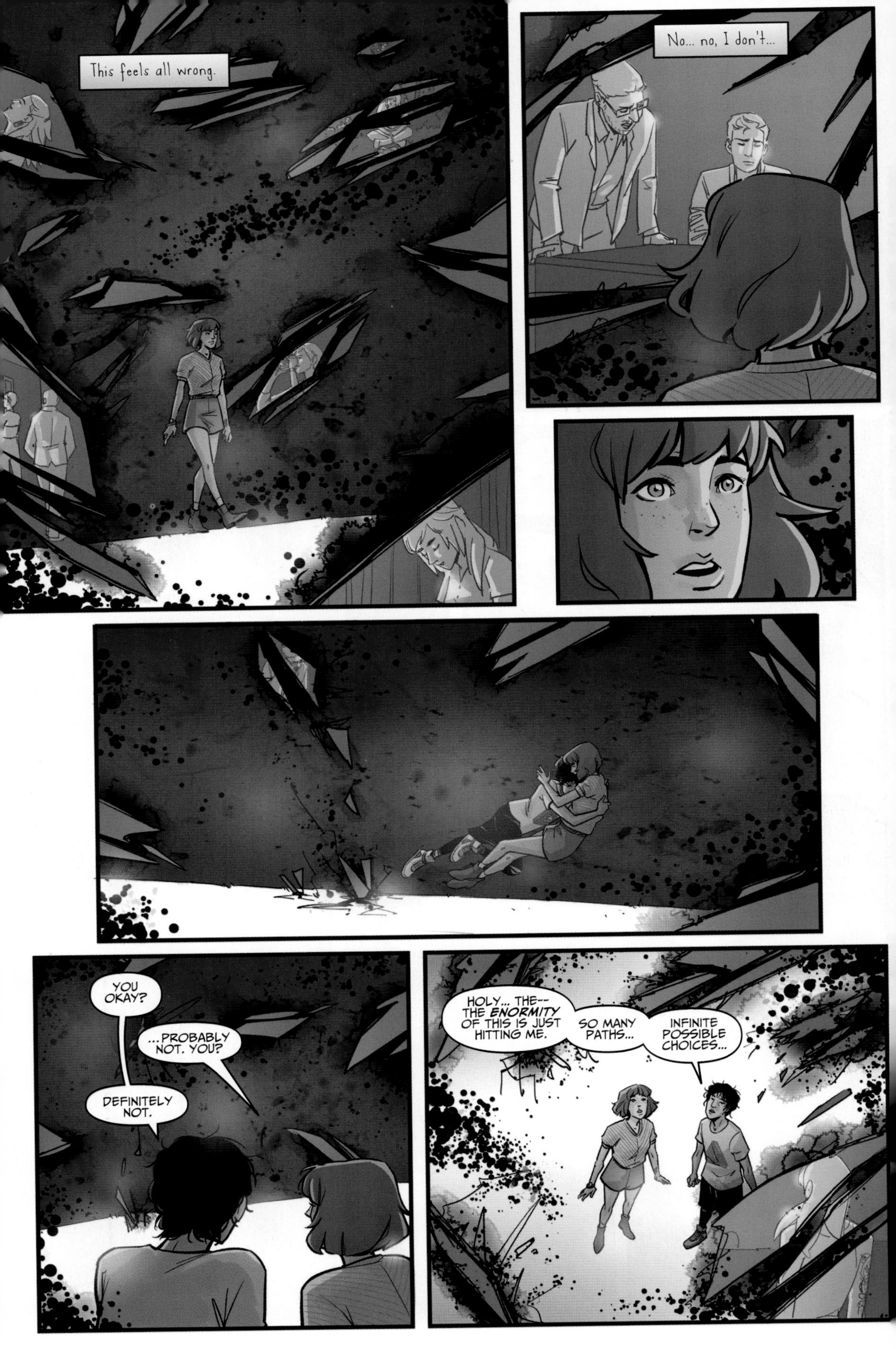
This feels all wrong.
No... no, I don't...
YOU OKAY?
...PROBABLY NOT. YOU?
DEFINITELY NOT.
HOLY... THE-- THE ENORMITY OF THIS IS JUST HITTING ME.
SO MANY PATHS...
INFINITE POSSIBLE CHOICES...

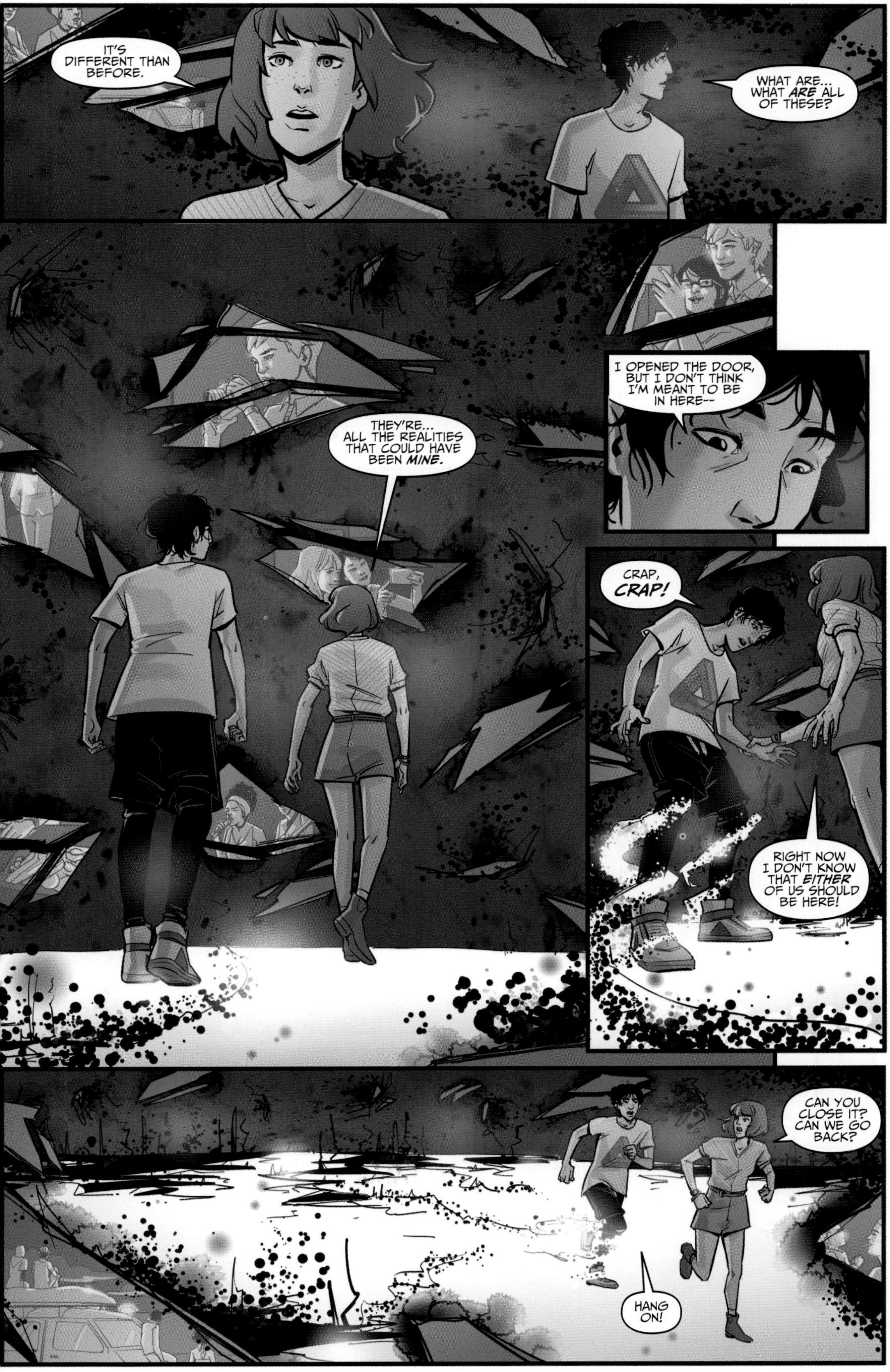
IT'S DIFFERENT THAN BEFORE.
WHAT ARE... WHAT *ARE* ALL OF THESE?
THEY'RE... ALL THE REALITIES THAT COULD HAVE BEEN *MINE.*
I OPENED THE DOOR, BUT I DON'T THINK I'M MEANT TO BE IN HERE--
CRAP, *CRAP!*
RIGHT NOW I DON'T KNOW THAT *EITHER* OF US SHOULD BE HERE!
CAN YOU CLOSE IT? CAN WE GO BACK?
HANG ON!

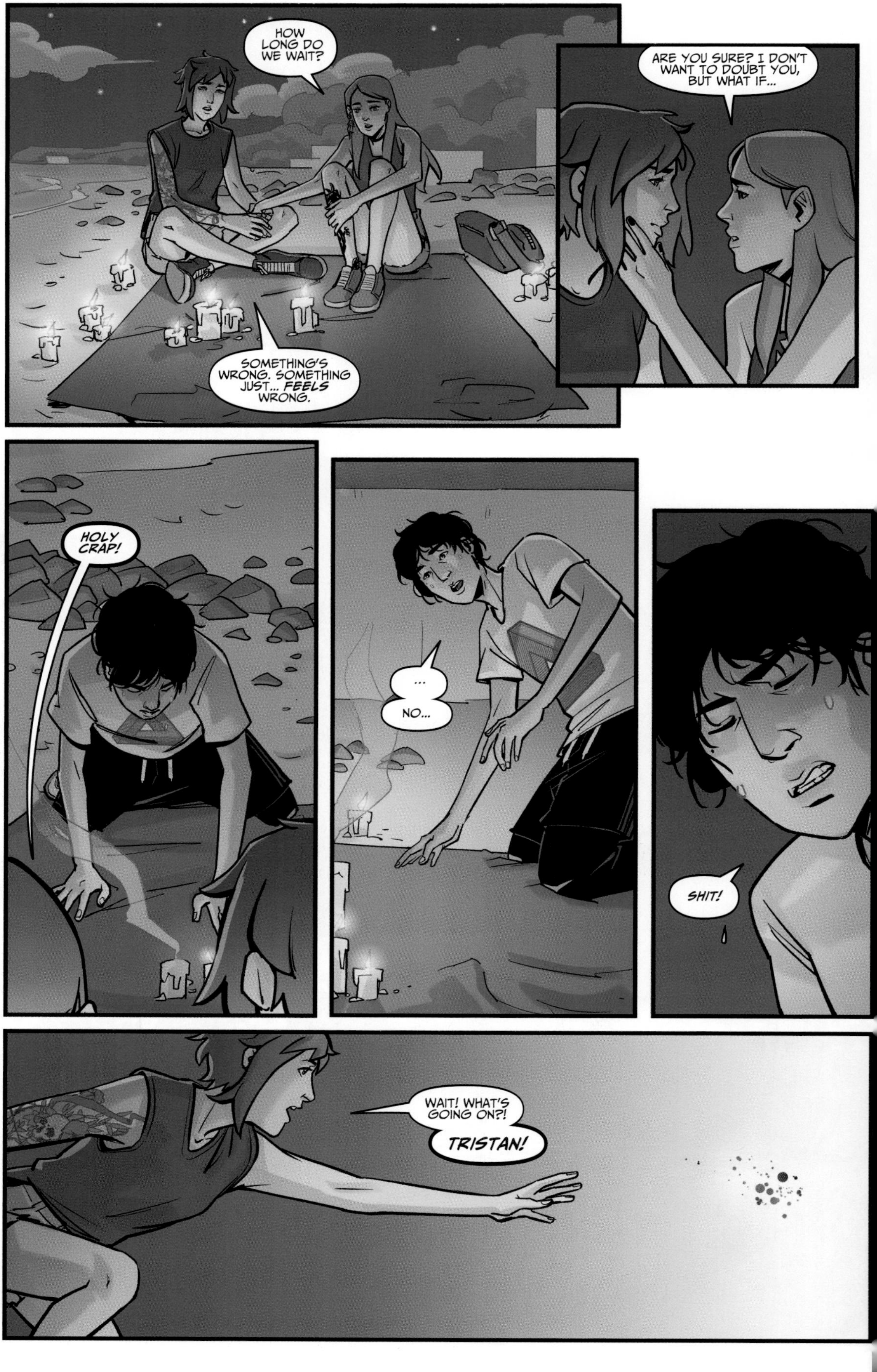
HOW LONG DO WE WAIT?
SOMETHING'S WRONG. SOMETHING JUST... FEELS WRONG.
ARE YOU SURE? I DON'T WANT TO DOUBT YOU, BUT WHAT IF...
HOLY CRAP!
...
NO...
SHIT!
WAIT! WHAT'S GOING ON?!
TRISTAN!

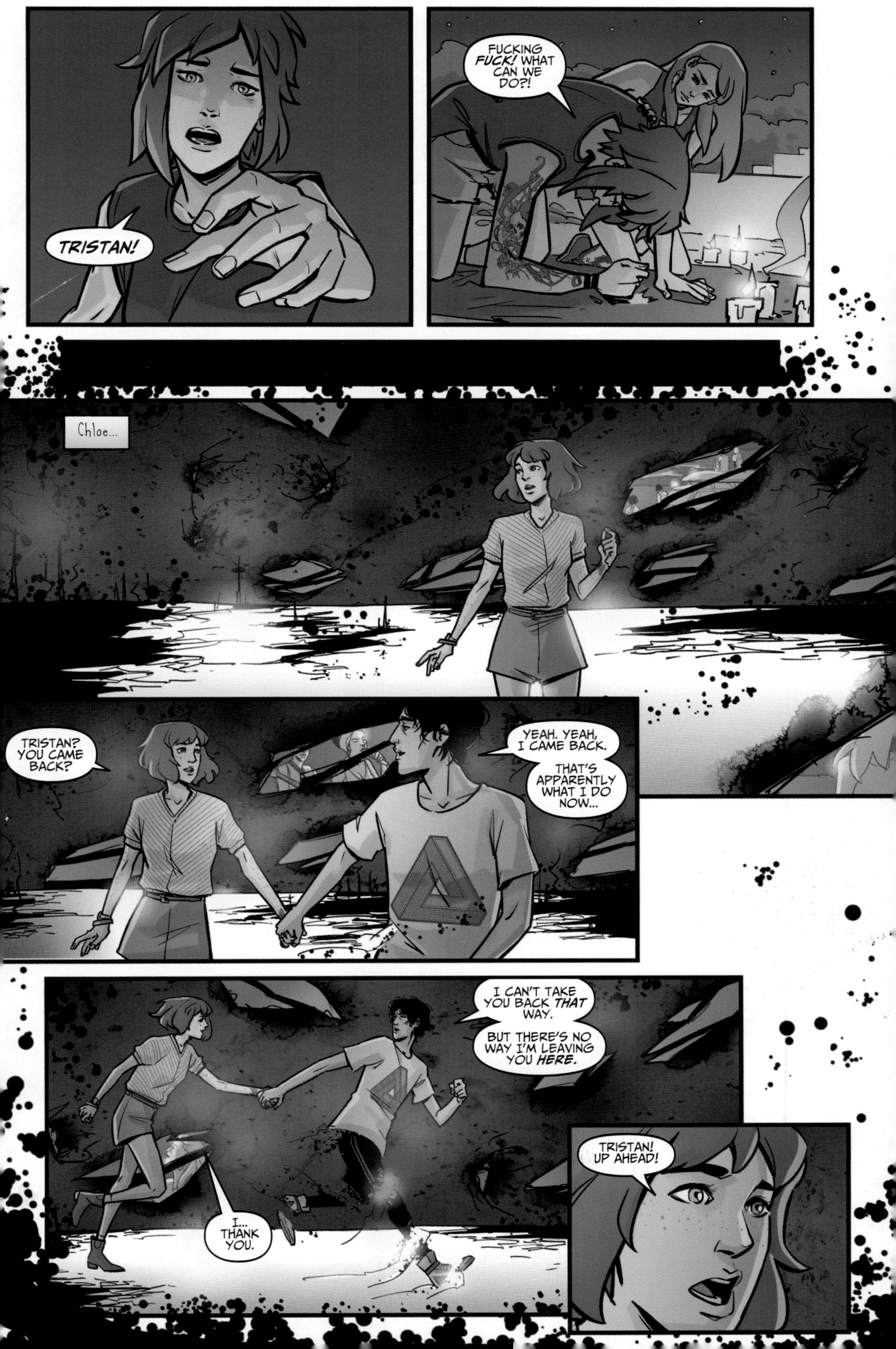

TRISTAN!
FUCKING FUCK! WHAT CAN WE DO?!
Chloe...
TRISTAN? YOU CAME BACK?
YEAH. YEAH, I CAME BACK.
THAT'S APPARENTLY WHAT I DO NOW...
I CAN'T TAKE YOU BACK THAT WAY.
BUT THERE'S NO WAY I'M LEAVING YOU HERE.
I... THANK YOU.
TRISTAN! UP AHEAD!

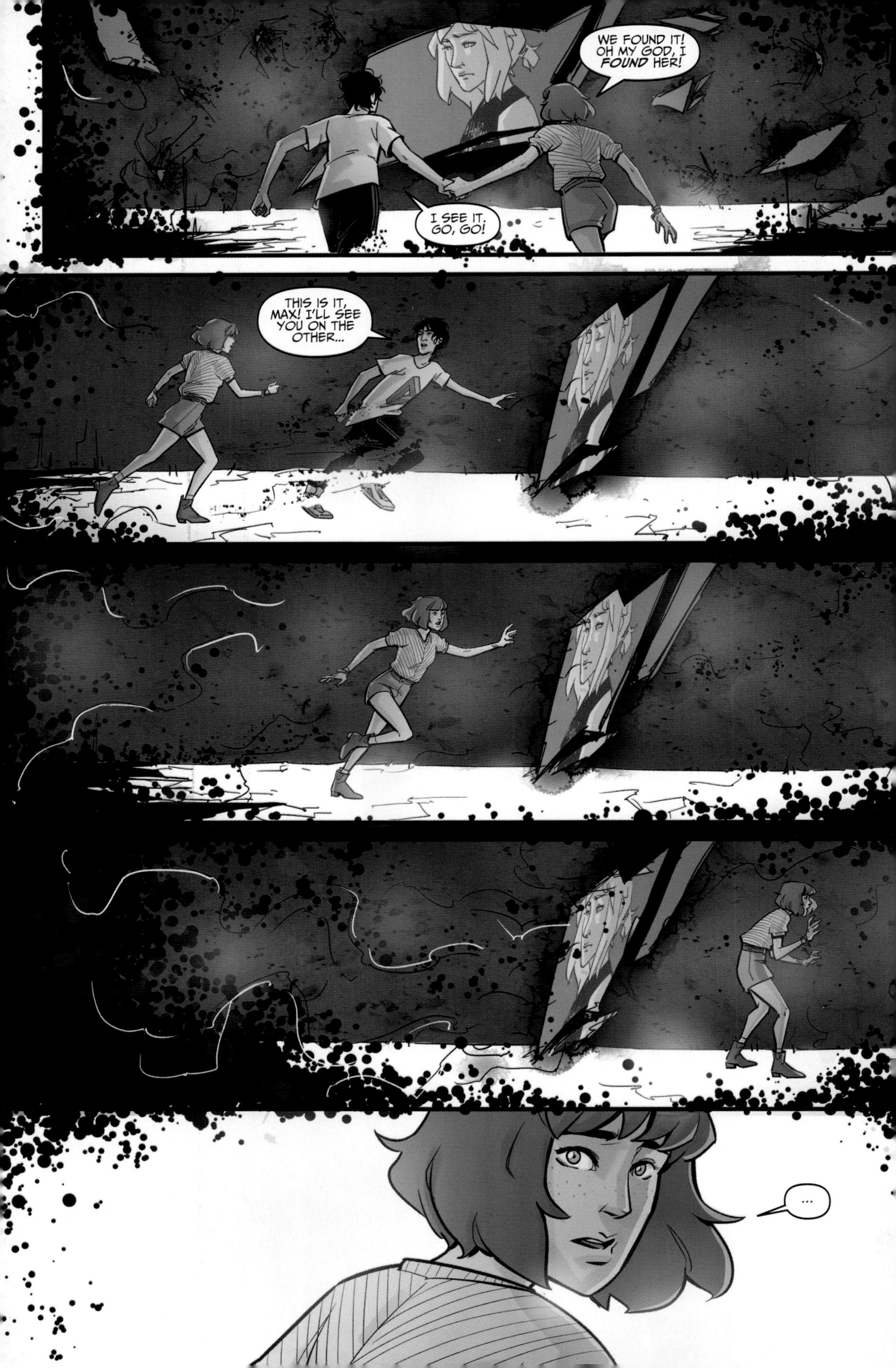
WE FOUND IT! OH MY GOD, I FOUND HER!
I SEE IT. GO, GO!
THIS IS IT, MAX! I'LL SEE YOU ON THE OTHER...
...

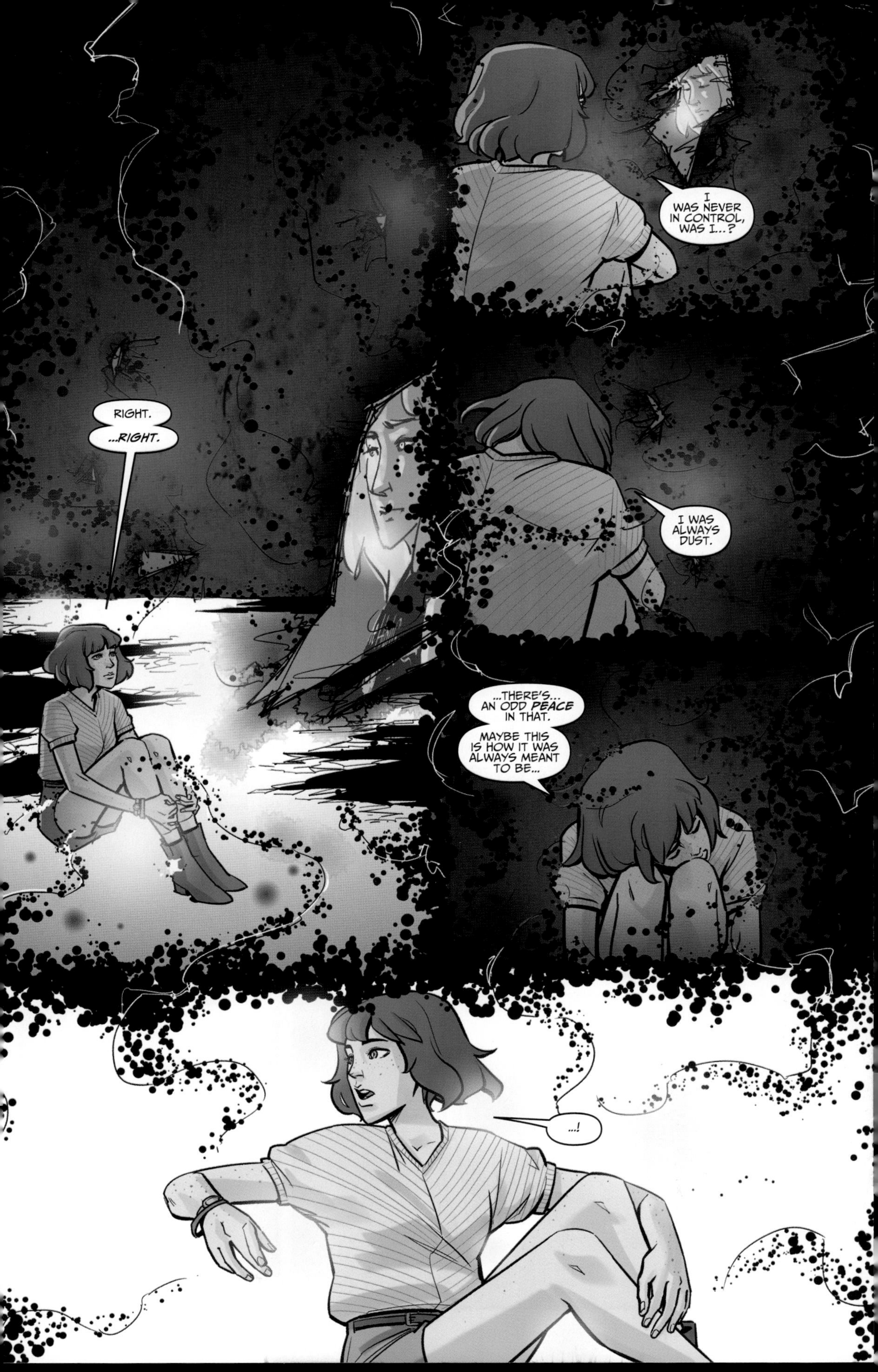
I WAS NEVER IN CONTROL, WAS I...?
RIGHT.
...RIGHT.
I WAS ALWAYS DUST.
...THERE'S... AN ODD PEACE IN THAT.
MAYBE THIS IS HOW IT WAS ALWAYS MEANT TO BE...
...!

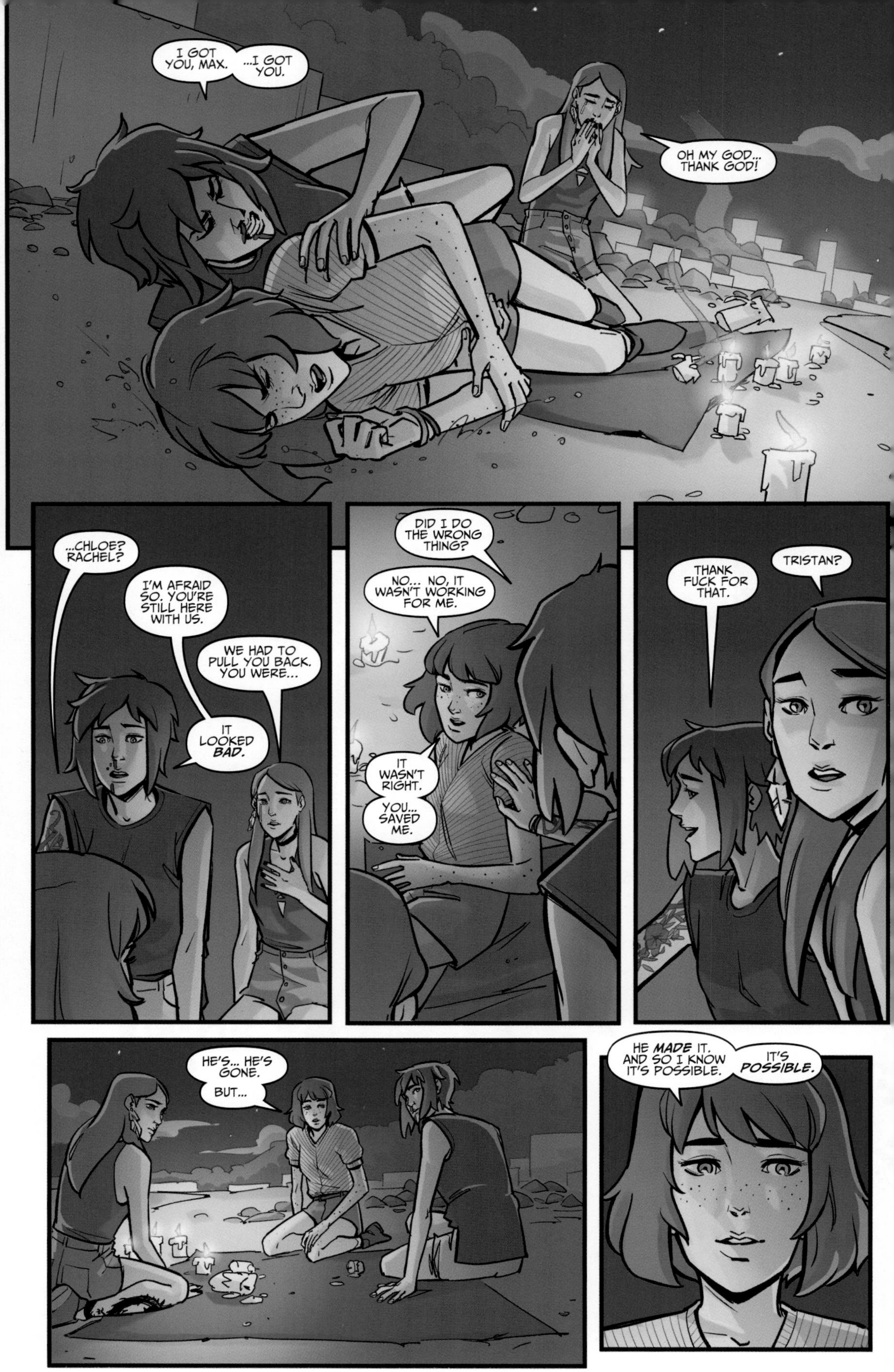

I GOT YOU, MAX.
...I GOT YOU.
OH MY GOD... THANK GOD!
...CHLOE? RACHEL?
I'M AFRAID SO. YOU'RE STILL HERE WITH US.
WE HAD TO PULL YOU BACK. YOU WERE...
IT LOOKED *BAD.*
DID I DO THE WRONG THING?
NO... NO, IT WASN'T WORKING FOR ME.
IT WASN'T RIGHT.
YOU... SAVED ME.
TRISTAN?
THANK FUCK FOR THAT.
HE'S... HE'S GONE.
BUT...
HE *MADE* IT. AND SO I KNOW IT'S POSSIBLE.
IT'S *POSSIBLE.*

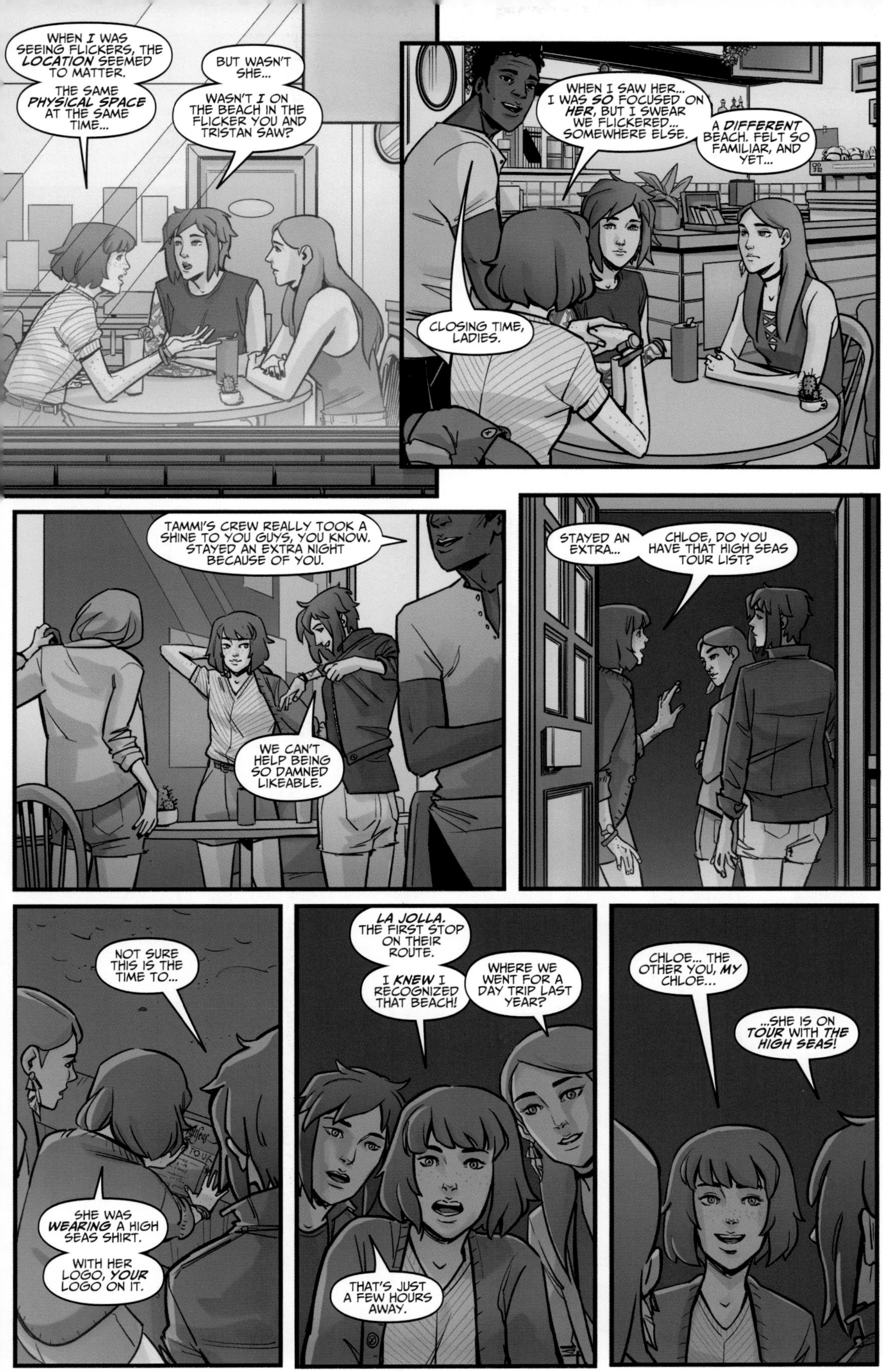
WHEN I WAS SEEING FLICKERS, THE LOCATION SEEMED TO MATTER.
THE SAME PHYSICAL SPACE AT THE SAME TIME...
BUT WASN'T SHE...
WASN'T I ON THE BEACH IN THE FLICKER YOU AND TRISTAN SAW?
WHEN I SAW HER... I WAS SO FOCUSED ON HER, BUT I SWEAR WE FLICKERED... SOMEWHERE ELSE.
A DIFFERENT BEACH. FELT SO FAMILIAR, AND YET...
CLOSING TIME, LADIES.
TAMMI'S CREW REALLY TOOK A SHINE TO YOU GUYS, YOU KNOW. STAYED AN EXTRA NIGHT BECAUSE OF YOU.
WE CAN'T HELP BEING SO DAMNED LIKEABLE.
STAYED AN EXTRA...
CHLOE, DO YOU HAVE THAT HIGH SEAS TOUR LIST?
NOT SURE THIS IS THE TIME TO...
SHE WAS WEARING A HIGH SEAS SHIRT.
WITH HER LOGO, YOUR LOGO ON IT.
LA JOLLA. THE FIRST STOP ON THEIR ROUTE.
I KNEW I RECOGNIZED THAT BEACH!
WHERE WE WENT FOR A DAY TRIP LAST YEAR?
THAT'S JUST A FEW HOURS AWAY.
CHLOE... THE OTHER YOU, MY CHLOE...
...SHE IS ON TOUR WITH THE HIGH SEAS!

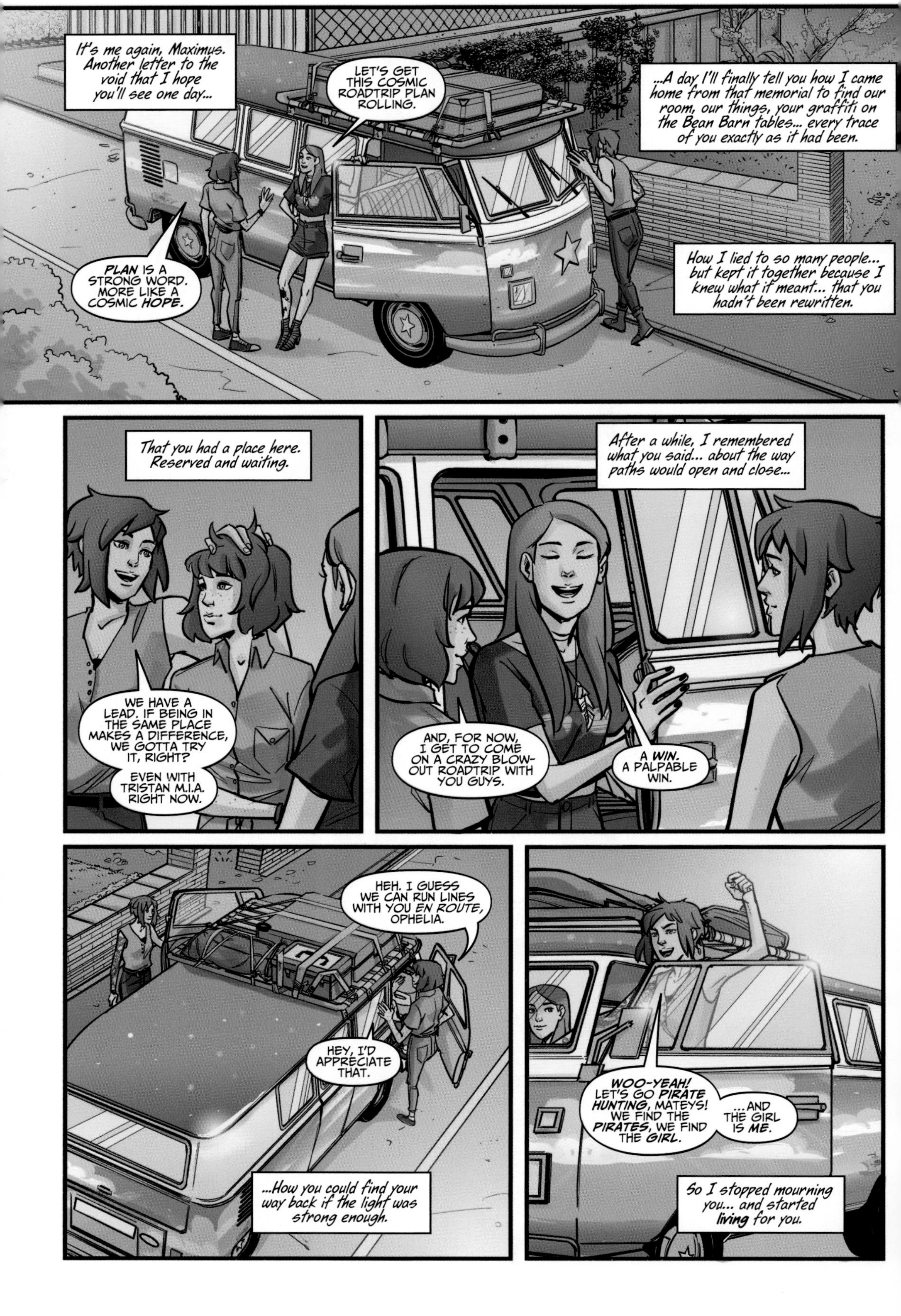
It's me again, Maximus. Another letter to the void that I hope you'll see one day...
LET'S GET THIS COSMIC ROADTRIP PLAN ROLLING.
PLAN IS A STRONG WORD. MORE LIKE A COSMIC HOPE.
...A day I'll finally tell you how I came home from that memorial to find our room, our things, your graffiti on the Bean Barn tables... every trace of you exactly as it had been.
How I lied to so many people... but kept it together because I knew what it meant... that you hadn't been rewritten.
That you had a place here. Reserved and waiting.
WE HAVE A LEAD. IF BEING IN THE SAME PLACE MAKES A DIFFERENCE, WE GOTTA TRY IT, RIGHT?
EVEN WITH TRISTAN M.I.A. RIGHT NOW.
After a while, I remembered what you said... about the way paths would open and close...
AND, FOR NOW, I GET TO COME ON A CRAZY BLOW-OUT ROADTRIP WITH YOU GUYS.
A WIN. A PALPABLE WIN.
HEH. I GUESS WE CAN RUN LINES WITH YOU EN ROUTE, OPHELIA.
HEY, I'D APPRECIATE THAT.
...How you could find your way back if the light was strong enough.
WOO-YEAH! LET'S GO PIRATE HUNTING, MATEYS! WE FIND THE PIRATES, WE FIND THE GIRL.
...AND THE GIRL IS ME.
So I stopped mourning you... and started living for you.

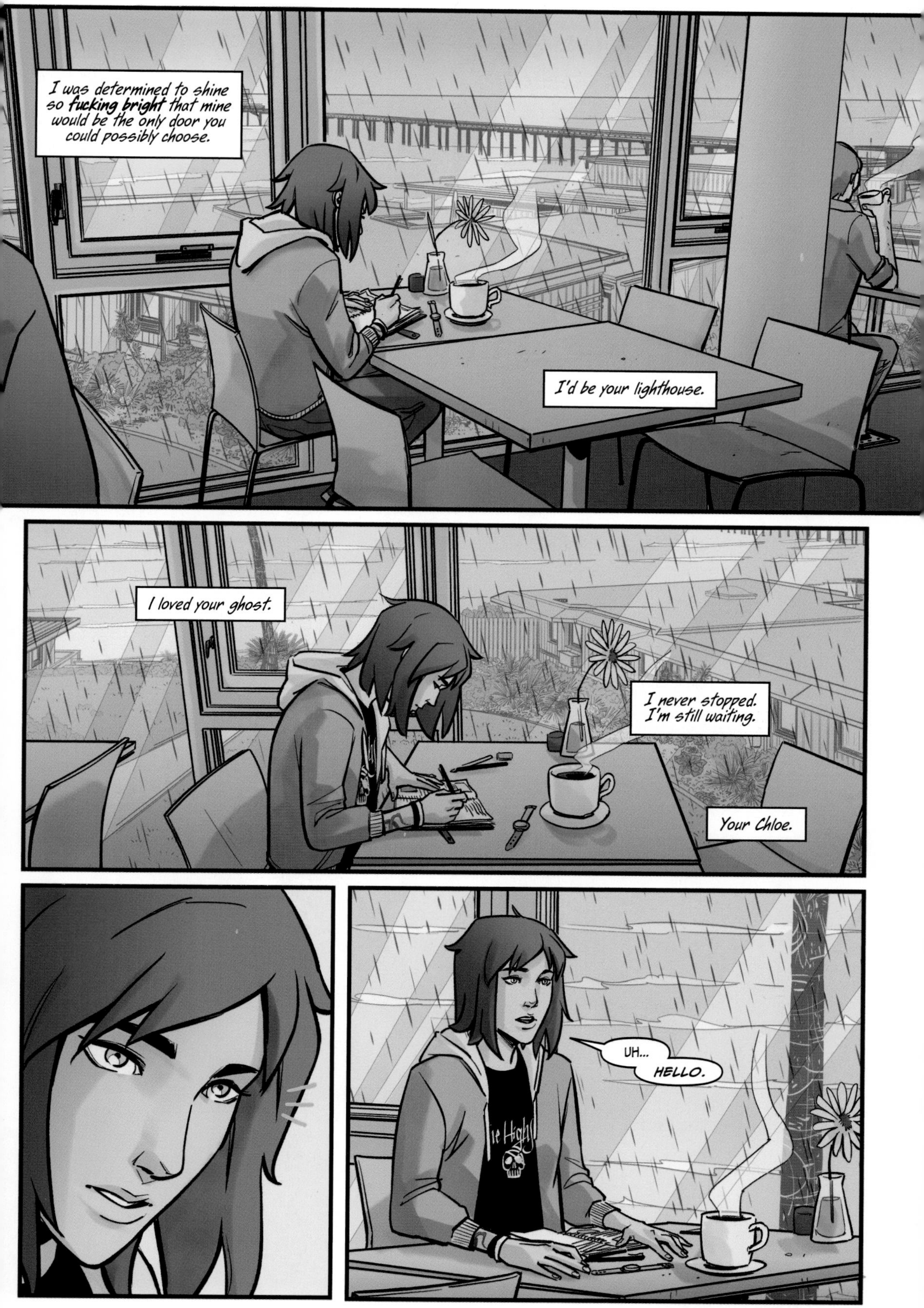
I was determined to shine so **fucking bright** that mine would be the only door you could possibly choose.
I'd be your lighthouse.
I loved your ghost.
I never stopped. I'm still waiting.
Your Chloe.
UH... HELLO.

TO BE CONTINUED...

COVER GALLERY

ISSUE #9

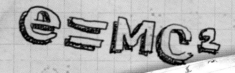

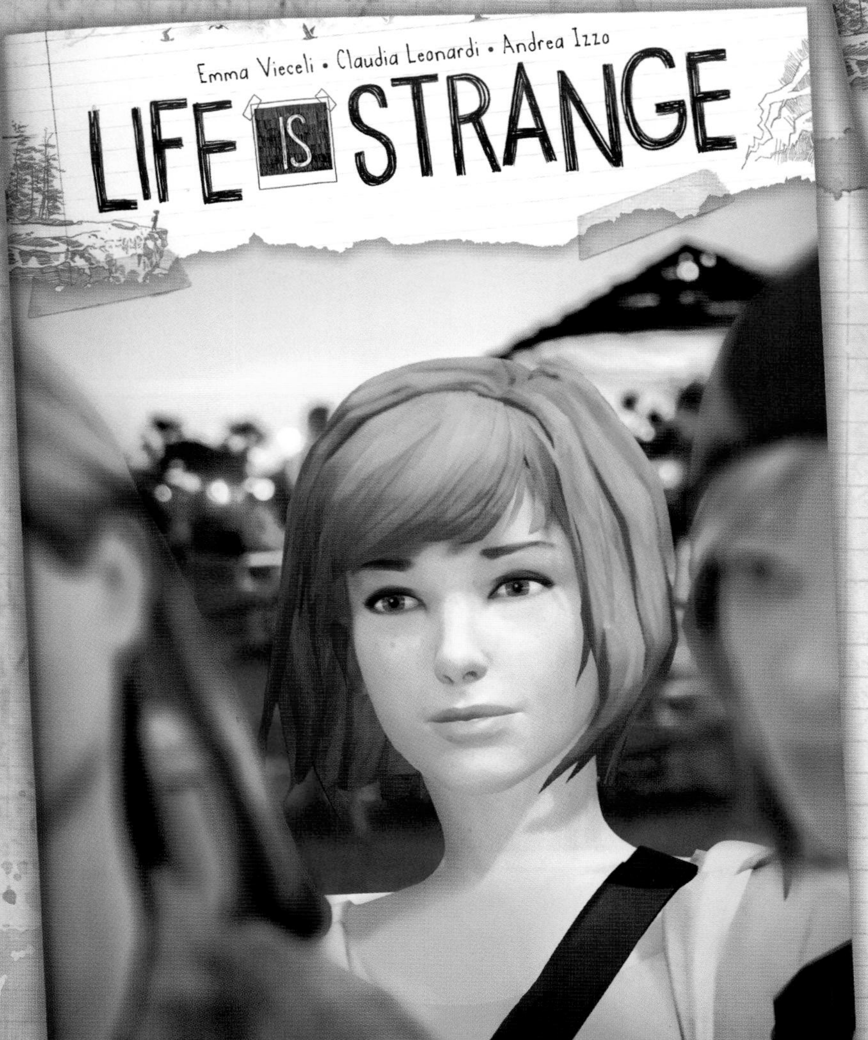
Emma Vieceli • Claudia Leonardi • Andrea Izzo
LIFE IS STRANGE

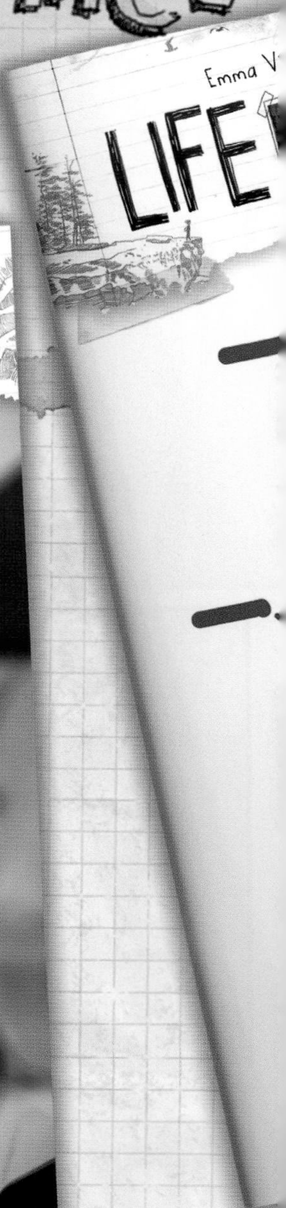
LIFE

COVER B - WILL OFFER

COVER C -
T-SHIRT ART

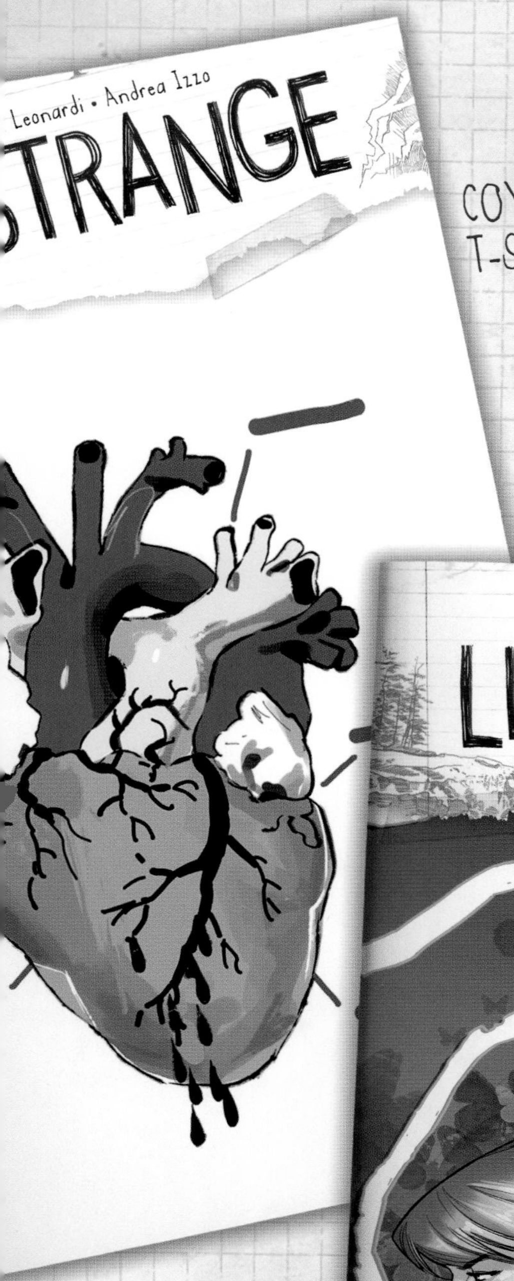
Leonardi • Andrea Izzo
STRANGE

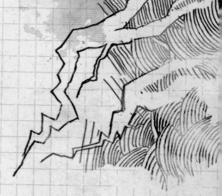

COVER D - ROBERTA INGRANATA

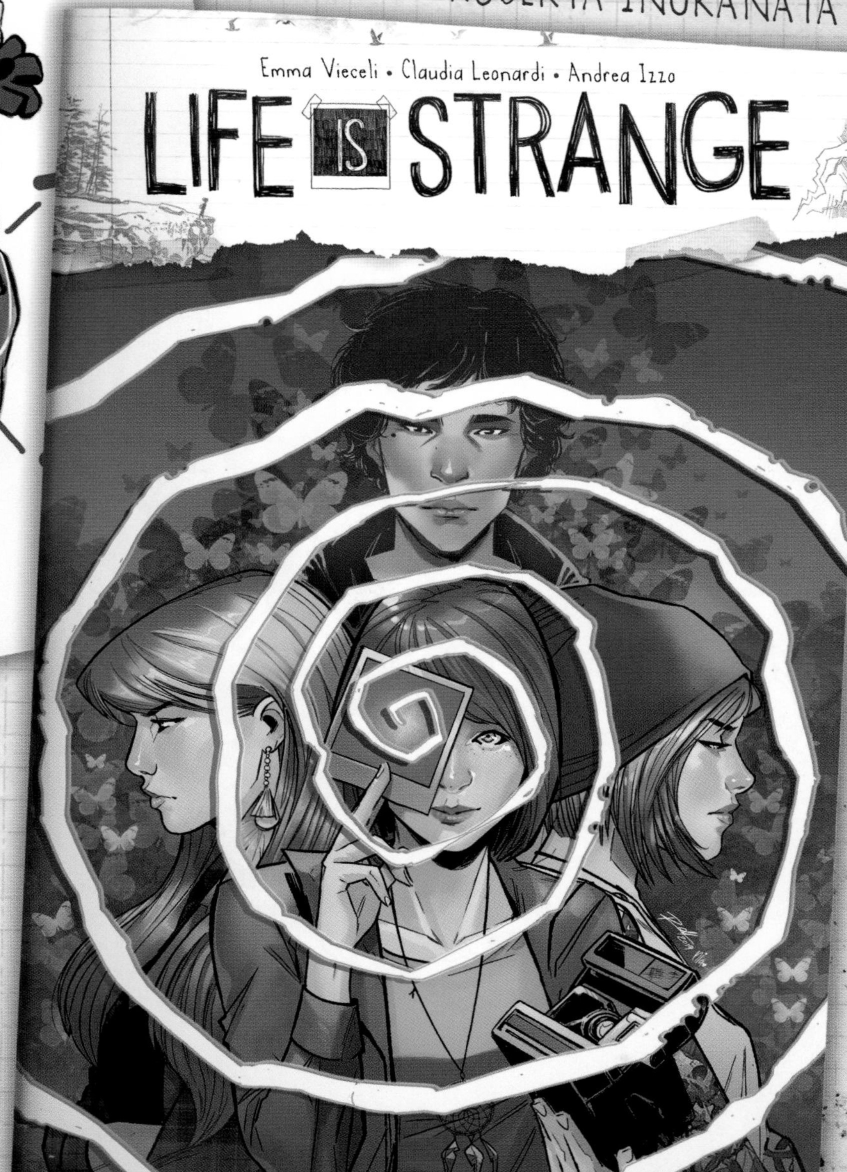
Emma Vieceli • Claudia Leonardi • Andrea Izzo
LIFE IS STRANGE

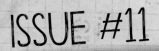

ISSUE #11

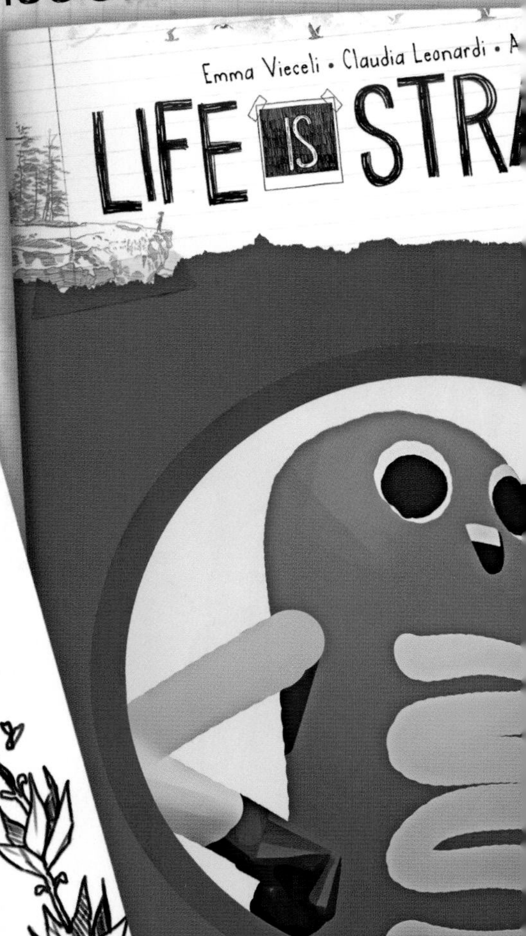
Emma Vieceli • Claudia Leonardi •
LIFE IS

COVER C - T-SHIRT ART

ISSUE #10

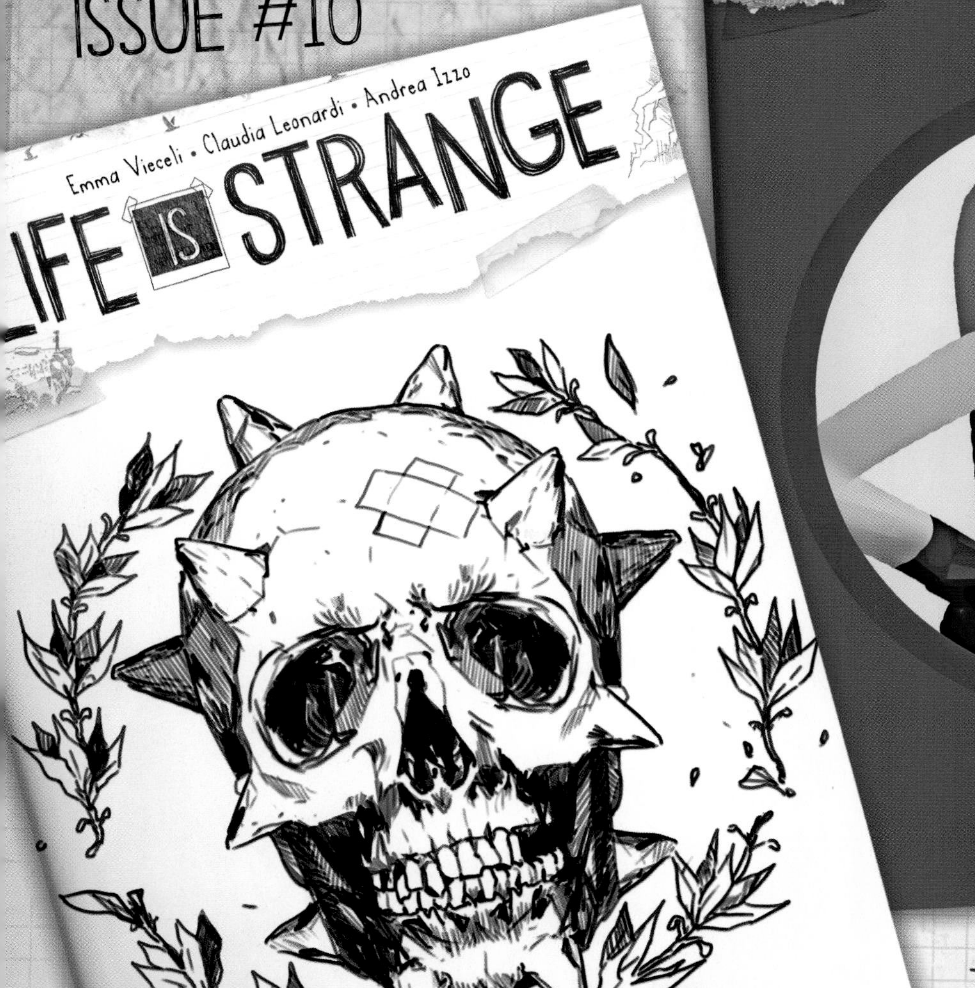
Emma Vieceli • Claudia Leonardi • Andrea Izzo
LIFE IS STRANGE

COVER C - T-SHIRT ART

ISSUE #12

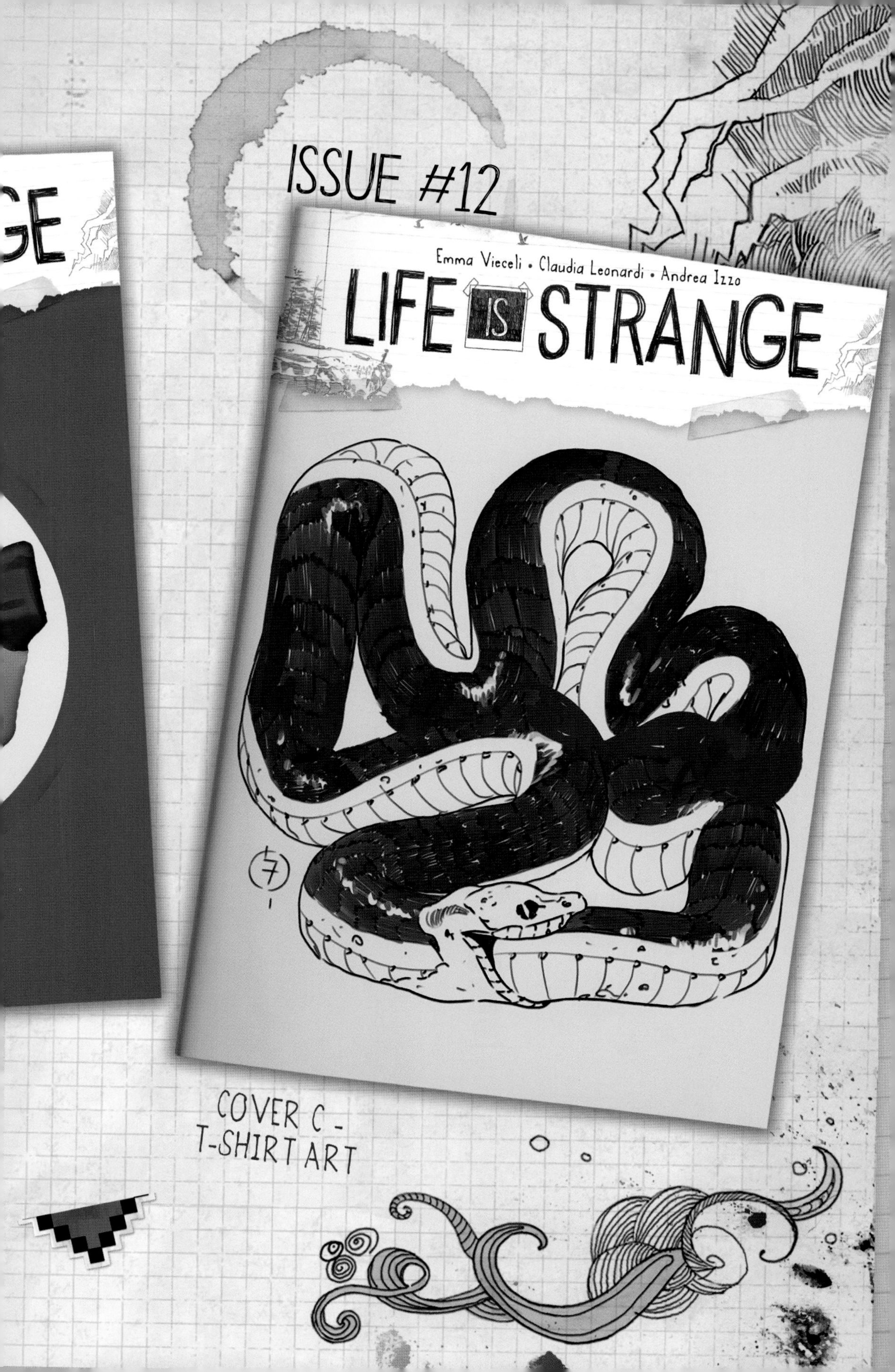
Emma Vieceli • Claudia Leonardi • Andrea Izzo
LIFE IS STRANGE

COVER C -
T-SHIRT ART

COVER DEVELOPMENT

Follow Claudia Leonardi's cover for #10 from concept to completion!

Any cover starts with a rough concept, or in some cases a brief from an editor using existing artwork, as here. Spirals are a strong motif in Life is Strange, and the original concept had photographs spiralling around Max as she reached out to grab one.

(Bonus points if you can guess which panel this image of Max is from! Hint: It's in Life Is Strange Volume 2: Waves)

STEP 1

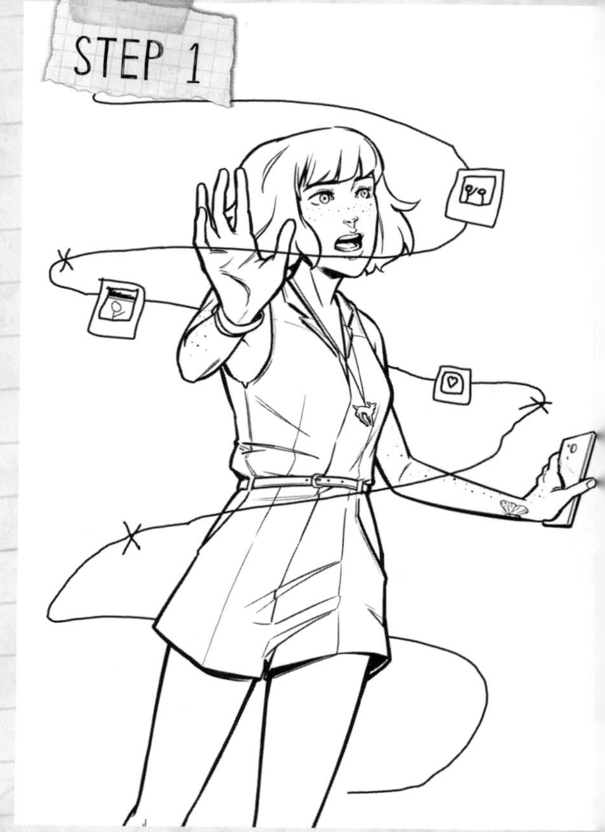

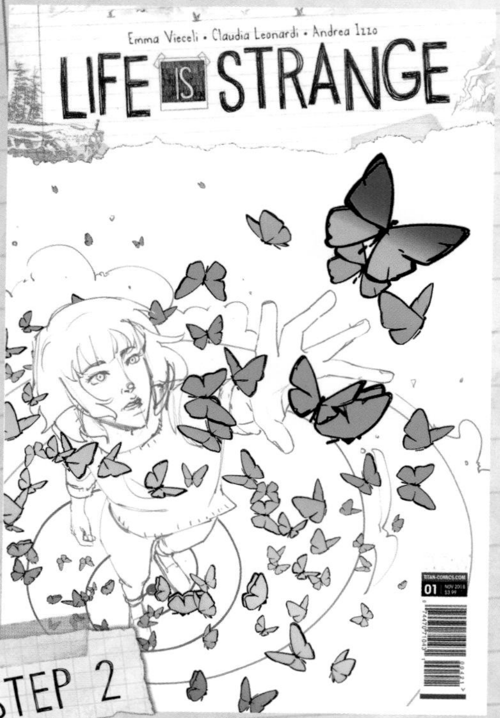
Emma Vieceli • Claudia Leonardi • Andrea Izzo
LIFE IS STRANGE
01

STEP 2

Butterflies were swapped in for photographs at the rough pencil stage, and the angle was changed, both to create a more visually dynamic composition and to centre the spiral itself. The result gave a visual sense of rising, emphasizing the butterfly effect (pun intended).

STEP 3

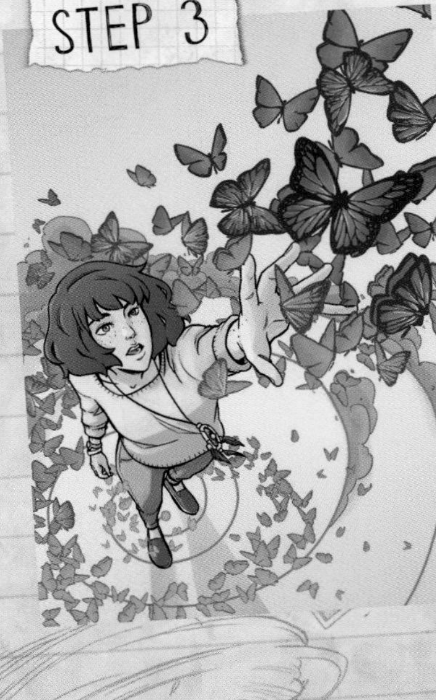

The autumnal tones of the butterflies matched the background color too closely on the first color pass, drawing t much focus from the central blue butterfly.

Claudia's original roughs contained the key - bringing in a rainbow effect to the swarm allowed the palette to sweep up from hot reds at Max's feet to cool blues at her fingertips, while still keeping the blue butterfly distinct.

STEP 4

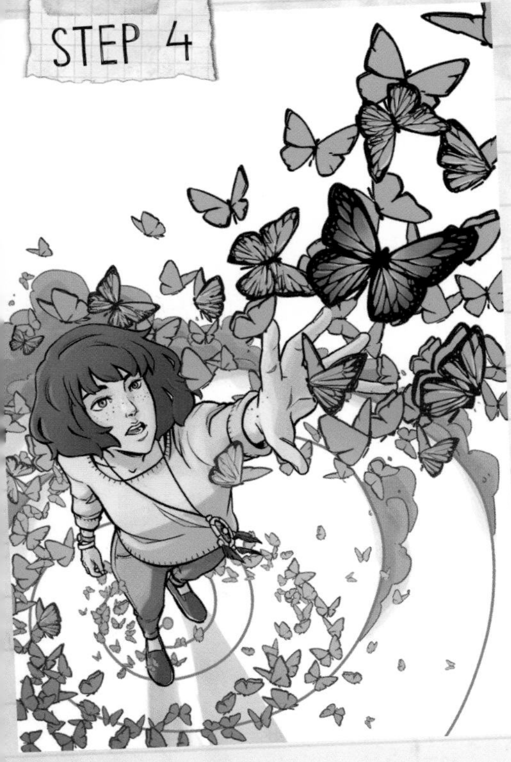

STEP 5

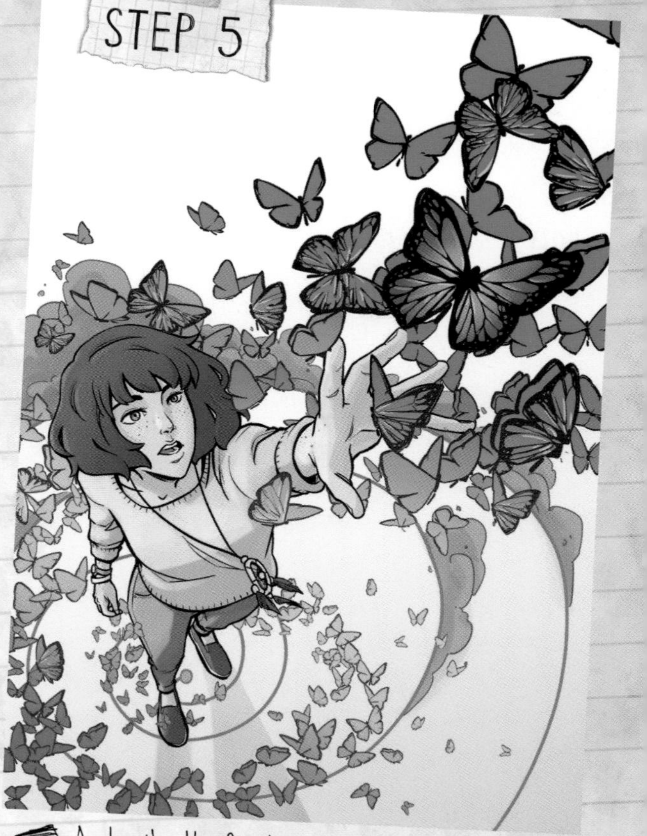

And voila, the finished cover! Bringing in some of the orange hue at the base of the image gave it back some depth, and emphasising the height to which Max is reaching.

CALLBACK COVER

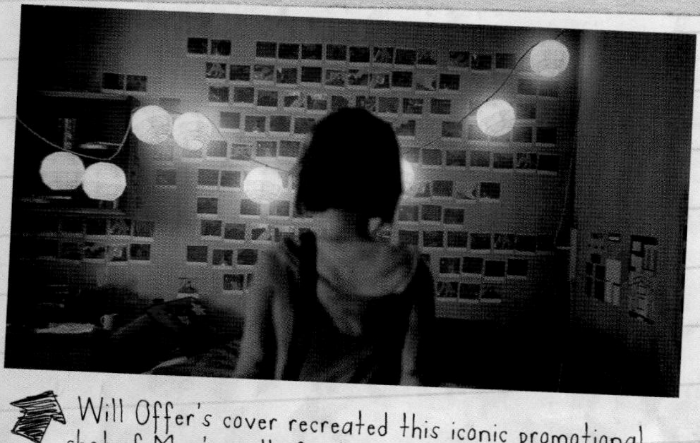

Will Offer's cover recreated this iconic promotional shot of Max's wall of polaroids, this time updated with shots and events from all across the first game - reminding us, and Max, of everyone she lost in Arcadia Bay.

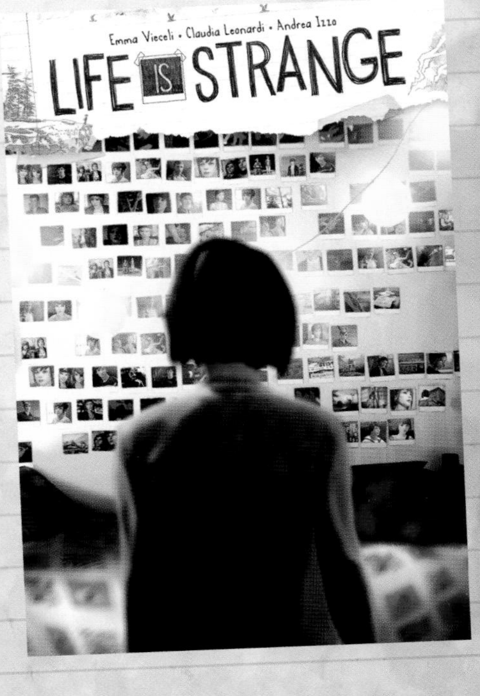
Emma Vieceli • Claudia Leonardi • Andrea Izzo
LIFE IS STRANGE

CHARACTER SKETCHES

BY CLAUDIA LEONARDI

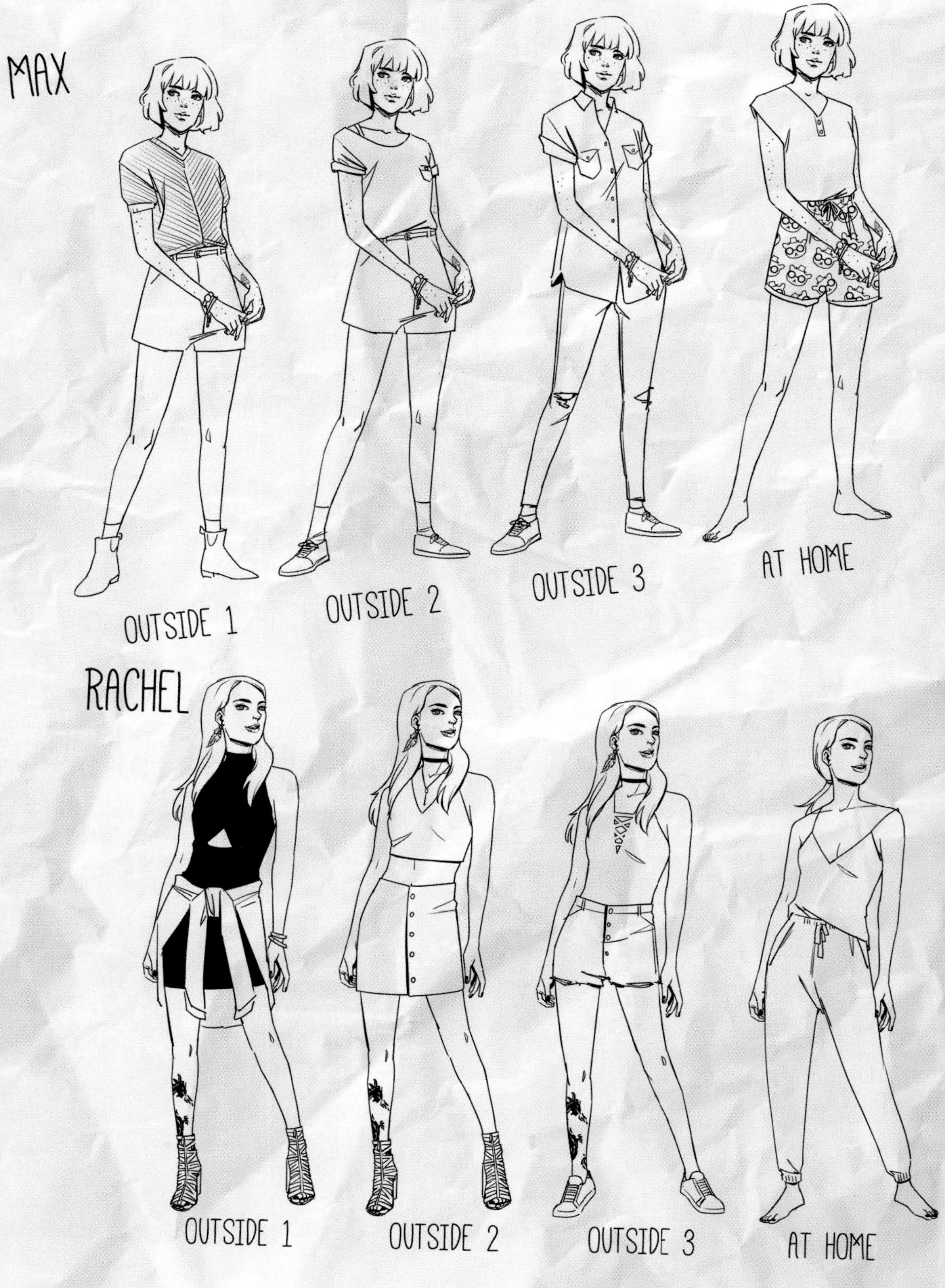
MAX
OUTSIDE 1
OUTSIDE 2
OUTSIDE 3
AT HOME
RACHEL
OUTSIDE 1
OUTSIDE 2
OUTSIDE 3
AT HOME

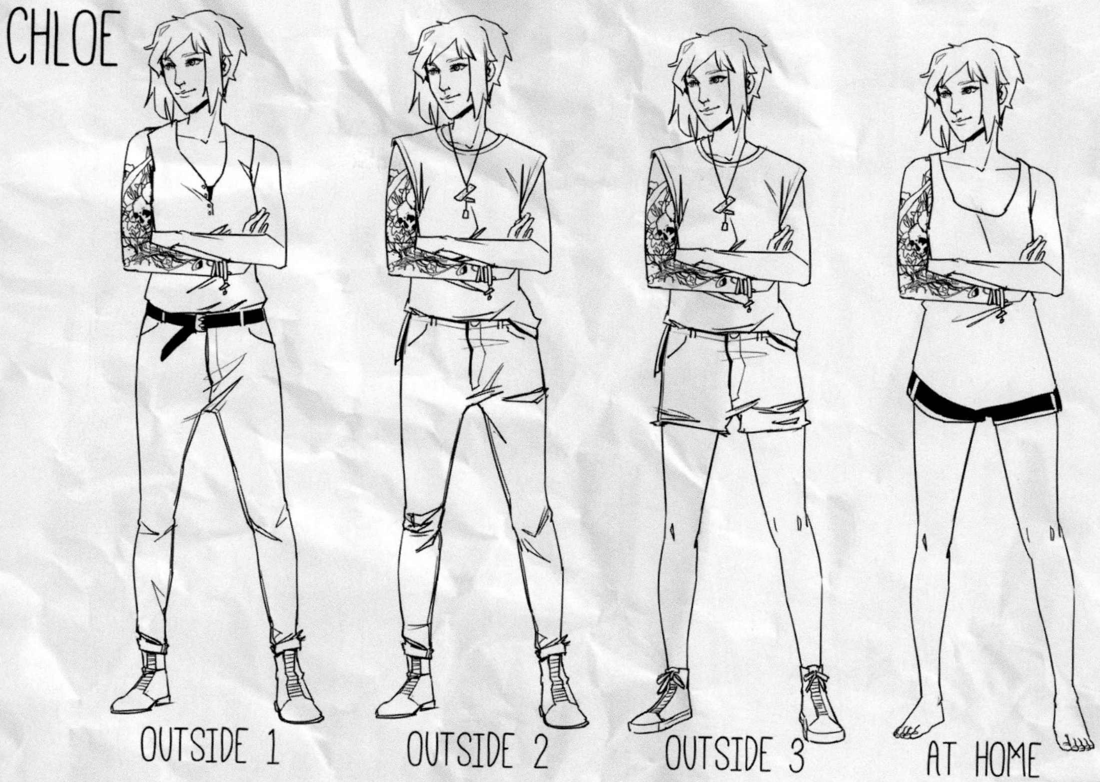
CHLOE
OUTSIDE 1
OUTSIDE 2
OUTSIDE 3
AT HOME

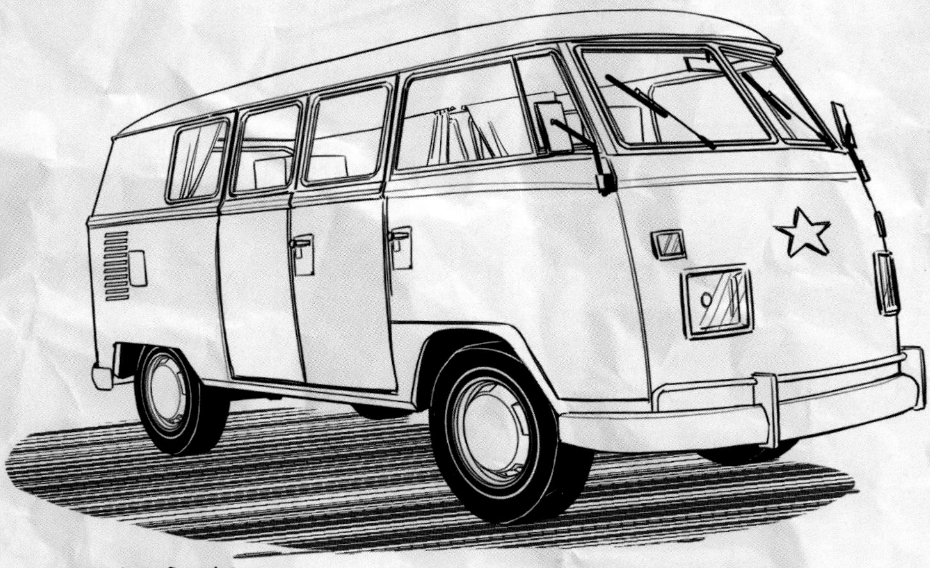
GLADYS

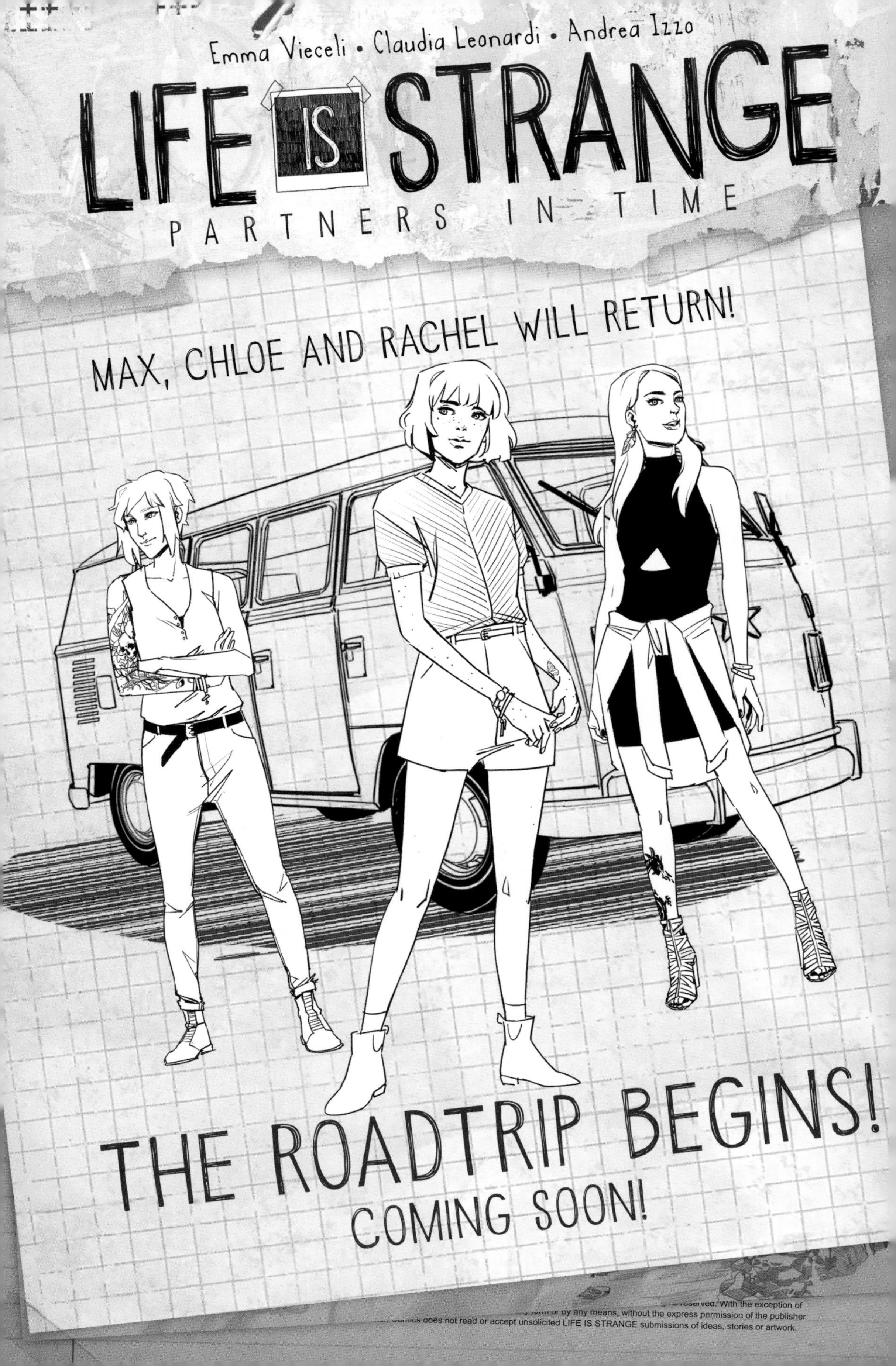
Emma Vieceli • Claudia Leonardi • Andrea Izzo
LIFE IS STRANGE
PARTNERS IN TIME
MAX, CHLOE AND RACHEL WILL RETURN!
THE ROADTRIP BEGINS!
COMING SOON!
reserved. With the exception of
by any means, without the express permission of the publisher
does not read or accept unsolicited LIFE IS STRANGE submissions of ideas, stories or artwork.

Welcome to HELL BLACKWELL ACADEMY

The student guide to Blackwell Academy and Arcadia Bay

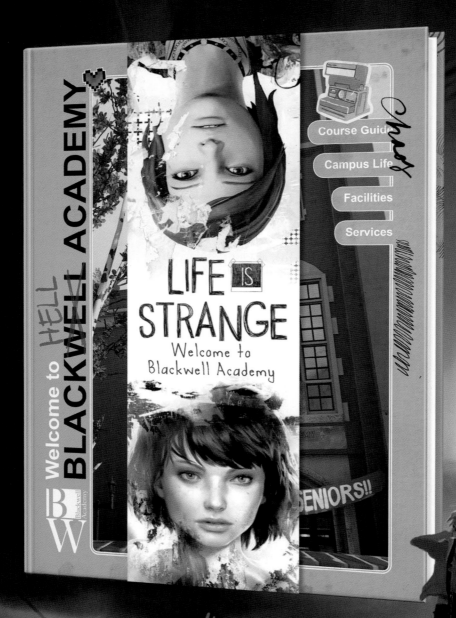

As defaced by Max and Chloe

OUT NOW!

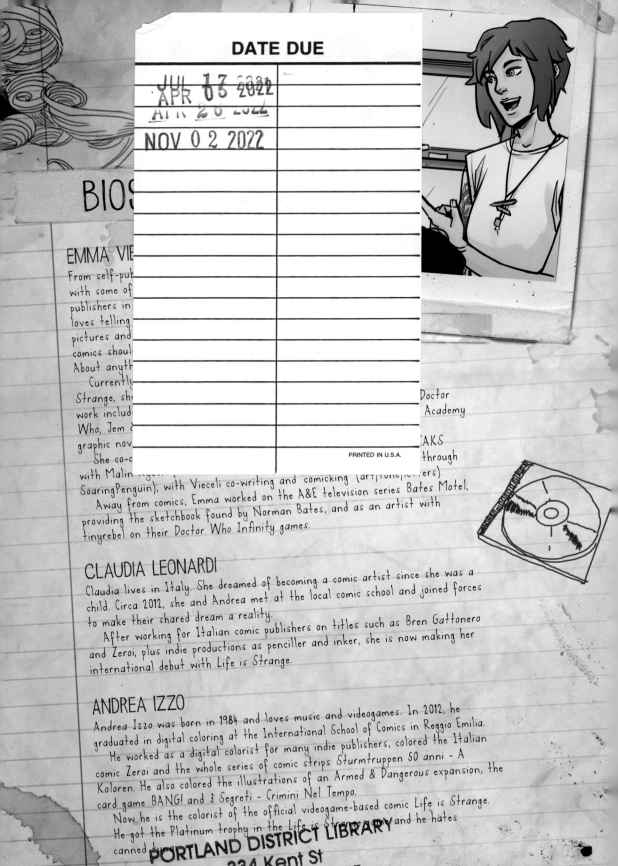

BIOS

EMMA VIE...

From self-pub...
with some of...
publishers in...
loves telling...
pictures and...
comics shoul...
About anyth...
    Currently...
Strange, sh... Doctor
work includ... Academy
Who, Jem &...
graphic nov... ...AKS
    She co-c... through
with Malin ... (art|text|letters).
SoaringPenguin), with Vieceli co-writing and comicking
    Away from comics, Emma worked on the A&E television series Bates Motel,
providing the sketchbook found by Norman Bates, and as an artist with
tinyrebel on their Doctor Who Infinity games.

CLAUDIA LEONARDI

Claudia lives in Italy. She dreamed of becoming a comic artist since she was a
child. Circa 2012, she and Andrea met at the local comic school and joined forces
to make their shared dream a reality.
    After working for Italian comic publishers on titles such as Bren Gattonero
and Zeroi, plus indie productions as penciller and inker, she is now making her
international debut with Life is Strange.

ANDREA IZZO

Andrea Izzo was born in 1984 and loves music and videogames. In 2012, he
graduated in digital coloring at the International School of Comics in Reggio Emilia.
    He worked as a digital colorist for many indie publishers, colored the Italian
comic Zeroi and the whole series of comic strips Sturmtruppen 50 anni - A
Koloren. He also colored the illustrations of an Armed & Dangerous expansion, the
card game BANG! and 3 Segreti - Crimini Nel Tempo.
    Now he is the colorist of the official videogame-based comic Life is Strange.
He got the Platinum trophy in the Life is Strange game and he hates
canned tu...